Western and Eastern Rambles

JOSEPH HOWE

Western and Eastern Rambles: Travel Sketches of Nova Scotia

EDITED BY M.G. PARKS

UNIVERSITY OF TORONTO PRESS

Toronto and Buffalo
Reprinted in paperback 2017
ISBN 978-0-8020-5283-4 (cloth)
ISBN 978-0-8020-6183-6 (paper)
LC 72-97424

Contents

INTRODUCTION 3

WESTERN RAMBLES

I Thoughts on travelling 47

II Leaving Halifax 52

III The road to Windsor 59

IV Windsor 66

V The Gaspereau, Horton, Kentville 74

VI Cornwallis Township 81

VII Kentville Falls 88

VIII The road to Bridgetown 93

IX Bridgetown 97

X Annapolis 102

XI Digby and Clare 106

EASTERN RAMBLES

I Getting under way 117

II The road to Truro 123

III Truro and neighbourhood 129

IV The Truro Falls 135

V The road to Pictou 139

VI A general view of Pictou 144

VII Reflections on Pictou and the Highland Scots 149

VIII Pictou Academy 154

IX The Albion Mines 159

X New Glasgow to the French River 168

XI Merigomish and the Gulf Shore 174

XII Antigonish 182

XIII The St Mary's road and Lochaber Lake 187

XIV The Forks of St Mary's and Sherbrooke 192

XV The road to Guysborough 196

XVI Guysborough 200

INDEX 205

Illustrations and Maps

Joseph Howe 1

Plan of the town of Halifax, 1830 8

Nova Scotia 12

The western trip 48

William H. Eager, ruins of the Duke of Kent's lodge, circa 1836 56

Terfry's Inn, Newport Corners 63

William H. Eager, view of Windsor, circa 1836 67

Front Street, Windsor, circa 1829 (artist unidentified) 71

William H. Eager, view from the Horton Mountains, circa 1836 77

The eastern trip 118

View of Halifax, circa 1836 125

R. Carpenter, view of Pictou, circa 1841 145

All illustrations are from the Public Archives of Nova Scotia and are reproduced by permission.

The portrait of Joseph Howe is taken from an engraving in the Public Archives of Nova Scotia. The original is undated but appears to be a copy of the portrait of 1851 painted by T. Debaussy.

Introduction

The Joseph Howe of the history books and popular imagination is well exemplified by his magisterial bronze statue which stands high on a stone pedestal outside the Province House in downtown Halifax. The erect, frock-coated figure grasps his lapel with his left hand and extends his right in a declamatory gesture as if in the midst of impassioned political oratory. Here is indeed the 'tribune of Nova Scotia,' the political leader and statesman, in all the formal dignity of Victorian sculpture, a stylized but not inaccurate image of the grandiloquent and shrewd orator whose eloquence was as persuasive among the farmers and fishermen of the countryside as before the more literate and cynical audience of his peers in Halifax.

The picture is not false, but it is partial. It is not a very close likeness of the Joseph Howe of twenty-three who began his travels throughout his native province and wrote of his experience in his own newspaper, the *Novascotian*. Howe the inquiring traveller and familiar essayist is much less statuesque and much more the man he must have been to his friends and acquaintances – loquacious and friendly, warmly emotional but intellectually penetrating too, vital and exuberant but quick to be moved by the dark forces of sorrow and tragedy, even sentimental when confronted by the grand themes of mutability and death or by the grandeur of nature.

Howe bought the *Novascotian* from George Young late in 1827, after he had spent that year editing another newspaper, *The Acadian and General Advertiser*, in partnership with James Spike. As editor, manager, and owner of the new venture, he soon became a very busy man. His unremitting labour was not in vain, for by the end of his first year he had about 800 subscribers, 300 in Halifax and the rest, nearly 500, throughout the Maritime provinces. In 1828 he began the series of excursions into the countryside of Nova Scotia which resulted in *Western Rambles* (published in the *Novascotian* from 23 July to 9 October 1828) and *Eastern Rambles* (17 December 1829, to 19 October 1831). In these years when he had not yet entered politics, his immediate purpose in travelling was the mundane business of making his newspaper a financial success. He travelled thousands of miles in order to get new subscriptions and, above all, to collect subscriptions due, in a constant struggle to keep ahead of his own creditors and gather the cash essential for the support of his family and business. An incidental result of his frequent trips, though of immense value to his subsequent career, was the intimate knowledge of the province thus gained.

From the published sketches, or, as Howe called them, the *Rambles*, we learn something of his actual life on the road. They have other purposes, however, than the recital of his day-to-day experiences in journal fashion. For that factual background, for the actual history of his life as a traveller with exacting business to transact, one may turn to a series of personal letters written to his young wife, Catharine Susan Ann (McNab) Howe, during and after the period when the sketches were being published in the *Novascotian*.[1] Besides showing clearly that the sketches are literary distillations of his experiences which he thought fit to present to the public, the letters reveal the frequency and extent of Howe's journeys, the nature of his business, his doings in parts of the province not reached in the sketches, and of course something of his private rather than public personality.

Although Howe may have made a few excursions beyond the Halifax area before 1828, particularly to Windsor and into the Annapolis Valley, it was in that year that he began his extended business trips which were to take him to every part of Nova Scotia, over many a road beyond the confines of the *Rambles*, and into New Brunswick and Prince Edward Island. In the early summer of 1828 he visited the western counties. In 1829 he was on the road in earnest, being away from home for most of June and early July, and then again from mid-August to the end of October. His first tour of that year was a routine trip through the Annapolis Valley, but his second was ambitious indeed – to Truro, Pictou, and over to Charlottetown; then back to Pictou and on through River John, Tatamagouche, Wallace, Pugwash, Londonderry, and back to Truro; then to Amherst and into New Brunswick, and finally

1 The original letters are in the Harvard University Library. A complete microfilm copy of the collection is in the Public Archives of Nova Scotia (reel 23, Joseph Howe Papers, 1830–73). Portions of the letters are reproduced here by permission of the Harvard College Library.

by ship to Boston and New York. In 1830 he left Halifax on 23 May and did not return until 18 July, travelling over 500 miles on horseback. The first stage of his route was down the South Shore through Chester and Lunenburg to Liverpool, cross-country to Annapolis, through the Annapolis Valley to Kentville and finally to Windsor. Instead of returning to Halifax, he then cut across to Truro, and rode to Pictou and through Antigonish down to Guysborough, where he took the sailing packet to Arichat in Cape Breton. From there he rode to Sydney, then back along the Bras d'Or Lakes to the Straits, returned to Pictou, took the packet to Charlottetown, and finally returned home by way of Pictou and Truro. Few letters seem to have survived to record his journeys in 1831, and a diary entry that has him travelling from mid-August to early November, going as far afield as Philadelphia, may well be misdated. In 1832, he was through the Annapolis Valley and over to New Brunswick and Prince Edward Island. In 1833, besides the more normal trips, he went on horseback through the Musquodoboits and St Mary's to Antigonish, and in 1834 was on the road by late April throughout the Maritime provinces.

The letters furnish abundant evidence that Howe had no easy time collecting the accounts due him. All too often he must express regrets that he has not been more successful: 'I send you a few pounds and am sorry they are so few but really I fared worse at Liverpool than at Lunenburg, scarcely collecting sufficient to pay my expenses' (Annapolis, 1829); 'though I have been four week days here, and have left no stone unturned, my collections have been only £3' (Miramichi, 1834); 'the country is miserably poor. You can scarcely have an idea how scarce money is among persons who have valuable properties worth hundreds of pounds, and almost all the comforts of life about them' (Kentville, 1834). In a letter from Guysborough (1830) he gives his wife a graphic sketch of his trials:

> Although I have not five bad names in this County, still the difficulty of raising money at a short notice is such that I have been signally unsuccessful. To give you an idea of my daily labors, I need only describe the operations of one. I left Pictou on Monday afternoon and got to the Mines [Stellarton] that night, where I had to stay, on account of the weather, nearly all the following day.

I got, however, to Copeland's, about 12 miles from New Glasgow, in time for supper. The next morning I found that one of my subscribers lived off the main road, on an Island. Not caring to miss him, I got a man and a canoe and paddled over, a distance of a mile – found him a respectable man, a magistrate and a farmer, but no cash – retraced my course – mounted my horse and rode on six miles to another – he was in the woods, setting a bear trap – waited an hour and a half for his return – the Paper was not for him but for a person three miles off the road – rode to his house – found him a respectable man, with a mill and a fine stone house, but no money – another subscriber lived 2 miles further, upon a short cut towards the main road – met with the same success, and continued on about a mile more, to the house of a magistrate and merchant, sure of receiving the needful – he had started the day before to Pictou, and I had again to mount the saddle. My next stopping place was Priest Grant[?], at the Gulf Shore. He gave me a bottle of good wine and – a promise to have his Bill paid in town. So that I got into Antigonish after a ride of 50 miles, without collecting a dollar.

Sometimes a trip that he had planned to complete in two weeks had to be extended to three and then to four, as he struggled to collect enough money to enable Susan Ann to meet bills that were piling up at home.

Though troubled sorely by such constant frustrations, Howe evidences in the letters flashes of the *joie de vivre* and the ebullient zest that one finds in the sketches, and often forgets his troubles in the pleasure of new experiences. He is mightily pleased over his developing stamina as a horseman: 'There is one thing that I am not a little proud of – which is that I can now sit a whole day on a horse's back and feel no more wearied than my neighbours ... Already the uttermost parts of the earth seem a great deal nearer than they did. Constantinople appears only about a day's ride off and any place to which there is land all the way seems as though it came within the reach of myself and Poney.' At times he writes as entertainingly for Susan Ann as for the readers of his newspaper. A Presbyterian minister he encounters at Musquodoboit is succinctly characterized: 'His discourses were not altogether uninteresting, but he every now and then got into the wide ocean of theology without compass or chronometer'; the same gentleman, being poorly paid and being inclined to the life of the farmer, 'cultivates the Lord's vineyard one day in the week, and his own the other six.' The delights of the open air in fine weather, the never-ending fascination of the human comedy, the exploration on horseback of the byways of his province, the sense of elation when he is received warmly by strangers who know him only through the written word or when he sees evidence that his newspaper is becoming influential – all these compensate in part for the toil, worry, and long absences from wife and children.

The irksome business of collections and subscriptions would by itself have exhausted a less energetic man, but Howe also managed to continue some of his editorial duties while travelling. Many of his evenings were spent in writing articles for the *Novascotian*, among them being several chapters or numbers of the *Rambles*, and he also collected whatever interesting material was forthcoming from local contributors. His wife, it is interesting to note, performed many editorial duties in his absence. As the Howe residence was at that time next door to the *Novascotian* offices, she could do so without neglecting her household. She was entrusted with proofreading in all stages the copy which Howe mailed to her; she was expected to keep an eye on 'the Boys,' as Howe calls his pressmen in the *Novascotian* offices, and to look after the make-up of the paper. When she complains about the carelessness of her husband's handwriting, he replies 'as to the writing, I shall need a few lessons from Massey [a teacher of calligraphy in Halifax] to make my hand intelligible if I stay in the country much longer. However, as an Editoress you ought to be accustomed to bad manuscripts.' Indeed she seems to have served him well in that capacity, for he frequently praises her efforts and diplomatically makes his criticism a mere afterthought: 'The last paper was capital – the selections and arrangement were very good, and the article was very correct – there were a few errors in spelling but they were not material.'

Reading the sketches, one realizes that Howe knows well and understands fully what he is describing and reflecting upon. What one cannot realize is the extremely arduous life out of which they grew. The comparative ease of the stagecoach travel so prominent in the *Rambles* was in reality only occasionally available to Howe, for most of the time he

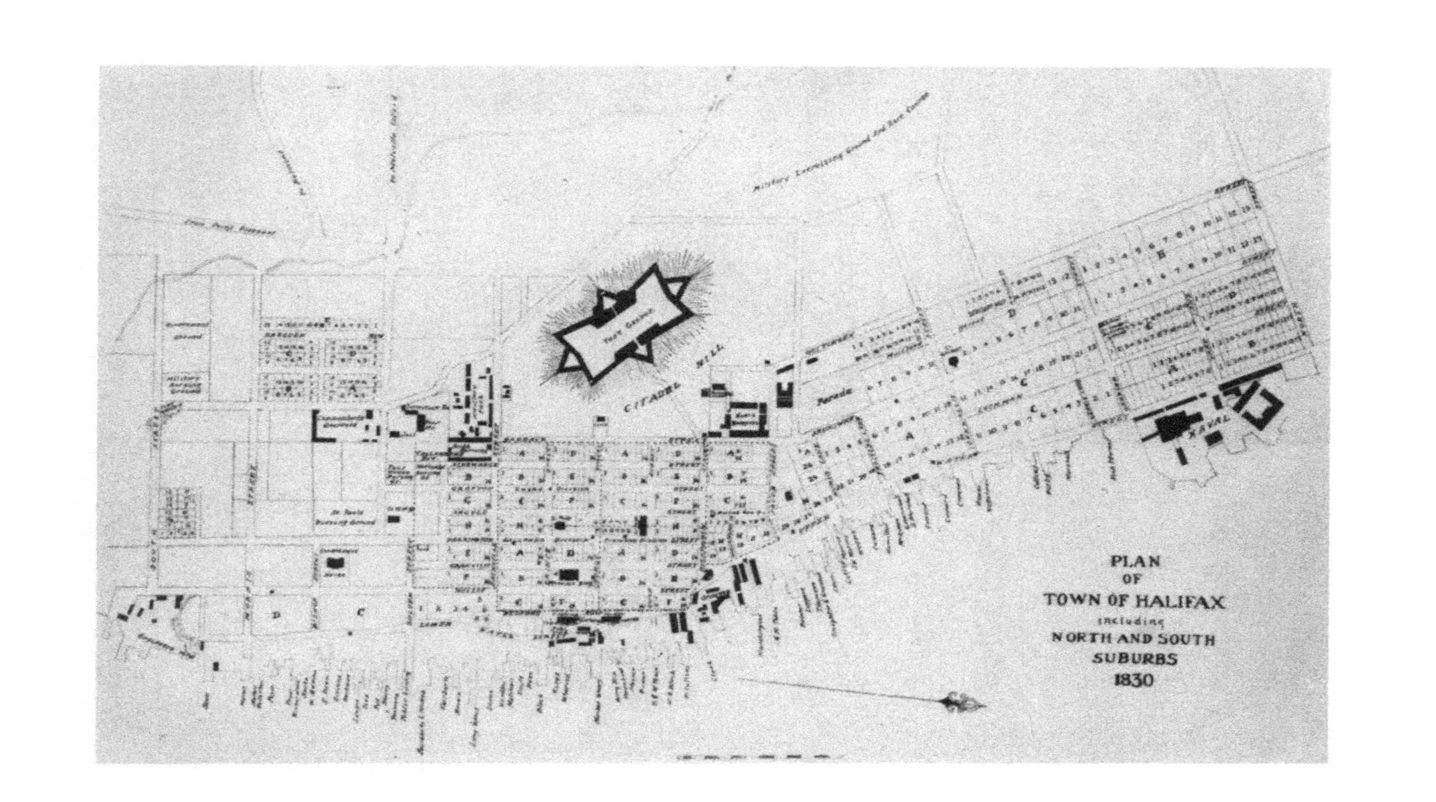
PLAN
OF
TOWN OF HALIFAX
including
NORTH AND SOUTH
SUBURBS
1830
CITADEL HILL
NAVAL

travelled where no stagecoach could possibly run, often where his horse was slowed to a gingerly walk or brought to a halt by bogs or windfalls. The physical demands upon him were so severe that only a man of powerful physique and unbending purpose could have endured them. 'Since this day week,' he tells his wife, 'I have, besides stoppages, ridden over 200 miles – yesterday I was on horseback from 5 till 8 o'clock in the evening. I could do more, but the horse must be saved a little.' When he lacked a horse and was unwilling to waste a day or more waiting for the stage to come his way, he walked. On one such occasion, being stranded in Windsor on a Sunday and impatient to be on his way, he thought nothing of trudging the twenty-five miles to Kentville on the Monday.

Halifax, Howe's home and starting-point, was in 1828 a considerable colonial town with a population of nearly 14,500, of which about 1800 were members of the garrison. In area it covered not much more than part of the present 'downtown' section, lying parallel with the harbour in the shape of a narrow rectangle about half a mile wide and, with the straggling northern suburbs, two miles long. Most of it lay on the slope below Citadel Hill, except for a small area in the south end extending for two blocks off Spring Garden Road (Queen Street, Birmingham Street, and Dresden Row) and the north suburbs enclosed by Gottingen, North, and Water streets. The rest of the Halifax peninsula was covered by fields and pastures, broken here and there by country lanes and thinly dotted by farmhouses, cottages, and, mainly in the southern part, a few 'country' estates of wealthy Haligonians. A contemporary description of the town by Captain William Moorsom, the author of *Letters from Nova Scotia* (1830), brings part of the picture into focus:

Picture ... to yourself Macadamized roads garnished with buildings mostly of wood, some of brick, and others of stone, of all sizes, shapes, and dimensions, from one story to three; some neatly painted, others setting the ingenuity of the colourist at nought: here, a line of shops ... followed by a row of good dwellings; then an interval; a garden, or the gable end of a temple of Vulcan; a fine stone edifice standing apart, evidently for public purposes; and opposite, a little wooden structure, setting at defiance all the rules of perspective, and looking as if ready to give up the ghost, with fear at the august appearance of its lordly neighbour. (pp 11–12)

The waterfront was busy, especially from May to October, when vessels were daily sailing out with cargoes of lumber, fish, and warehoused goods, while others were tying up at the wharves to discharge produce for the capital and the many imported goods required by the young province. Captain Moorsom thus describes the bustle of the little port:

the wharfs are then crowded with vessels of all kinds discharging their cargoes or taking in the returns. Signals are constantly flying at the citadel for vessels coming in; merchants are running about, in anticipation of their freights; officers of the garrison are seen striding down with a determined pace to welcome a detachment from the depôt, or a pipe of Sneyd's claret for the mess; and ladies, tripping along on the tiptoe of expectation, flock into two or three *soi-disant* bazaars for the latest *à-la-mode* bonnets. (pp 47–8)

Such was Howe's metropolis, his personal epitome of urban life which he contrasted, in the fashionable Romantic manner, with the unspoiled nature so abundantly available beyond the town limits.

The province that Howe traversed in his rambles then had a population of only 143,000, according to the census of 1827. Long stretches of wilderness were broken intermittently by settlers' cabins, farms, quiet little villages, or, much less frequently, by settlements with the dignity of towns – Windsor, Liverpool, Lunenburg, Pictou, Yarmouth, Digby, Shelburne. Kentville and Truro were mere villages in size, though the centres of well-settled farming areas; the once-prominent Annapolis Royal had become a quiet place of 300 people; New Glasgow had only recently been established and was as yet only a hamlet; Bridgewater in 1828 was a tiny settlement off the main South Shore road; Antigonish and Guysborough were small centres of surrounding farming districts; Sydney, which Howe visited but did not include in his *Rambles*, was still only a mere village reached overland by nothing better than a rough blazed trail.

The landscape through which we are taken in the *Rambles* exemplifies some, though by no means all, of the variety to be found in Nova Scotia. As the 'Western Rambles' end at Church Point in Digby County, the picturesque South Shore from Yarmouth to Halifax is not described. Neither is the ruggedly austere landscape of the Eastern Shore from Halifax eastward to Canso; in 'Eastern Rambles' Howe merely pauses at Sherbrooke before turning inland again. Cape Breton, which he visited as editor of the *Novascotian*, is also not touched, though it possesses some of the most striking scenic features in the province. No doubt the northern highlands sheering steeply into the sea and folding inland in peaks and glens would have inspired Howe to a romantic rhapsody more intense than any here recorded if he had had occasion to visit what was then the most remote fastness of the province. With these notable exceptions, Howe traverses the major land forms of Nova Scotia.

His western tour first takes him across the centre of the province through the forested area which stretches irregularly the length of the peninsula and is invaded by pockets of fertile farmland in the interior of Queens, Lunenburg, and Halifax counties. Long stretches of his route from Bedford to Windsor, which he found dull, are still forested and have little to offer the sightseer. On the western side, however, the route enters the rich farmland of the Annapolis-Cornwallis Valley. This extends from the dyked lowlands around the mouth of the Avon River and along the Minas Basin through the long and narrow valley itself, which runs for some sixty miles between two continuous high ridges, the North Mountain on the Fundy side and the South Mountain on the other. From Digby to the end of Howe's recorded journey at Church Point, the landscape is marine, with the salt tides of St Mary's Bay on the one side and farms, pasture-land, and forest on the other.

The eastern route from Halifax through Truro and Pictou to Antigonish, and then cross-country to Sherbrooke and eastward again to Guysborough, begins by crossing the peninsula diagonally through a low and then gently undulating countryside of mixed forest and cultivated land. The farmland, though more extensive now than in 1829, is still concentrated in the region some distance off to the right of Howe's route, in the Musquodoboit Valley where he was to spend some pleasant years in the 1840s. Not far beyond Truro the land rises as the road passes over the rolling hills which extend from Cumberland and Colchester counties into eastern Nova Scotia. That portion of the Gulf

NEW BRUNSWICK
Saint John
PRINCE EDWARD ISLAND
Charlottetown
CAPE BRETON ISLAND
N
BAY OF FUNDY
Chignecto Bay
GULF SHORE
AMHERST
Amherst
WALLACE
CUMBERLAND
Tatamagouche
ECONOMY
PARRSBORO
Parrsboro
LONDONDERRY
ONSLOW
Minas Basin
Pictou
PICTOU
DISTRICT OF PICTOU
EGERTON
MAXWELTON
Antigonish
NORTH WESTERN DISTRICT
NORTH
EASTERN
DISTRICT
Sydney
Bras d'Or Lakes
SOUTH
DISTRICT
MAN-CHESTER
Guysborough
GUYSBOROUGH
SYDNEY
ST MARY'S
CORNWALLIS
KINGS
Wolfville
HORTON
AYLESFORD
WILMOT
GRANVILLE
ANNAPOLIS
Annapolis Royal
Digby
CLEMENTS
DIGBY
ANNAPOLIS
SHERBROOKE
FALMOUTH
WINDSOR
KEMPT
DOUGLAS
HANTS
RAWDON
TRURO
COLCHESTER
HALIFAX
PRESTON
Halifax
HALIFAX
LUNENBURG
CHESTER
Chester
NEW GERMANY
LUNEN-BURG
Mahone Bay
Lunenburg
La Have
NEW DUBLIN
CLARE
QUEENS
LIVERPOOL
Liverpool
GUYSBOROUGH
Yarmouth
SHELBURNE
SHELBURNE
Shelburne
SOUTH SHORE
ATLANTIC OCEAN
County boundary
Township boundary
0
20
40
60
80 MILES

Nova Scotia

Shore which Howe briefly describes is of a less rugged aspect than much of the Atlantic coast, as his reference to the many seaside farms would suggest. His final traverse of the province from Antigonish to Sherbrooke carries him again over the central hills, here more gradual in rise and fall. This is still mainly wooded land, and, contrary to Howe's prophecy, even the beautiful Lochaber Valley has not been developed into the rich agricultural district which he envisioned. The country of river and forest to Sherbrooke and then east to Guysborough, though it presents no extraordinary features, was probably seen in its worst light by Howe, harassed as he was by its then abominable roads and the soaking downpour through which he had to ride. His eastern trip fortunately ends on no such dismal note, as the prospect of Guysborough pleased him as it does the modern traveller.

In 1828, Nova Scotians still depended heavily on the sea for transport of both goods and people. Many of the early settlers had naturally chosen sites along the 4,000-mile coastline, indented as it is for much of its length by dozens of harbours and hundreds of sheltered coves and inlets, and had developed settlements which looked outward to the sea rather than inward to the wild land behind them, where thick forests and swamps, and all too often rocky terrain, made travel and farming equally laborious. Exceptions to this general pattern of coastal settlement were few, the main one being the Annapolis Valley, a good farming region shut off by the North Mountain from the Bay of Fundy coastline. For many decades the sea continued to be the unobstructed highway for towns, villages, and hamlets which felt no pressing need for land links with other communities, at least for nothing more elaborate than well-marked trails that could be easily followed by a man on foot or on horseback. We need look no further to account for many a rough trail of the 1820s and 1830s, such as the 'post road' so heartily cursed by travellers having to take the coastal route west of Liverpool. Even the town of Lunenburg was a thriving port long before it was linked to Halifax by anything better than a notoriously rough bridle path.

Although the great days of the clipper ships, when Maritimers built and sailed their fast square-riggers to all parts of the globe and made

Canada fourth among ship-owning countries of the world, were yet to come, even in 1828 sailing packets were running along the Nova Scotian coast and farther afield to neighbouring provinces, to the United States, Bermuda, and the West Indies. Local traffic in freight and passengers was handled by a variety of craft ranging from the inshore fisherman's small sloop to the large coasting schooner. These craft, and small brigs, brigantines, and barques as well, were built in shipyards large and small from one end of the province to the other – at Yarmouth, Wilmot, Pictou, Tatamagouche, River John, La Have, Lunenburg, Shelburne, Liverpool, and numerous other places. Despite what we now think of as their slow pace and despite their dependence upon wind and weather, these sailing vessels could carry heavy cargoes much more readily and cheaply than any land conveyance developed before the coming of the railway. Even the steamboat, which by 1828 was just beginning to attract interest in Nova Scotia, did not seriously jeopardize the dominance of sailing craft until fairly late in the century. In 1828 the only local steamship service challenging sail was that of the *Saint John*, a schooner-rigged as well as steam-propelled vessel which crossed the Bay of Fundy to Digby and Annapolis on a regular schedule. The situation is well summed up by Captain Moorsom: 'The internal trade of the province has not arrived at such a state, as to deserve particular mention; the facility of water carriage round the coast compensates, in great measure, for the want of good communications across the country' (*Letters from Nova Scotia*, p 55). As he testifies, 'clouds of small craft, from petty shallops to schooners of 120 tons, annually emerge from the sequestered inlets, all around the shores of the province ...' (p 60).

It is not surprising, then, that land routes in Nova Scotia were in a relatively early stage of development and that only a few good roads existed when Howe recorded his experiences. In 1828 only two provincial roads, known as the 'Great Roads,' were well enough constructed and surfaced to carry heavy stagecoaches drawn by four horses: the 'Western Road' from Halifax via Windsor to Annapolis (the present route 1), and the 'Eastern Road' from Halifax via Truro to Pictou (much of the present routes 2 and 4). (The 'Northern Road' from Truro to Amherst and New Brunswick had no stage service until 1842.)

A few other sections of roads were fit for small carriages or waggons drawn by one or two horses: from Annapolis through Digby to Yarmouth and, in summer, as far as Shelburne (the present routes 1 and 3); parts of the road from Liverpool to Chester via La Have and Lunenburg (the present 3, 331, and 332); Antigonish to Manchester township and the Straits of Canso (now an unpaved road far off the main highway). Some roads in the immediate vicinity of towns and villages were fit for carriages but they gradually degenerated into rough tracks passable only by horsemen as the built-up areas were left behind. Such was the cross-country road from Windsor to Chester (now route 14) – fairly good for the first nine miles, then degenerating into a stony cart-track on which one struggled with windfalls, tangled roots, and decayed bridges for ten miles, and finally improving from the half-way point until, near Chester, it became a decent carriage road. Nearly impassable stretches could ruin a route which was otherwise practicable for at least a farmer's rough waggon. Such was the sad experience of a man encountered by Moorsom in Liverpool. This farmer had driven a horse and cart to Liverpool from Horton, following the road from Windsor to Chester and then westward along the South Shore. After he had sold his cartload of cheeses, he could not face the bone-jolting return journey over the same road, but astutely sold his cart, saddled his horse, and rode back to Horton over the bridle path to Nictaux (now route 10).

Even the Great Roads left much to be desired in unfavourable seasons. During the summer months they were usually in good enough condition to be compared favourably with the better secondary roads of England, and in winter they were often smooth highways for the sleighs that replaced the carriages of summer. At other seasons, however, particularly during the long Nova Scotian spring, their low-lying stretches frequently became morasses of rutted mud. As late as the 1840s, by which time roads and coach service had been much improved, a Great Road could degenerate into a quagmire in the month of April. Colonel Sleigh, in *Pine Forests and Hacmatack Clearings* (1852), gives a graphic account of his trials on such a stretch of road outside Halifax on the way to Windsor. The heavy coach in which he was riding plunged so violently into the muddy ruts that the thick leather straps supporting it gave way, the coach overturned, and the trapped passengers had to be pulled through the window. A pole was inserted in place of the broken straps and the coach drove on – but only a short distance. Again it broke down, this time beyond repair, and the shaken travellers were forced to plod five miles through rain and mud to reach the next stage.

Once off the Great Roads and those portions of secondary roads which were fit for carriages or waggons, a traveller in 1828 went on horseback or on foot. There were many such routes in the province. Some were well-trodden bridle paths following old Indian trails or the paths of early settlers and soldiers; others were 'new cuts,' cleared swathes through the forest in which the trees had been cut down and thrown to the side, leaving the stumps to threaten horses' feet until enough time had passed for roots and stumps to rot and be cleared away.

The Truro-Amherst road (now not a complete route), though even in 1828 styled the 'great Northern road,' could not live up to its grand title until the 1840s, when its troublesome eighteen-mile stretch over the Cobequid Mountains was at last made passable for two horses abreast, pulling a light coach. It ran through Onslow (the present route 2) and Londonderry, and then turned inland, pursuing, according to Moorsom, 'an extremely hilly and ill-constructed course for eighteen miles' over the Cobequid Mountains before it resumed a more even line through heavy forests to River Philip and Amherst. Travellers to Amherst avoided it whenever possible by taking the ferry from Windsor to Parrsboro and then the shorter and less hilly route from Parrsboro to Amherst.

In the eastern part of the province the principal or 'post' road led from Pictou by way of Arisaig to Antigonish and then through Manchester township to the Straits of Canso. As has been noted, this was the only road beyond Pictou fit for wheeled vehicles. The coast road from Antigonish through Pomquet and Tracadie to the Straits (now a dirt road) was of a very different order, being described by Moorsom as 'an infamous track covered with rocks and loose stones.' Also from Antigonish horse-trails ran to Sherbrooke and St Mary's (now route 7), to Country Harbour (now route 316), and to Cape

George (now route 337), trails which at their worst widened into the infamous 'new cuts.' The present Eastern Shore route (7) did not exist, but there was an interior trail from Dartmouth through the Musquodoboits to the St Mary's River (now incomplete), a route which Moorsom characterizes as alternating between being 'a rough horse-path' and a 'new cut.' Howe also found it 'miserable enough': 'The only pleasant reflection the road afforded was that every step brought you nearer to the end of it. I could not think or even dream, for the roughness of the path kept me constantly on the watch to guard my own neck and also that of my horse – and at almost every hundred yards I had to alight to wade through a puddle or lead the beast around a windfall' (Letter to his wife, September 1833). Moorsom's description of the 'new cuts' which he encountered frequently in the undeveloped parts of eastern Nova Scotia makes clear that they were worse than the narrower horse-paths:

My evil stars led me over those lines which for great part of their course had been formed only a few months previous. The forest trees had been cut down, and the trunks piled on each side so as to form an avenue of about thirty feet in width. Stumps and tangled roots were left as nature had given them growth, amid stones, or masses of half-decayed vegetable matter; to which occasionally a profusion of brushwood, or a treacherous slough, afforded some variety. From five to ten or a dozen miles may be passed in this manner, without meeting any signs of habitation ... (pp 338-9)

West and south-west of Halifax, in addition to the Windsor-Chester road and the bridle path from the South Shore to Nictaux already mentioned, a coastal road of very uneven quality ran from the capital along the South Shore through Chester, Lunenburg, La Have, and Liverpool to Shelburne (the present routes 3, 332, 331) and onwards to Yarmouth to merge with the Western Road. The section from Halifax to Chester was denounced by Moorsom as a 'miserable horse-path' full of rocks and morasses. Howe's testimony is similar: 'From the head of Margaret's Bay till you get within five or six miles of Chester the road is nothing better than a cow path – in some places scarcely so passable as some of the sheepwalks upon the Island – and in others you have to ride along the beach' (letter to his wife, 1830). It was so bad that many travellers preferred to add forty miles to their journey by going all the way to Windsor and across country again to Chester rather than attempt the direct shore route. From Mahone Bay to Liverpool the road became much better, although in 1828 rough enough in places to damage waggon springs and wheels. From Liverpool to Shelburne it degenerated into a track which all travellers who went that way denounced; even the normally patient Moorsom singled it out for particularly acid comment:

> The line of route from Shelburne to Liverpool bears the palm of vileness from all 'post-roads' I ever saw, except one. The natives described this to be the 'post-road to Halifax'; I was therefore simple enough to ride my own mare; but any man who has a regard for his cattle would never trust his own cow upon such paths. Being in company with three or four others, we marched in Indian file, each taking the lead by turns as a wider space in the path admitted his passing to the front: this arrangement was but fair play for the horses. The passage of so formidable a cavalcade attracted hosts of mosquitoes and other winged plagues of Nova Scotia, who came buzzing about our ears to the tune of 'what can the matter be', and seemed so well satisfied with the replies they extracted from the carcase of the leading horse, that those following were but little troubled with their inquiries ... To wander a little from such a path as that we have been upon is surely excusable: in this instance, however, such wandering brings its own punishment, there being on both sides a deep bog, into which a horse, if once plunged, would run no small risk of remaining till doomsday; while, by carefully keeping the middle of the track, I was assured, by way of consolation, my horse would not sink above his knees. (pp 284-6)

Other routes in the western part of the province were merely forest trails linking the Atlantic seaboard with settlements in the Annapolis Valley: one could ride a horse from either Liverpool or the La Have-Lunenburg area to Annapolis or to Nictaux, as Moorsom's farmer had done. Elsewhere some of the commonly used horse trails were those which led from Windsor to Shubenacadie (now partly route 14, partly a dirt road), from Onslow to Tatamagouche (possibly the present dirt road), and from Halifax via the Musquodoboits to Pictou (now a dirt road beyond Newton Mills).

Two other hazards for travellers remain to be mentioned – the wooden bridge and the 'corduroy' road. In a province so interlaced with rivers and streams as Nova Scotia, bridges were of necessity numerous. To build them of stone was normally out of the question; wood, the material closest to hand, had to suffice. They were perfectly adequate for a few years until they rotted and had to be repaired or replaced. As not nearly enough money was available for this purpose, travellers in the 1820s and 1830s frequently complained about decrepit and even impassable bridges. Haliburton's Sam Slick is reminded of one of his yarns when his fast-stepping horse takes a bridge too incautiously: 'There goes one of them are everlastin rottin poles in that bridge; they are no better than a trap for a critter's leg' (*The Clockmaker* I, chapter 20). Captain Moorsom complains of a decaying bridge near Annapolis: 'one on the outskirts of this town was very nearly the occasion of your being deprived of an invaluable correspondent, whose precious person ran no small risk of being engulphed, while "threading the needle" in the dark, between some dozen fractures that yawned in every plank, like traps to catch the unwary' (p 247). Even Howe, who is much less given to complaining about the roads of a young and sparsely populated country than were British visitors or temporary residents, tells in a letter of his horse being injured by falling through a rotten bridge near Musquodoboit and, in the *Rambles*, cannot smother his indignation when he finds a bridge over the French River impassable on foot or on horseback, and has to cool his heels waiting for a scow to ferry him across the fifty yards to the other side.

Everyone at all acquainted with the history of pioneering on this continent has heard of the 'corduroy' road, a surface of logs placed side by side across the road to enable wheeled vehicles to pass over swampy ground without getting stuck in the mire. By 1828 there seem to have been no such sections on the 'Great Roads' of Nova Scotia, and indeed no considerable number on the lesser roads. Certainly execrations upon them are much less frequent than in the travel literature of early Ontario, where they were a mixed blessing hardly appreciated by travellers. Perhaps corduroy strips turned up more frequently a little later when road-builders tried to improve swampy portions of 'new cuts.' Moorsom does mention them, however, and explains their deficiencies in his usual florid style: 'the wheels, jolting over the interstices, beat hollow the vilest French diligence over the vilest *pavée* of France. However well the interstices may be filled with gravel, the wear and tear soon carries it down below, and the corduroys remain in their pristine simplicity, alike insensible to the maledictions of all impatient travellers, and to the furious assault of their waggon-wheels' (p 246).

This relatively primitive road system is hardly to be wondered at, however strange it may seem to a generation accustomed to swift travel over smoothly paved roads which defy such acts of nature as the once-dreaded spring thaw. In the early nineteenth century, Nova Scotia was a young province with a history of widespread settlement dating back only a few decades. A sparse population in a country crisscrossed by rivers and streams, dotted with ponds, lakes, and swamps, with sea coasts rocky and incessantly indented and an interior heavily forested could perhaps have done little better even if the sea had not offered an alternate way. Moreover, it is well to remember that good roads were very late to appear even in highly developed European countries. In England road-building was haphazard before 1750, and even in the last decades of the century had not greatly improved. In 1770 Arthur Young, describing his tour of northern England, complains frequently and sharply of turnpikes that were 'a scandal to the country,' 'infamously stony,' or 'cut into ruts that threaten to swallow one up.' It was not until the beginning of the nineteenth century that good roads became a really serious concern of government and people in England. Even then, and indeed until the end of the coach-era in the 1840s, Englishmen complained about the condition of British roads and unflatteringly compared them with the roads of Holland and Switzerland, despite the obvious success of such great nineteenth-century road-makers as Thomas Telford and John Macadam in creating thousands of miles of durable and well-surfaced highways. At any rate, what the mother country had only recently accomplished would hardly be duplicated by a raw colonial society, a fact fully appreciated by British travellers in the province in the same breath as they complained of the hardships of colonial land travel.

The progress of road-making was naturally impeded as well by forces other than those imposed by intractable nature in a new country. Fault can easily be found now, and was found then, with the whole system of road construction and maintenance before 1850. The main faults seem to have been in the institution of statute labour, the system of local road commissioners, and the Assembly's handling of grants.

According to a provincial statute, every able-bodied man was required to work a specified time on the roads each year (six days, or four days if he supplied a team as well as his own labour). Many a settler, however, so begrudged the time thus lost to his own work that he did as little as possible. A man could avoid roadwork entirely by paying four shillings for each day required of him and so deplete an already insufficient work force without contributing much to the provincial treasury. Even more inadequate was the lack of any distinction between the large and small landowner: the man whose property bordered the road for a mile or two was required to do or pay no more than his neighbour with a frontage of a hundred yards. Worst of all, the statute exempted absentee landlords from both work and pay. Taken all together, and compounded by the presence of extensive land grants lying unsettled for decades, these provisions inevitably resulted in many roads or sections of roads being entirely deprived of statute labour.

Local road commissioners were appointed each spring, one for each small stretch of road. Many of them knew nothing about efficient ways of building or repairing roads, and, since their appointments were for one year only, even the zealous among them no sooner had acquired some knowledge than they were likely to be replaced by new men. The system was made even more inefficient by the actual conditions of road use. Wherever coaches, waggons, or carriages were driven over muddy roads, the narrow wheels cut into the surface and left a series of ruts which gradually deepened and spread from ditch to ditch as drivers made new ruts in trying to avoid the old ones. The commissioners, who were appointed in May, might manage in late May and in June to repair the rutted surfaces left from the spring thaws of March and April and make the roads passably good for summer traffic. But by November the roads would be cut up once more and not attended to until the next May. By April they would be at their worst again, with no money left even to fill gaping holes. Clearly they went untouched at the very times (spring and late autumn) when they needed repair most urgently.

Finally, the Assembly as a body showed no clear grasp of the need for a better system and apparently allowed political considerations and patronage to outweigh common sense. It was urged, to no avail, by critics, indeed by provincial governors, to spend its road allocation more wisely – specifically, to stop dribbling away thousands of pounds in numerous small grants which produced hardly discernible results, and to appoint at least some supervisors who knew how to repair roads.

The annual grants for roads could certainly have produced better results, but one wonders how much improvement there could have been in the circumstances. Probably a massive expenditure of money would have been necessary to make even the Great Roads excellent highways in the muddy seasons. The annual allocation for roads in 1828 was £15,000, a sum which increased to £22,000 in 1829 and £25,000 in 1830 and 1831. Before 1828 it had been £12,000 for a number of years; after 1831 it held steady at around £20,000 for several years, then was halved from 1835 to 1838. These were considerable sums for the times. It is chastening to note, moreover, before one utterly condemns either the parsimony of the government or the inefficiency of the system, that in England at the time the cost of three miles of a Telford road was about £10,000. In short, the whole Nova Scotian grant for 1830, at English rates for material and labour, would have produced no more than some eight miles of first-class highway.

Travel by stagecoach, which in England had begun in the seventeenth century but had entered upon its heyday only when good roads had become common in the early nineteenth century, was naturally impossible in Nova Scotia for many decades. In 1816 two enterprising men decided to set up stage services on the two Great Roads. First in the field was Isaiah Smith, who equipped himself with coaches, sleighs, and horses for the Halifax-Windsor run even before he had been granted the sum of £100 for which he had petitioned the Assembly. His first coach left Halifax on 14 February, with room for six passengers at a fare of one pound ten shillings each. Smith's horses averaged five miles an hour, covering the forty-five miles in nine hours. This was a weekly service, but in May, as the roads improved and more travellers appeared, Smith began a bi-weekly schedule.

A second stage service was begun by Ezra Witter in the same year from Halifax to Pictou. Witter's first coach left Halifax on 1 July. His service was weekly and slower than Smith's, as it took two days for him to make the 100-mile trip. His one-horse coach was also smaller, being either a simple four-wheeled carriage or a waggon. As the Pictou line attracted fewer passengers than the stage to Windsor, Witter was probably forced to use simple equipment accommodating perhaps two passengers and certainly not more than four.

It should be noted that both Smith and Witter were actually running mail coaches with accommodation for passengers, and also that these early vehicles were a far cry from the colourful Royal Mail coaches that were by this time rolling along the turnpikes of England at ten miles per hour. Even Smith's coaches, which were soon carrying eight passengers each, could not have been much like the lordly Dickensian masters of the road which come to mind when one thinks of the coaching days as romanticized by so many British writers.

Witter's coaches kept running to Pictou and back through the 1820s. On the Halifax-Windsor line, Isaiah Smith remained in business in spite of a competing service being started in 1825 by a Mr Todd. But in 1828 both Smith and Todd were over-shadowed by the formation of the Western Stage Coach Company, which gained an Assembly grant and established a regular line from Halifax via Windsor to Annapolis Royal, extending the scope of the old service by some eighty-five miles. The new line sent its first coach drawn by four horses out of Halifax on 3 June 1828, to initiate what was to be a tri-weekly service at a fare of £2/10s per passenger. Since this was the coach line that carried Howe as far as Annapolis on his 'western rambles,' its exact schedule is of particular interest: the coach left Halifax at 5:00 AM, reached Windsor at 12:00 noon, left Windsor at 1:00 PM, and reached Kentville at 6:00 PM. Travellers going to Annapolis spent the night in Kentville and left at 5:00 the next morning; they reached Bridgetown at 1:00 PM, left Bridgetown at 2:00 PM and arrived in Annapolis at 4:00 PM. The average speed on the road, taking into account the brief stops for changing horses and the longer stops for meals, was a little over six-

and-a-half miles an hour for the 130-mile trip. It appears that the well-established stretch of road from Halifax to Windsor was in considerably better condition than the road from Windsor to Bridgetown, for the schedule allows for decreased speed on the Valley section of the line – except on the fifteen-mile stretch from Bridgetown to Annapolis, where the average speed rose again to seven-and-a-half miles per hour.[2]

A year later, in 1829, service on the eastern line to Pictou was also improved. A proferred grant by the Assembly was taken up by the newly-formed Eastern Stage Coach Company, which established a bi-weekly four-horse coach service from Halifax to Truro and a similar service, but with two horses, from Truro to Pictou. The schedule was thirteen hours from Halifax to Truro, and eight hours from Truro to Pictou (a total elapsed time of thirty-five hours, including an overnight stop at Truro). The coach left Halifax at 6:00 AM and reached Truro at 7:00 PM on the same day; after an overnight stop, it left Truro at 9:00 the next morning and reached Pictou at 5:00 PM. The average speeds of these coaches, slightly under 6 miles per hour for the 64 miles to Truro and five-and-a-half miles per hour for the 38 miles from Truro to Pictou, suggest that the Great Eastern road was not quite as good as the Great Western.

As ridiculously low as these average speeds appear now, they were not at all bad for a new service over what in England would have been no better than good secondary roads. The average rate of seven-and-a-half miles per hour attained on parts of the Western line should be compared to the average of ten miles per hour that was normal for the fastest lines in England at the height of coaching; indeed, the English mail coaches were by law forbidden to exceed that speed. As an historian of English coaching points out, a galloping team of coach horses could go faster than horses moving at the normal trot, but the increase was only to thirteen miles an hour, and they could maintain that higher speed for only four miles. Consequently the horses were driven at a

2 The average speeds were approximately 7 1/2 mph from Halifax to Windsor, 5 1/2 mph from Windsor to Kentville, 6 mph from Kentville to Bridgetown, and 7 1/2 mph from Bridgetown to Annapolis.

trot, except when steep hills slowed them to a walk or when a particularly smooth and straight stretch of road tempted the coachman to enjoy a short gallop. The more leisurely pace of the Nova Scotian coaches may be attributed not only to the inferior roads but also to the absence of the heavy traffic and consequent sharp competition among owners of stagecoach lines that was so evident in England, to the considerably longer stages of the colonial system, and perhaps even to poorer horses.

In Nova Scotia, the stages – that is, the sections of road covered by one team before another team was substituted – seem to have averaged about fifteen miles in length, in contrast to the ten-mile stages of England. They were shorter if a particular stage was very rough or hilly, and longer over level terrain and good roads. The Western line to Windsor, for example, was divided into three stages, and as the distance was forty-five miles, the average length of stages was exactly fifteen miles. Actually, however, the first stage (Halifax to Hiltz's Inn) was twenty-one miles long, much too great a distance for horses to be kept at a steady trot as they were over the ten-mile stages of England. Over such long stages an average speed of seven miles per hour would be all that the horses could possibly maintain without becoming exhausted miles before they reached the next stage. If one wonders why ten-mile stages were not therefore instituted so that the service would be much faster, the answer is simply that the trade could not bear the expense. Five stages to Windsor would have added so much additional outlay in horses, stablemen, and equipment that the coach line, in these early days always in financial difficulties and dependent upon government grants and mail contracts to supplement income from passenger fares, would have been forced out of business. A system that was profitable and highly competitive in densely populated England could not possibly have been feasible in Nova Scotia at the time.

At each changing place there would be a stable with attendants and usually dining facilities for the passengers. The changing places which were also regularly scheduled stops for meals – on the Western line, Hiltz's Inn where the passengers had breakfast, Mrs Wilcox's inn at Windsor where the coach stopped for dinner, Mrs Fuller's inn at Kentville where the evening meal awaited travellers, and another dinner-stop at Bridgetown which Howe does not name – these especially must have benefited from the coaching trade.

The coaches used on the two routes at the time of Howe's excursions are not clearly described by Howe or other travellers. From the bits of available evidence, however, one can assemble a picture that is probably close to the reality. Captain Moorsom observes to his British readers that a coach of the Western Stage Coach Company was hardly a counterpart of the Oxford *Regulator* or the Cambridge *Times*, two examples of the fast but heavy public stagecoaches running in England in the 1820s, the decade when coaching reached its peak. He adds, 'It resembles rather the light vans of the Isle of Wight, with canvass awning for wet weather' (p 213). From this remark we might assume that he is describing a roofless vehicle equipped with some kind of canvas frame that could be raised and collapsed. That he can mean nothing of the kind becomes clear when we note what Howe has to say about the Western coach. He tells us that he rode on the 'Stage top' from Halifax to Horton and refers to setting his foot 'more firmly upon the dickey' (that is, on the back of the coachman's seat) while he dashes his 'clenched fist on the top of the coach, to the terror and amazement of the insiders.' Moreover, when later explaining why the Western stage has been so much more successful than the Eastern, he remarks that the students at King's College in Windsor are frequently visited by friends and relatives from Halifax bearing gifts, 'bundles of boots, breeches, hats, shirts, pound cake ...,' which are loaded on top of the coach. The coach, then, must have had a solid wooden roof strongly supported by pillars or by the coach body. The 'canvass awning for wet weather' mentioned by Moorsom would seem to refer to window awnings or curtains. Probably the coach had a solid front and back but open sides from about the level of the seats to the roof, with side curtains rolled horizontally along the roof-edge. In cool or wet weather they could be let down and secured. Such a coach would indeed have had a lighter body than the usual English stagecoach, which had solid sides broken only by a small window in each side door. The Eastern coaches, however, were apparently more primitive, for Howe wishes that the company could get a higher legislative grant in order to buy 'a better class of vehicles'; he also complains that there was 'no back to the front seat of the waggon.' The very word 'waggon,' which he never applies to the coaches of the Western line, speaks for itself.

Like most stagecoaches in England, those on the Western line and the Halifax-Truro run were 'four in hand' – that is, drawn by teams of four horses. The coaches on the less busy run from Truro to Pictou apparently required only two-horse teams, at least most of the time. As for capacity, it is likely that the Western coach carried seven or eight 'insiders,' the Eastern coach perhaps six. Apparently the passengers occupied two coach-width seats as in first-class British railway carriages, and faced each other, those occupying the front seat having their backs to the horses. A third or middle seat, which certainly was standard in the coaches of the 1840s, was probably not built into this earlier coach. Judging from Howe's remarks, one gathers that, at least on the Western coach, there was also a roof seat outside, just behind the coachman's box, from which lordly perch Howe surveyed the passing countryside. Although the Western Stage Coach Company declared in its advertisement that its coaches were 'easy and commodious,' it is likely that the passengers sometimes disagreed with the first term. In these days before steel springs, the coach body was supported and cushioned by the thorough-braces, long and thick belts of tanned hide made up of multiple layers riveted together. These heavy leather 'springs' extended from front to rear on each side and supported the body of the coach above the axles. While the thorough-braces absorbed shocks and bumps fairly well, they created a less dangerous but nevertheless unpleasant side effect, a series of oscillations all too likely to have dire effects upon passengers with queasy stomachs. When the horses were allowed to break into a wild downhill gallop, the gyrations of the coach can be imagined. Howe's alarm at such a breakneck dash down the Horton mountains should not be ascribed to timidity.

The inns of the young province were as varied in quality as its roads. In the towns and larger villages on the coach lines, such as Windsor, Kentville, Annapolis Royal, and Truro, efficient inn-keepers served travellers good meals and offered overnight guests comfortable rooms. Howe's testimonies are echoed by other travellers of the period. The inns of Mrs Wilcox at Windsor, Mrs Fuller at Kentville, and Mrs Davis at Annapolis Royal are commonly praised for their good food, attentive service, and comfortable bedrooms. Howe also remarks that Fultz's near Bedford is well-known for its meals and that Blanchard's at Truro offers 'a bounteous board, handsome accommodation, and a pleasant Veranda,' but adds that such comforts 'are not always to be expected in travelling in the interior of a new country like this.' Moorsom finds a few excellent inns even in smaller settlements, mentioning specifically those at Petite Riviere and Mahone Bay, but generally country inns were much less dependable. Their proprietors were usually farmers who catered to travellers in order to supplement the income of their farms; the inns themselves were usually farmhouses or cottages. Howe is pleasantly surprised when one such inn on the Stewiacke River serves not the expected ham and eggs or broiled fowl or veal cutlets, but delicious fresh salmon. Too often the bill of fare in country inns consisted, according to Moorsom, of 'sinewy hens and hard bacon' which only the strenuous exercise of riding over bad trails could render palatable and digestible. It was Moorsom's misfortune to spend the night at perhaps the worst in the province when he was travelling in the undeveloped Guysborough region. The house was a shabby one-storey cottage with broken window-panes, the innkeeper an unshaven and sinister-looking backwoodsman, the main dish broiled salt mackarel and potatoes, and the captain's bed-chamber a draft-swept cell with a filthy truck-bed for his slumbers. Such places were probably uncommon. One was much more likely in country districts to come upon 'brown sugar houses,' second-rate inns which unconsciously symbolized their inferiority by serving brown sugar rather than the white loaf-sugar found as a matter of course in good inns. The term served handily as a rating device among Nova Scotian travellers, for a 'brown sugar house' would usually be mediocre in all ways. Lowest on the scale, and only rarely encountered, were the houses which served no sugar at all, only molasses.

One characteristic of the country inns was commonly remarked upon by English travellers – the independent attitude and familiarity of the innkeeper. As Moorsom explains, this person was 'a very different being from his accomplished prototype in England':

I know of no occasion more likely to arouse the choler of an aristocratic Englishman than his arrival at one of these inns, before he has become acquainted with the character of the country. The last crack of the whip, which, in England, places, as if by magic, a stable-boy at the head of each leader and a waiter at the door, here dies away unheeded in an echo among the woods. He looks round with surprise – surmises that he may have mistaken the house – descends to inquire. By this time, a countryman makes his appearance from the field, announces that the host will 'be here after fixing the next load', and coolly begins to unharness. *Milord Anglais* may walk in if he pleases, – for though there is no one to invite, there is no one to forbid his entrance: a neat little parlour will then receive him; perhaps even the 'mistress' will be sufficiently on the alert to perform the office of introduction in person. Woe betide him if any symptoms of dissatisfaction or *hauteur* express themselves! If he has the address to conceal his impatience, – to open the heart of the good lady by a few civil inquiries, – all will be well; his wishes will be attended to with all the ability in her power; but if the costume of Boniface from the hayfield shock his sensibility; if his pride takes offence at the *nonchalance* and the familiar style of conversation opened by his host in the shape of question and answer, – adieu to his expectations of attention and speedy refreshment ... (pp 248-9)

T.C. Haliburton also remarks on the same subject, defending Nova Scotians against what was apparently a common misreading of their motives:

The people are accounted civil in their manners, and hospitable. This liberal feeling has had its effect on the Inns, which in very few instances afford a subsistence, without the aid of agriculture. Most Innkeepers, therefore, in the country are farmers, and the entertainment or accommodation of the public is not their occupation, but one of their resources. From this [liberal] feeling, so creditable to the country, [comes the charge that] though the roads are good the inns are indifferent, which circumstance, as the cause is not obvious to strangers, is often unjustly attributed to the ignorance and poverty of the people, or to a republican spirit of levelling, which prompts the landlord to consider the ordinary attendance upon his guests as beneath the dignity of a free man. (*Historical and Statistical Account of Nova Scotia* II, pp 294-5)

The attitude of Moorsom's 'aristocratic Englishman' was of course very different from that of the native-born Howe, who accepts the casualness of country innkeepers as normal and obviously plays the game of guest and host according to provincial rules. Indeed, the sketches are strongly marked by the author's identification with the people he encounters, by his sense of pride in the province, and by his constant awareness that he is writing primarily for Nova Scotians. Here is no observer from an older and richer civilization naturally comparing what he sees with what he has left at home and just as naturally finding it wanting or, while knowing that in all fairness he cannot pit the stripling against the mature man, nevertheless allowing condescension to creep into his tone. At times Howe sounds as if he were deliberately righting the balance, for critical though he is of some aspects of provincial life, he passes over many a rocky road in silence, so to speak, and finds much to praise. He enjoys with hearty grace the simple fare of a country inn, observing that only the fastidious traveller would complain of 'a clean bed, a good cup of tea, a hot johnny cake, and excellent butter, with perhaps a saucer of preserves.' He even half-seriously dons rose-tinted glasses now and then, as when Horton becomes an Arcadia where nature and man – especially woman – blend in a vision of beauty. Warm hospitality seems to encompass him wherever he goes. If he meets unpleasant people, we do not hear of it: the good people of Bridgetown, he tells us, are completely free of the vain airs, 'the ludicrous assumption of dignity and importance,' which 'have been laid to the charge of some of our western villages,' but we recall that he had not mentioned encountering such pompous people in the other Valley towns. Even Windsor, that country-seat of would-be aristocracy, gets no more censure than is carried by such offhand and reported remarks as that above or by a passing reference to current stories of the Windsorians' 'inhospitality and pride' – stories which Howe does not repeat, having no inclination 'to paint people worse than we find them.' The harsh party spirit of Pictonians, he reflects, may lead the visitor to fear that he can expect no warmth from them, but Howe finds that such fears are groundless, for 'if he be disposed to accept the civilities of the people in the same spirit of frankness in which they are proferred,' all doors are open to him. So goes Howe through the province, a man whose warm appreciation and optimistic propensity to see the best side of everything doubtless drew a similar response from others. It is noteworthy that the letters to his wife, though of course not, like the sketches, built upon the complementary themes of pride in provincial virtues and criticism of forces undermining those virtues, are also generous in spirit and never cheaply critical of persons or places. By nature he seems to have been perfectly suited to the task of revealing to Nova Scotians why they should take pride in their province.

Howe's sketches of Nova Scotia reveal considerably more of their author's distinctive qualities than do his correctly conventional poetry or even his magnificent speeches. The medium of the travel sketch naturally accounts in part for the increased intimacy, as the familiar essay, the form in which he writes, places less distance between speaker and audience than Howe's other forms of public utterance – specifically the heroic verse couplet of his most ambitious poems and the conventions of the classical oration upon which he built his speeches. The poetry of the period written in the Maritimes so strictly adhered to conventional modes of style and thought that it is characterized by a bland anonymity. Howe's verse suffers from the same fault: it is more competently written than most of the verse turned out by the numerous provincial bards of the day, but it bears no individual stamp. The pervasive weaknesses identified by Fred Cogswell in *Literary History of Canada* – 'impersonality' and 'sameness of expression ... joined to a sameness of attitude and theme' – limit Howe as a poet; the qualities which made him an outstanding person are not mirrored in his verse.

When they turned to prose, and especially to the more informal kinds, even writers of modest talents spoke more characteristically in their own voices. Thus two writers of travel sketches covering much the same ground would be expected to produce very different accounts. The point is well illustrated by a comparison of Howe's *Rambles* and Moorsom's *Letters from Nova Scotia.* Captain Moorsom reveals that, despite his good intentions, his considerable common sense, and his genuine knowledge of the province, he was somewhat of a military dandy, larding his pretentious and sometimes pompous prose with bits of French and Latin, and frequently affecting an air of amused but kindly tolerance. His attitude is not as condescending as one might expect, but it is basically that of a self-assured young aristocrat who had passed through Sandhurst and whose father was an admiral. 'I love to stroll around the neighbourhood wherever I am quartered,' he confides to the reader, '– to enter the dwellings of those who form the mass of the people; to converse with them upon all their little daily concerns, and draw them out upon their petty topics of importance' (p 8). Howe's sketches reveal just as clearly some of the distinctive characteristics of their author. They are discursive in structure and vary in tone from the intimate to the elevated, drawing the reader into fellowship with an amiable and hearty conversationalist who seldom stands upon ceremony or holds back from taking the listener into his confidence. Neither Moorsom nor Howe is above the desire to impress his audience, but each does so in a characteristic way. The young soldier presents himself as a man of mode at ease in the fashionable world, revealing with studied nonchalance the marks of the gentleman – superficially in the bits of schoolboy Ovid and drawing-room French, and more profoundly by his pervasive air of superiority. The young editor likes to parade his familiarity with literature and history by numerous quotations and allusions, as if to demonstrate that he has more than overcome his lack of formal schooling. However, Howe's little display of vanity, if it can be called that, becomes valid as an integral part of his expression: his quotations are aptly chosen to illuminate his thought, unlike the tags of Moorsom which at best merely embellish in the dubious manner of affectations. It is clear too that Howe is much more the conscious literary artist in a wider sense: his sketches combine description and reflection while holding to the framework of a journey that itself is composed of selected elements of many actual journeys. This is particularly true of *Eastern Rambles*, which is based upon repeated trips to eastern Nova Scotia.

Above all, Howe's sketches demonstrate how the prevailing concepts of a literary culture can find root in and help to form what was no doubt fundamentally an imaginative and even poetic temperament. His response to external nature, though encouraged and nourished by his reading of pre-Romantic and Romantic poets, appears to be no mere parroting of current intellectual fashion but as natural to him as breathing. In comparison, Moorsom observes but is unmoved by the beauties of nature. Though no doubt he was much inferior to Howe in his knowledge of contemporary literature, he also seems temperamentally immune to the imaginative and meditative appeal of nature. All that Moorsom has to say about the Nictaux Falls (near Middleton), which he describes as 'the principal cascade yet discovered in Nova Scotia,' is that it is 'a mere pailful of water thrown over a rocky barrier about twenty feet in height' – a description hardly to be surpassed for matter-of-factness. To Howe a similar scene, that of the Kentville Falls, is 'romantic and lovely,' infused with 'a wildness and singularity ... that nothing can surpass.' He wishes that he could 'linger around it for hours, to give full current to the feelings which it engenders,' and he imagines it as the retreat of a hermit whose 'evening hymn might mingle with the falling waters, and his knee bend in adoration of him whose power and beauty were ever before his eyes.' Howe expresses the usual regret that such Nova Scotian scenes unfortunately lack the Old World enrichment of historical or legendary associations, but he can readily imagine the Falls as a setting for romantic moments in Scott's *Rob Roy*. Just as sharply contrasting are the two writers' descriptions of the view from the Horton Mountains. This, says Moorsom, is 'the finest view in Nova Scotia,' and he proceeds systematically to catalogue what may be seen from the eminence – the 'rich valley of the Gaspereau River studded with farms,' the 'large masses of forests hanging on the hills,' the level farmland of Cornwallis, and Cape Blomidon 'boldly uprearing its cliffs against the turbulent tide-waves of the Basin of Mines.' Again Howe is not merely impressed by the beauty of the scene but is deeply moved to exclaim 'This is my own, my native land' and to advise his readers to 'indulge the feeling ... and don't be ashamed of it.' Moorsom quickly passes on from his brief notice of the landscape to the mundane matter of distances between settlements and the absence of useful milestones. Howe takes the reader to the deep ravine of the Gaspereau River, impresses upon him the sublimity of the place and the insignificance of man 'surrounded by the awful handicraft of the Diety,' and significantly reveals how his attitude to nature has been influenced, perhaps formed, by literary associations: 'You bethink you of all the sublime passages which you have heard or read, and pant for language to display the images which the wild sublimity of the scene has impressed upon your soul.' Although the terms used by three generations of landscape poets are also part of Moorsom's vocabulary, they seem to be dropped casually into his sketch of a scene and never confirmed by any personal reaction. Howe seems incapable of such detachment: 'nature, wild, unsophisticated and sublime' never fails to move him to rapturous prose in which the whole gamut of Romantic wonder is expressed. The ardent temperament that was so obvious to his contemporaries and so frequently evident in his later public life is well exemplified in many such passages in the *Rambles*. Evidence that these passages are not mere literary posturing in a fashionable mode is afforded by his letters, in which, for example, one finds him remarking to his wife that 'truth – and religion – and philosophy – pass into the heart from the constant communicating with nature.'

The sketches help us to see Howe more clearly in another way too: they give more definite clues to the nature of his education than his published verse or even his speeches. That Howe was an 'educated' man is obvious. It is true, of course, that he attended school only sporadically, that he went to work in 1818 at the age of thirteen, and that, unlike T.C. Haliburton, he never attended a university. Yet the judgment of Colonel Sleigh, pronounced in 1853, is far from the mark: 'In ... Howe we recognize considerable native talent, which would have shone more resplendently, had early education refined the thought and speech, and taught that elegance of expression and gentlemanly suavity of manners are more valuable in a public man than rude and reckless sarcasm.' Sleigh's remark, however much moved by political antagonism, is not only snobbishly condescending but basically misleading as well. Howe indeed on more than one occasion, and even in the House of Assembly, used earthy language that his more staid compatriots (and especially his political rivals) considered coarse and vulgar. But in both thought and speech he could be as refined and elegant, when he chose, as his conventionally educated friend Haliburton. By 'early education' Sleigh means the drilling in Latin language and literature which took up most of the schoolboy's time. The truth is not that Howe had no early education, but rather that it was of a different kind. His father, John Howe, played the role of schoolmaster as well as adviser in all things for his son. So effective was the father's influence in forming and encouraging his son's fondness for reading that Joseph Howe, aided by the tremendous energy that characterized all his activities, reached through self-education a remarkably high level of literacy and knowledge. He was a voracious reader from childhood on, and at the age of nineteen, he tells us, was regularly spending his evenings, until midnight or later, in reading and writing. Three years later he was apparently concentrating on the reading of poetry, plays, and novels, having neglected them for a period in which he had tried to suppress his strong interest in literature and even to root out his taste for verse-making. By the winter of 1825–6, however, he had given up his three-year 'warfare with the Muses,' as he called it, and was again trying his hand at verse, writing, besides some short pieces, the longer descriptive-narrative poem, 'Melville Island.'

It is a matter of conjecture whether or not Howe's informal and unconventional education developed his natural Romantic temperament more significantly than the usual schooling of the times would have done. At any rate, while other boys were labouring in Latin grammar and slowly working their way through passages of Livy and Caesar, or Vergil and Horace, Howe was reading and digesting book after book in English. We know by his own testimony and by the numerous echoes in his own writing that he became intimately familiar with the King James version of the Bible and with the plays of Shakespeare. Though he did not know Latin (at least up to 1824), he probably knew many of the Greek and Latin classics in English translations (he mentions having read Homer, and asks his wife to send him his two-volume edition of Herodotus, as 'it is dull travelling with nothing to read of a night') and had probably studied classical mythology – much of his own writing suggests this, although it is likely that he would deliberately play down this area of knowledge among his classically educated acquaintances. Above all, he was unusually well read in the poets, essayists, orators, dramatists, and historians of the eighteenth and the earlier nineteenth centuries.

In enlarging one's awareness of Howe's intellectual background, the travel sketches also testify to his powers of retention. If his display of learning had been spuriously based on some pre-Bartlett treasury of quotations, of course nothing would be demonstrated except intellectual charlatanism and skill in choosing and integrating borrowed spoil. The evidence, however, is to the contrary: when quoting from another writer, Howe is much more often slightly inaccurate than accurate. It is obvious that he was drawing upon his remarkable but by no means photographic memory. His frequent errors are exactly those likely to be made in such a recalling of specific passages: prepositions and articles are changed, punctuation slightly altered, synonyms introduced.

Of the writers quoted from or referred to, Shakespeare seems to have been Howe's favourite source of memorable lines. He recalls passages or incidents from several plays and incorporates fragments from others in the tissue of his prose. Of the other Elizabethans, only Spenser turns up, but Howe's quotation, perhaps significantly, is from the deep recesses (book v) of the voluminous *Faerie Queene*. As one would expect, he quotes from *Paradise Lost*; as early as 1827, when writing in *The Acadian*, he had revealed his knowledge of that poem. His breadth of reading in Restoration and eighteenth-century literature is reflected by the number and variety of references – to Pope, Prior, Blair, Smollett, Erasmus Darwin, William Combe, Gray, and Burns; to Sterne; and to Goldsmith, Farquhar, Sheridan, Gay, Colman, and Garrick. The writers of his own time are represented by Coleridge, Byron, Scott, Campbell, Moore, Felicia Hemans, and James Montgomery. Among foreign authors, Howe gives evidence of knowing a minor work by his contemporary Chateaubriand, the major work of the sixteenth-century Italian poet Torquato Tasso, and Cervantes' *Don Quixote*. Though we do not find him quoting in foreign languages, it is well to remember that he could have done so. As early as 1824 he tells his sister Jane that he has acquired a reading knowledge of French to the point of being able to read the 'lighter works' of French writers with 'tolerable ease,' and that he is beginning the study of Spanish.

Such evidence by itself is too random to support many conclusions, but it does tell us something about Howe's interests. Although it seems unlikely that many other Haligonians of 1829 had read Tasso's *Jerusalem Delivered* or even book v of Spenser's *Faerie Queene*, Howe's inquiring mind may not at this period have taken him much beyond the conventional intellectual fare of a well-read but not scholarly man. Perhaps most revealing is his taste in contemporary writers. Sir Walter Scott, who by the mid-1820s enjoyed remarkable popularity and prestige, appears to have been the one Romantic novelist to impress Howe deeply for, besides several references in the sketches to Scott's novels, in the columns of the *Novascotian* one frequently finds him reprinting chapters from the Waverley novels and reviewing them with enthusiasm; moreover, he asks his wife to send him several of Scott's novels when he finds himself on the road without anything to read. That other Romantic luminary, Lord Byron, whose popularity – and notoriety – lasted long after his death in 1824, seems to have been one of Howe's favourites; he had read *Childe Harold's Pilgrimage* and *Don Juan*, and probably many of the other poems. One can only wonder if Howe's reputed inclination to women and wine made him particularly, if surreptitiously, fascinated by the unconventional morality of the Byron of *Don Juan* and, perhaps, by the Rabelaisian earthiness of Sterne's *Tristram Shandy*. It may be that the tension between Howe's undeniable moral idealism and his supposed hedonistic tendencies – if the latter have indeed been rightly ascribed to him – offers a lively problem for the biographer. The *Rambles* in no way clarify or even introduce such a conflict.

Of the other great Romantic poets, only Coleridge is represented in the sketches. The absence of quotations from Wordsworth is surprising, for many lines of that poet's shorter works (*The Prelude* was not published until 1850) would have fitted very aptly into Howe's rhapsodies on nature, but it is clear from a letter of 1830 that he knew Wordsworth's poetry. Shelley too was of some interest to him, for as early as 1828 he reprints 'Stanzas written in dejection, near Naples' in the *Novascotian* and in 1834 extols 'The Cloud' as a 'highly imaginative production' well worth the study of provincial bards. His apparent unawareness of Keats is to be expected, as that poet was not widely read until the mid-1830s, even in England. Two poets who were very popular at the time but were destined to become minor figures in literary history, Thomas Moore and Thomas Campbell, seem to have been Howe's particular favourites. He quotes from Moore several times, and was impressed not only by Moore's songs but also by the long poem *The Loves of the Angels*. A year earlier (1827) he had also written appreciatively of Moore in *The Acadian*, specifically praising *The Loves of the Angels*, *Lalla Rookh*, and *Evenings in Greece*. Although he does not appear to quote from Campbell in the sketches, in *The Acadian* he had highly commended that poet's *Pleasures of Hope* and *Gertrude of Wyoming,* and had even gone so far as to call Campbell 'the greatest of our modern poets,' placing him above Byron in both range and height of achievement. It is clear too that he had a high regard for the more questionable talents of Mrs Felicia Hemans. In *The Acadian* he had twice singled out her poetry for praise and had reprinted 'Edith'; in the sketches, besides quoting from her verse, he calls her 'the dazzling Hemans'; and in the *Novascotian* he frequently chooses a Hemans poem as an example to inspire local writers.

Although nothing short of a thorough examination of all of Howe's pronouncements on literature would be needed to make a definitive statement, perhaps some tentative implications may be drawn from these indications of Howe's taste. First, he seems to have fallen in step with contemporary opinion, which placed Moore and Campbell very high among the poets of the time – an opinion, one should note, held by many literary critics as well as the reading public. Probably, bent on self-improvement, he followed the accepted guides and formed his tastes according to their recommendations. Secondly, in spite of his deep appreciation of Shakespeare, his approval of Mrs Hemans reveals that he was capable of greatly over-estimating tawdry, or at least mediocre, verse. The inconsistency may be easily enough explained by supposing that Howe's aesthetic judgment, like that of many of his generation, could be blinded by noble sentiments, by an authorial sensibility that appealed to shared moral ideals and widely approved emotions – in much the same way as a modern Marxist may grossly overvalue a novelist or poet who follows the party line. Mrs Heman's fame in her day rested on just such a conventional foundation and was probably enhanced by a wholly unliterary consideration that would certainly have moved Howe to admiration: she was a woman of blameless character who, deserted by her husband, wrote verse to support her children. Howe's rhapsodic eulogy of Grieselda Tonge in the 'Western Rambles' comes to mind as a closely related example of sentiment overcoming critical judgment. Judging by her surviving verse, one can hardly be more complimentary than to say that Miss Tonge wrote competently in conventional styles on conventional subjects. But to

Howe she is a female Lycidas, a figure evoking the deepest tones of romantic pathos from the sensitive lover of the muses. Young, beautiful, talented, indeed a paragon of provincial maidenhood, she sailed to fever-ridden Demerara to visit members of her family and there was struck down like 'some sweet flower, whose bloom and fragrance, had it lived, would have cheered and brightened the age.'

Howe reveals the strategy of his sketches in his own half-bantering words: he takes his readers through the province 'admiring the beauties of nature, laughing, crying, and moralizing by turns.' His descriptive writing is skilful and effective, but much of the charm of the sketches lies in the extended and frequent commentary to which a place, person, or scene gives rise. His reflections on nature have already been noticed. As for the 'laughing,' it is often what raises these sketches above the commonplace. Howe has the useful gift of perceiving varieties of human folly without falling a victim to humourless self-unction; his normal tone is lightly ironic, whether he is saying that far too many women degrade themselves in the gossiping round of social chatter, that the Legislature is inept in its allocation of grants for public works, that the fierce party spirit in Pictou is the curse of that place, or that a 'rural bower' at Truro was once the site of a much-frequented still. Even though he is sometimes found 'crying' over the misfortunes of others or 'moralizing' on the 'awful handicraft of the Deity' or the propensity to idleness among the Cornwallis farmers, his solemnity is hardly overbearing or tedious, and is either lightened by humour or soon succeeded by it.

Certainly he does not involve himself in solemn disquisitions on those two most contentious and favourite topics of the day, politics and religion. Generally he avoids these subjects in the *Rambles,* and even when they must be brought up – as in his description of Pictou and his encounter with a ruined bridge at the French River – he avoids serious discussion of the principles at issue. The near-silence, especially on political matters, may seem odd for a man who was soon to be so ardent a political reformer and campaigner and was even now becoming more and more critical of the established power structure in the province.

One may reasonably conjecture that Howe considered the *Rambles* no suitable forum for even dispassionate treatment of provincial politics. He wanted to describe and interpret the province to his fellow Nova Scotians, not to thresh again the grain already winnowed in his own editorials and extensive reports of Assembly debates and in the political columns of other Halifax newspapers. Therefore the *persona* he assumes in the *Rambles* is not that of Joseph Howe the political critic but rather that of the urbane and sympathetic observer of places and human affairs. A brief comment such as he makes on the inefficiency of government could naturally come from any traveller annoyed over an impassable bridge that should have been replaced long ago. Howe is content with that in the *Rambles,* knowing that he has other and more suitable means of publicizing political neglect and inefficiency.

On religious controversies Howe is equally reticent. When he must introduce the touchy subject in his sketch of Pictou, he treats the factionalism of the Presbyterians as a deplorable aberration from common sense best spoken of in the deflating language of ironic humour. He does not take sides on the issues of church doctrine behind the conflict over Pictou Academy or even say what the issues are; he does not even declare his own opposition to a principle accepted by both factions, that of state support for church schools. Yet even by this time Howe was an opponent of denominational education and on principle disagreed with Dr McCulloch's attempts to obtain a perpetual government grant for his Presbyterian academy – as he was later to oppose the continuance of a legislative grant to the Baptist academy at Wolfville which eventually became Acadia University. This particular conviction was probably deeply rooted in Howe and grew out of his early training by his father in Christian doctrine. John Howe was a Sandemanian, and that minor offshoot of Scottish Presbyterianism held as its chief tenet the absolute separation of church and state. Indeed the sect had broken away from the parent church on that very question, denying that the state had any right to dictate or even involve itself in any way in matters of faith. In this context, attempts by Presbyterians of any faction to gain financial support from the legislature in order to teach, among other subjects, their particular version of Christian theology would be seen as a spreading of the unscriptural doctrine already established in the province by Anglicanism. In short, on this question Howe has definite views founded on religious rather than political principles, but still chooses to keep his distance and express only generally his distaste for squabbles among Christians.

His reasons for saying so little about this or any other dispute over religion, as over politics, are no doubt partly literary, in keeping with the tone and purpose of the *Rambles.* His purpose is not that of Haliburton in *The Clockmaker,* to expose and ridicule the follies of the Bluenoses and, in matters of religion, to urge his own beliefs; likewise Howe's tone is the opposite of Sam Slick's outrageously biased diatribe and is considerably more tolerant than even the voice of the Squire, Haliburton's more sober mouthpiece.

As it happens, however, what suits the tone Howe establishes in the *Rambles* also reflects something of his own personal attitude to the practice of religious faith. The 'cordial and proper spirit' that he finds sadly lacking in Pictou is close to his own ideal; in effect, Howe holds to the principle of toleration in religion. For him this does not appear to mean that, being devoid of faith himself, he can all the more readily decry the uncharitable rancour to which it can be perverted in others. His belief in basic Christian principles seems sincere enough, and his letters suggest that he is no scoffer at true piety and worship. He can even say, after a marathon of church-going in Musquodoboit where he attends morning, afternoon, and evening services, that 'The ... day was one to me of real inward enjoyment' (letter to his wife, 1833). One gathers, nevertheless, that Howe was considerably more liberal and less puritanical than was characteristic of his time and place. Perhaps the elements of eighteenth-century deism which are observable here and there in his writings partly explain his attitude. The rigid patterns of social behaviour accepted by many people in the name of religious piety he seems to have held in low esteem, and consequently could act unconventionally unless restrained by his own prudence or the advice of others. On one occasion, as he confides to his wife, he was all set to walk from Windsor to Kentville on a Sunday and was dissuaded from his purpose only when Haliburton and other friends warned him that he would create a scandal 'by journeying on the Sabbath past half a thousand persons going to and from church.' To such a man, disagreements over religion which could not be conducted moderately and prevented from issuing in social strife were deplorable. His distaste for the bickering of Pictonians reflects his own wider conception of religion.

His actual advice to the province does not differ markedly from the judgments of his compatriots who had recently looked or were now looking at Nova Scotia with critical eyes – notably John Young ('Agricola') in a series of epistolary articles on provincial agriculture published in *The Acadian Recorder* beginning in 1818, Thomas McCulloch in *The Letters of Mephibosheth Stepsure* which had appeared serially in the same newspaper in 1822–3, and T.C. Haliburton in *The Clockmaker*. Like them, Howe believes in a staunch agrarianism unweakened by the vices of luxury and idleness and built upon a spirit of proud independence. Like Haliburton, he encourages Nova Scotians to take pride in their British tradition, and even more insistently preaches ardent devotion to the development of their province. Where the two friends differ is in the intensity of their local patriotism. Though Howe was later to declare that even Nova Scotia was not as important to him as the safety of Britain and British institutions, early and late his declarations and his actions suggest that the choice of Britain before his native province would have been hard; Haliburton, of course, allowed disillusionment with the political drift of his province to sour his later years and finally to play a part in exiling him to England. It is Howe's egalitarianism, however, that ultimately distinguishes his outlook from Haliburton's: in the sketches, as later in his speeches and editorials, Howe holds to a faith in the dignity and worth of the people that Haliburton would never share.

Howe's *Rambles* are not masterpieces of their *genre,* but they take a respectable place in the more modest context of the considerable body of colonial writing which appeared in Nova Scotia in the 1820s and 1830s. Their weaknesses are obvious enough. In structure they are incomplete, for Howe never took the trouble to round off either each tour or the whole series with proper conclusions. The mannered pretentiousness of the youthful editor bent on impressing people with his mastery of literary graces is at times heavy-handed, especially in the opening pages of each set of *Rambles*, and his occasional flights of florid sentiment are equally overdone. He still had something to learn about the discipline of words. Yet, on balance, the defects are minor and the literary skill well above the reach of ordinary colonial journalism. The *Rambles* should be judged not as chronicles or journals given a veneer of art by their author's penchant for a literary style but as consciously conceived and executed literary pieces. Others could have reported more factually and thoroughly on the state of the province and produced accounts to delight the historian and antiquarian; only Howe could have written the *Rambles*.

Editorial note

Howe's *Rambles* first appeared in his newspaper the *Novascotian* on the dates indicated in this edition at the head of each chapter. The present edition is their first reprinting. The text is a faithful reproduction of the complete *Rambles,* except for corrections of obvious errors in spelling and a few changes in punctuation where it tended to obscure or confuse Howe's meaning. Otherwise, the original is unchanged.

The notes are intended to supplement Howe's text by explaining local references and supplying information on various matters less likely to be readily comprehended today than by readers in 1830. The identification of Howe's numerous quotations will perhaps not be looked upon as an exercise in pedantry, on the grounds that it is useful to know as much as possible about Howe's reading. Most of his quotations have been tracked down; the few that remained stubbornly obdurate have had to be left unidentified.

The introduction and notes draw information from a wide variety of sources: Halifax newspapers and periodicals of the 1820s and 1830s, especially the *Acadian* and the *Novascotian*; the Joseph Howe Papers, 1830–73, on microfilm in the Public Archives of Nova Scotia (original manuscripts in the Public Archives of Canada and Harvard University Library); maps, almanacs, and records in PANS; the books of Moorsom, Haliburton, Sleigh, and McCulloch as cited; the standard nineteenth-century histories, especially those of Haliburton and Murdoch; county histories, and various articles and monographs on local history; the modern histories of Halifax (Thomas Raddall) and Dartmouth (J.P. Martin), and various modern studies of historical subjects pertaining to Nova Scotia such as W.S. MacNutt's *The Atlantic Provinces* and J.M. Beck's *The Government of Nova Scotia*; relevant books and articles on Howe, especially those of Fenety, Logan, G.M. Grant, Roy, Harvey, and Beck; R.D. Evans' unpublished MA thesis on Nova Scotian roads; and numerous articles in *Collections of the Nova Scotia Historical Society*.

Special thanks for assistance are due to the Provincial Archivist, Dr C. Bruce Fergusson, to the staff of the Public Archives of Nova Scotia, and especially to the Assistant Archivist, Miss Phyllis Blakeley.

This book is published with the aid of grants from the Social Science Research Council of Canada, using funds provided by the Canada Council, and from the Publications Fund of the University of Toronto Press.

Western Rambles

I

23 July 1828

Nature I'll court in her sequester'd haunts,
By mountain, meadow, streamlet, grove, or cell.
Smollett[1]

Man was at one time defined to be a 'cooking animal,' but if asked for a definition, I should be inclined to pronounce man, at the present day, to be an animal who travels about. With the exception of the Chinese, who, as a nation, are singularly domestic, there is hardly another portion of the globe in which the principle of attraction is sufficiently strong to counteract the prevailing disposition for going abroad. If we look to the four corners of the earth, we see the men of the North, with their faces turned due south, broiling beneath a sun hot enough to cook a salamander, and those of the tropics wending their way to the neighborhood of the Arctic circle, to gaze with watery eyes, and chattering teeth, and shivering limbs, on mountains of ice; and to run, with an avalanche treading on their heels, into the embraces of a Bear. There is the same system of making and returning visits among the men and women of the eastern and western hemispheres; they keep travelling in opposite directions like the tide and eddies of the Shubenacadie, or as though they had caught the curse from the wandering Jew. The Englishman, who has toiled for a score of years, behind a counter in Cheapside, till he has gathered plenty of goods and plenty of children – has risen to the dignity of an alderman, and impressed upon the minds of the multitude, by the impression made on a sirloin of Beef and a Tureen of Turtle, that he is a man of great *capacity,* tires of strutting before his door, and looking big upon 'Change, and smoking his pipe in the back parlor; and, by the sweet persuasion of Mrs. Nutmeg, and the gentle blandishments of his eldest girl, and the coaxing importunity of Master Jacky, resolves to bid adieu to the smoke of

1 Tobias Smollett (1721-71), 'Ode to Independence' ll.105-6

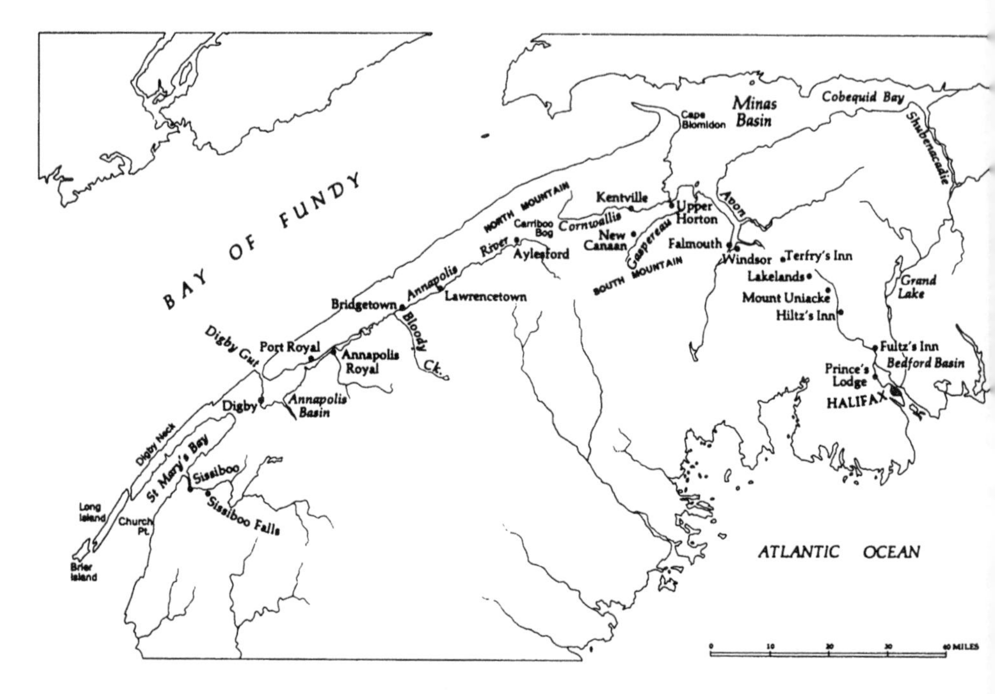

The western trip

the city, and make the tour of Europe; and after the necessary arrangements, the whole cavalcade rolls away, to enjoy all the pleasures of locomotion – to stare and be stared at – to bully innkeepers and Dilligence Drivers,[2] and get cheated by both; to sprain their ankles at St. Gothard, and bark their shins at Simplon[3]; to wonder that the Lake of *Geneva* should be in Switzerland, when it ought to be in Holland, and to speculate on the cause of there being so many Cantons in the former country, when they never heard of but one, and that was in the East Indies. But let them wander along – if I had not other matters in hand, I might follow them to advantage, and make the reader smile as the cavalcade of cockneyism winds over the hills and the vallies, getting upset in one place and robbed in another – alternately delighted with novelty, and tormented by the wish to get home; until at length they settle down in the City of Cities, and amaze the burgesses thereof with the *i*story of their ad*w*entures, while the whole street is bursting with envy at the dignity and importance of the Nutmegs.

The Scotchmen migrate to all quarters of the earth, travelling for wealth as prophets are forced to do for honor; and in the hope of lighting on some pleasant quarter of the Globe, where a man who has only one God, and one religion, is not forced to fatten more than one Priest, the Paddies go laughing and fighting, with their hats on the sides of their heads or their hands in the apertures of their breeches, into any country where the soil is favorable for the growth of Potatoes, and where there is a sprig to be cut, or a sconce to be broken. The Frenchman kindly sallies forth to teach the world to speak his national language, and cook their victuals as it becomes Christians to eat them; and cut their garments and dress their hair as it is essential that both should be worn. The Swiss goes forth to battle, and for any monarch, and in any cause, will cut the throats of mankind for so many shillings a day. The Savoyard[4] is a kind of Musical Missionary, who, like the cuc-

2 A public stagecoach was called a *diligence* in France.

3 These are both high Alpine passes in Switzerland. St Gotthard Pass is in south-central Switzerland, the Simplon Pass in the Lepontine Alps on the Swiss-Italian border.

4 Savoyards were natives of Savoy, a duchy in northwest Italy which formed part of the Kingdom of Sardinia. Then as now, musical talent was considered a characteristic national trait of Italians.

koo, 'sings as he flies', until after wandering over the fairest and loveliest portions of the earth, he returns to spend his days and his money upon his native hill, and recline his head on the lap of one of his juvenile playmates, who, from sundry glances and tokens, had long expected him back. The new world copies the old in travelling, as in almost everything else; the Georgian and the Carolinian run away from the sun, and, while sipping the waters of Saratoga, snap their fingers at the fever, and set colera morbus at defiance; and brother Jonathan,[5] during the winter, steals from his wharf and his store, and getting into the stage, rolls off to Washington to see the doings of Congress; that great ark of his political safety, into which all manner of animals have been crammed.

But whither tends this speculation and rumination on the migratory habits of the bipeds? saith the pleasant reader; and I answer thus – that having myself a disposition to take a fortnight's ramble, and being desirous of good company on the way, I want, if I can, to coax the gentle reader aforesaid to be of the party; and, supposing him, like Sterne, willing and ready to do anything with any body, 'provided there be no sin in it',[6] I am disposed to show that if travelling be a sin, there are a goodly number of equestrians and pedestrians to keep us both in countenance. But to what strange land are we going, and what is the object of the jaunt? asketh my fellow traveller again – shall we ascend Dhawalegeri,[7] and gaze on the wonders of Asia – shall we rove on the borders of the Garonne – explore the city of the Dead, or plunge into those living focusses of business and iniquity, Paris and London? – shall we recline in the shade of the Pyramids, and imagine that the armed legions of Napoleon and the dextrous Mamelukes are wheeling and curvetting before us in all the splendour of battle array? or go on a pilgrimage to the Holy Land, and like Chateaubriand,[8] steep our imagi-

5 'Brother Jonathan' was then a common personification of a citizen of the United States or of the country itself. Its exact origin is apparently unknown, as there is no evidence for the legend that it originated with a remark of George Washington concerning the governor of Connecticut, Jonathan Trumbull. It seems to have been first used by British soldiers in derision of American patriots.

6 Laurence Sterne *A Sentimental Journey through France and Italy*, 'Montriul'

7 Probably Mount Dhaulagiri (26,800 ft) in the Himalayas

8 Chateaubriand (1768–1848) travelled to the Near East, Africa, and Spain in 1804–7 and recorded his experiences in *Itinéraire de Paris à Jérusalem* (1811).

nations in its sublime and sacred recollections? Not so fast, if you please, gentle Traveller, not so fast – we are only to be a fortnight gone, and cannot go quite so far. But your error is common enough – for who, of the great moving multitude, ever thinks of travelling at home, if he can get abroad; or cares a straw for beauties and peculiarities which cost him but little trouble to see? Sandy of Glasgow may be found in Egypt, who never went to Bervie[9] – and Paddy from Cork may be seen digging at the Canal, who cares very little and knows less about the land of Paddy in Wexford. This error is of both genders – for males and females are afflicted with it; and it is observable in other matters besides travelling, for how often do we see Ladies who have an accurate knowledge of the concerns of every house in the neighborhood, but their own – and who are better informed of the doings in the distance, than they are of what occurs under their own roofs.

But, give me the man who will go rambling over his own country, and find in its features a fund of interest – who will clamber over its rocks, and plunge into its forests; who will dip his digits in its streams, and tear his breeches with its brambles; and, from some mountain height, survey the landscape of cultivation spread in beautiful luxuriance before him, and feeling the warm current of life flowing more freely through his veins, and bubbling up to his heart, and mantling upon his cheek, and the tear of joy and pride trembling in his eye, will thank his God for the fertility and beauty before him, and break the head of any man who attempts to affirm that there ever was, or will be, such another Country on the face of the earth. If then gentle reader you are such a man, the sooner we join company the better, and wend our way over the *west countrie.* But stay – let me examine your outward man and see that you are sound in wind and limb; that the soles of your feet are not very tender; that you are not three years gone in a consumption, nor troubled with head aches nor back aches, nor any other kind of aches; for when a man looks at a prospect through the medium of disease he cannot discover a beauty – he sees gout in the horses, asthma in the cows, dyspepsia in the oxen, and the blue devils in every thing. And here let us make another pause, and thank Providence and

9 A town on the east coast of Scotland, about twelve miles north of Montrose. The main attraction would have been Bervie Castle.

the Proprietors for the establishment of the Stage Coach,[10] by which a man may get a look at the country, without having to hire a sorry gelding at the rate of a shilling a day for every ounce of flesh upon his ribs, and a waggon worthy of the spirited animal that draws it – being so composed that, like the Roman's ship, it falls to pieces the moment you get fairly embarked. Aye, and be thankful also, that you are exempt from the labor of beating the beast aforesaid – and watching him eat his oats for fear of being cheated by the ostler – and splicing the harness, and greasing the wheels and running for a mile to catch the horse, when getting out of pasture he turns his tail towards you and his head towards town; and, last not least, for the clear saving of fifteen or twenty pounds, which it might have cost you to pay for the slight accident of his dying on the road. For exemption from all these evils, I say again, put up prayers for the prosperity of the Stage, and having entered your name at the office, give yourself no uneasiness about the matter. We must walk the first twelve miles of the road, for although you may have seen the borders of the Basin[11] before – and have read some half dozen descriptions thereof both in prose and verse, it will be hard if we cannot find something on our way to laugh at or admire.

II

31 July 1828

If we had a load of hay at our heels, gentle Traveller, we would prefer the Kempt Road, as the most even and regular; but as we have not, and as the old road is the most picturesque, we who travel at our leisure

10 The Western Stage Coach Company was founded in 1828; its first coach left Halifax on 3 June of that year, just shortly before Howe set out on the tour upon which he bases *Western Rambles*. See the Introduction for details of the coach service.

11 Bedford Basin, the inner harbour of Halifax

must choose it of course.[12] There is no moment of a man's life when he feels a more thorough contempt for Towns and Cities, than when he is going out of one to enjoy the free air of the country. He turns up his nose at the bustling and busy hive, toiling to and fro, although albeit but a few hours before he was among the number. He sees them piling pound upon pound – and laying stone upon stone, until Death comes quietly along, and carries them far away from their treasures; and anon old Time approaches – and levels their bricks and tiles, and throws their money bags to their heirs, who scatter them all abroad; again to be gathered by the thrifty, and dispersed by the thoughtless. These are reflections which will intrude, perhaps for the first time in a man's life, while escaping from the crowd; and which are sure to be forgotten the moment he returns to mingle in its vortex. Having gained the high ground by the North Farm,[13] we wheel to the right about, and take a view of the scene from which we are escaping – it is varied and picturesque enough; on the west the high land beyond the Arm, with some of the clearings at Spryfield in the distance, bound the view; and on the east, Dartmouth and the fine strip of cultivation which skirts the Passage,[14] lye before us – the Peninsula, with its fields and its cottages on the one side, and its little city on the other – with the Citadel, like some giant sentinel placed there to keep order, rising between, form a varied and pretty picture, which is heightened by the calm placidity of the water, and the deep green of the Islands in the distance. To a stranger's eye all this would have a charm, but haply every object before

12 The Kempt Road was surveyed and built during the administration of Sir James Kempt (1764–1854), the lieutenant-governor of Nova Scotia from 1820 to 1828. As it was built in 1824–5, to Howe in 1828 it was the 'new road.' It was an alternate route for passage northward out of Halifax, being less hilly than the old Windsor Road (Windsor Street), the route of which had been cleared shortly after the city was founded in 1749.

13 The Governor's North Farm, in what was then the unsettled northern part of the Halifax peninsula, occupied the present area (just north of Fort Needham) bounded by Gottingen Street on the west, Duffus Street on the north, Campbell Road (now Barrington Street) on the east, and Richmond Street on the south.

14 Eastern Passage, the entrance to Halifax Harbour on the eastern side of McNab's Island

you brings to mind some passage of your early days – you have shot Plover on Camp Hill, and Snipe in the marshes, and sailed about the harbour and skated on the Ponds, and perhaps clambered up to the flagstaff, to watch for the signal of some friend who had long journeyed over the deep, and whom you hoped soon to welcome to his home. As one train of associations follows another, faster than the eye can take in the inanimate objects by which they are occasioned, you half forget the scene,

> While memory runs,
> Lifting the shroud which time had cast
> O'er buried thoughts,[15]

and the 30th minute finds you musing. We stand now, as it were, half way between Town and Country; and like the spirit when about to leave its earthly tenement, however bright and glowing the scenes we are about to view – and however pure the pleasures in which we hope to mingle, there is much to bid us linger on the way. And, as we may say and do many foolish things in the course of our journey, it is good to utter a wise saying when we can. You have been perhaps a great reader in your time, gentle Traveller, and have wasted the midnight oil over goodly tomes – and imagine that you are as wise as your neighbors, and I doubt it not. But have you ever studied the philosophy of nature? have you ever learned to gather wisdom from the expanded leaves of creation, and instruction where the Bookworm would search in vain? The artist who can copy a print, but cannot sketch a landscape, is not more deficient than is he who cannot learn a lesson out of book – who can read and ruminate only in his study – and heeds not the wisdom which is taught by the hills, and which a wise man may gather in the vallies. Every flower you see hath its instruction – every tree is waving in wisdom, and he who runs may read.

How boundless and beautiful is the prospect now before us; we can see on all sides, and take in at a glance hundreds and hundreds of objects, while those in the streets, and the lanes, and the low places, can

15 Thomas Moore *The Loves of the Angels* ll.65–7

see but a trifling distance; and although each may perhaps have a more accurate knowledge of the objects by which he is immediately surrounded, he cannot form so clear an idea of the *tout ensemble* as we can. It is thus that knowledge lifts man above his fellows – and enables him from the hill of science to look beyond the vulgar – to behold the relations which bind the great human family together – to judge of the general interest without prejudice – to controul, to govern and improve; and though gradual the ascent, though the path be rough and the obstructions many, who, to attain the summit, would refuse to climb? – Hah! Hah! saith the merry traveller; I thought I was to have a lively companion on the way, but you have all at once turned into a field preacher – and if the breeze was only strong enough to blow off your hat and dishevel your hair, you would make a most excellent ranter among the faithful.

The walk round the Basin, as everyone knows, is cool, shady and pleasant – on the left there are plenty of rocks and on the right plenty of water, and on the road we are generally certain to meet a number of gigs and waggons, loaded with bonnets and ribbons, and flounces and flats,[16] and lots of teams, loaded with more bulky articles, on their way to the country. And here too you are sure to encounter a goodly bevy of sable beauties, with their unsophisticated feet, and their woolly heads, adorned, not with 'the likeness of a kingly crown',[17] but with tubs and baskets of fair dimensions, from which, like so many dingy Pomonas, they have been pouring strawberries down the throats of the citizens – and having got their cornucopiaes replenished with Indian meal, and their pipes filled, are trudging along with their hearts a great deal lighter than their heads, and caring no more for the fashionable frivolities of their betters, than Miss Laetitia Lavinia would for Mrs. Dingy's wooden turban, and the Indian meal into the bargain. It has been the fashion to revile these poor devils, – man, woman and child, for lazyness, and for the heinous sin of not immediately accustoming themselves to a climate half a dozen degrees colder than it was where they were born. They are a burthen to the country, says Political

16 Flats were low-crowned, broad-brimmed straw hats for women.

17 Milton *Paradise Lost* II, l.673

William H. Eager
Ruins of the Duke of Kent's lodge, circa 1836

Economy – they are rogues and vagabonds, says the miser, who claps his hand upon his stick the moment they approach, for fear they might ask for a sixpence; they ought to be sent to Sierra Leone, or quartered on Sir Thomas Cochcran,[18] says every body. But suppose, good folks,

18 In 1791, the negroes who had fled northward to Nova Scotia during the American Revolution were offered free passage to Sierra Leone. Early in 1792 over a thousand of them accepted the offer and sailed to Africa. Howe's reference to Sir Thomas Cochrane is less easily explained. Sir Thomas (1789-1872) commanded the frigate *Surprise* on the North American coast during the War of 1812, served on the Halifax and West Indian stations after the war, and was governor of Newfoundland from 1825 to 1834. He seems to have had no prominent part, however, in the bringing of hundreds of American negroes from the Chesapeake Bay area to Nova Scotia in 1814 and 1815, although he was in the Bay during the British attacks on Washington and Baltimore. His father, Sir Alexander Cochrane (1758-1832), who became Naval Commander of the North American station in 1814, was in general command of the operation. Howe seems to have mistaken Sir Thomas for Sir Alexander. It is possible, of course, that Sir Thomas, in spite of his youth and relatively junior rank in 1814, had more to do with the removal of the negroes than the records indicate. Or Howe's report of popular feeling may mean that the 'sins' of the father should be visited upon the son who, as governor of Newfoundland, was conveniently at hand and master of an island with plenty of room for new settlers.

that you were suddenly caught up and cast into Maryland – stripped to your trowsers, and a hoe put into your hand, do you think that hoeing Tobacco and Corn would come a bit more easy to you, under the burning rays of the sun, than cutting down trees and clearing land is to the negro, in a country where every thing is opposed to his accustomed habits? The immediate descendants of the race brought here by Sir Thomas may be little better than their parents, as regards industry and intelligence – but there is nothing in their color to prevent them from eventually becoming as good farmers as your grandchildren would make hoers of corn, or eaters of hominy, on the banks of the Chesapeake. Therefore have a little patience, good people, and let the old leaven of ignorance and idleness work out of these gentlemen of color; and although they may never be able to pay the interest of the £300,000 which Brother Jonathan charged for them[19] – yet they may one day or other be hard-working and independent landholders, and do good service to the Country.

But we are approaching the Lodge;[20] and, like other Travellers, must loiter around it a while, and make our reflections on the mutability of human affairs – and hark to the wild strain of martial music that

19 After a prolonged controversy, Britain agreed in 1826 to pay the United States the sum of $1,204,960 in US currency as reparation for the negro slaves freed and transported by the British fleet during the previous war. Captain Moorsom (*Letters from Nova Scotia* 129) makes an interesting observation on this transaction: 'These are the people on whose account Great Britain lately awarded a donation of one million to the United States; a donation as unlooked-for as it is ridiculed by those very citizens who have tasted the cream of the jest – a donation bestowed by honest John, in compensation to the planters, whose slaves were carried off in order to enjoy the domestic comforts of political feedom and physical starvation, under British auspices in Nova Scotia!'

20 Prince's Lodge, on the western shore of Bedford Basin, had been the country residence of Prince Edward, the fourth son of George III, when he lived in Halifax. Edward came to Halifax in 1794 as Commander-in-Chief of the forces in Nova Scotia. In 1798 he returned to England in order to press claims for promotion. He was eminently successful, for when he resumed his duties at Halifax in 1799, he did so as Duke of Kent and Commander-in-Chief of British forces in North America. He held his new post only until August 1800, when he went back to England on leave and never returned to the site of his considerable triumphs as builder of fortifications and leader of Halifax society. By 1828, as Howe implies, the estate was deserted and in ruins, a fit object for 'reflections on the mutability of human affairs.' For a detailed description of exactly how the mansion and its grounds looked in the very same year Howe visited them, see T.C. Haliburton *The Clockmaker* 3rd series, chapter 1.

comes bursting from the wood, and see where the gay and the proud are roving beneath the boughs, and winding along the footpaths, while forms of fairy-lightness are hanging on their arms, and eyes, with a deeper tint than the raven bears upon its wing, are beaming upon them in love and gladness; while ever and anon the joyous laugh, or the silver sound of some warbler's voice blends with the stirring melody of the music. Waiters are flying to and fro, and carriages are crowded round the gates, and all seems gaiety and joy; and in the midst is the stately figure of the Royal Edward – the soul and spirit of the scene – around whom the glittering pageant revolves, administering to his pleasure and his pride. But 'a change comes o'er the spirit of our dream'[21] – and the dead is sleeping with the dead – and the music has ceased, and the crowd has vanished, 'And left us in lone woods and empty halls.'

But we must be moving onwards to Fultz's[22] – or the shadows of evening will be upon and around us. We have travelled but slowly so far, but when we mount the Stage in the morning we shall ride at a quicker pace. Slowly and majestically the sun goes down – and cold must be the heart that, while viewing his descent, does not sigh for a course like his. The commandment forbids us to covet whatever belongs to our neighbor; but surely one may envy the sun his glorious rising in the east – his high and proud career, with all the splendor of his noon-day beams – and then his calm and dignified decline; his rays still lingering to brighten and adorn the clouds that hang around the world.

21 A repeated line in Byron's poem 'The Dream,' slightly misquoted.

22 The inn of William Fultz, often called '12-mile House' to designate its distance from Halifax on the road to Windsor. It stood at the junction where the road from Halifax split into the two Great roads, one to Windsor and the other to Truro. This road to Truro is now known as the Old Cobequid Road, and the site of the junction is Lower Sackville. Fultz's Inn was well established by 1828. In the 1830s its good food and spacious ballroom attracted many Haligonians, among whom were the members of the Tandem Club who made it the outward terminus of their sleigh-rides. Fultz ran the inn until 1849; in later years it was used as a residence. It was destroyed by fire about 1900.

III

7 August 1828

'All the world's a *Stage*,
and all the men and women merely passengers.'
Shakespeare improved

The coward hates the bugle note that hurries him to the charge; the gallant Stag dislikes the sounding of the Hunter's Horn, and the Ferryman's Conch has a most provoking echo, when it warns the sot that he must leave his can, or the lovers that Boatmen, like time and tide, wait for no man – and who can tell with what a woebegone countenance the Passenger hears the infernal bellowing of the Triton's sea shell, when Neptune rises over the bow to 'shave him for god sake' with some old rusty cutlass, picked up from the bottom of the sea; but when we have arrived at the eighth hour of a long, deep slumber, which has borne us away on its wing of down, from the vexatious realities of this life, and carried our spirit aloft into the world of dreams, and, through the clear obscure of 'that rich twilight of the soul',[23] is showing us visions more varied and lovely than ever came 'over us in our waking hours', we think there is melody in all these sounds, compared with the blast of Peter's horn, which makes us start from one world back into the other, and gives us a 'taste of its quality' by bumping our head against the door which Fultz has opened to tell us the Stage is waiting.[24]

Perhaps, my friend, you have been accustomed to spend a few hours at your toilette – to loiter away your life in eradicating a freckle from your cheek, or a pimple from your chin – in curling a whisker or coaxing a moustache; or, mayhap, you have been reading the recent French

23 Thomas Moore *The Loves of the Angels* 1.838

24 As the Western stagecoach left Halifax at the early hour of 5:00 AM, it would have arrived at Fultz's Inn, twelve miles out, at about 6:30. The end of the first stage being at Hiltz's Inn, twenty-one miles from Halifax, the coach merely stopped at Fultz's to pick up passengers, like Howe, who had stayed there overnight. Peter was the coachman as far as Kentville, where he was replaced by a driver named Pat.

work, and practice diurnally the five and twenty ties upon your cravat,[25] but these will not do this morning – leap into your trowsers and boots, and gather your upper garments about you, and jump into the coach; and, for the first time in your life, reflect on the folly of wasting so much time in performing an operation which may be done so quickly. Crack goes Peter's whip, and you roll away on your journey, wondering at the rapidity of your motions, and the motion of the coach; and after having reconciled yourself to the idea that there is no danger of your neck being broken, you begin to examine your fellow passengers; and a goodly collection there are. First, your attention is drawn to a fat lady by whom you are flanked on the right, and who utters sundry murmurings about the folly of hurrying into a coach at the expense of people's corns, and as you protrude your elbow between her ribs in order to button your waistcoat, adds, by way of accompaniment, a small 'piece of her mind' about the indelicacy of gentlemen dressing in the Stage. Having appeased her wrath with half a score of apologies, and got her into a good humour, which, as fat ladies have generally a fair share of the milk of human kindness, is no difficult matter, you at once discover the motive for her pilgrimage, in the form of a frail and delicate girl beside her, whose pale cheek displays 'the rose whose root is death.'[26] Consumption's touch is upon her, and she is fading and withering beneath it, and in the hope that the country air may be of service, and check if not eradicate the disease, she has left home to breathe it during the summer months; and as your eye rests on her fragile form and her pale white brow, you curse yourself for treading on her mother's corns, and pray from the bottom of your soul that health may yet banish the hectic flush from her cheek, and the ashy paleness from her lip, and kindle her dark eye with a more natural lustre.

With his face like a full moon, and his cane in his hand, right opposite sits a country Postmaster; who is both a man of Peace and of War –

25 Howe is referring to a current fad encouraged by various French manuals with titles such as *L'Art de mettre sa cravate*.

26 A paraphrase of a line from Felicia Hemans' poem 'Edith: A Tale of the Woods': 'But her form wasted, and her fair young cheek/Wore oft and patiently a fatal streak,/A rose whose root was Death.'

being a Magistrate and Major of Militia. Now, either of these three offices of dignity and trust would be sufficient to give a person a tolerable notion of his own consequence, but they are like the three nobs of the Jack of Clubs – the three leaves of a clover; they are a kind of official trinity, which renders a country gentleman omnipotent, and omnipresent. His conversation is a compound of three languages; the technicalities of three professions are curiously blended together, and the consequence necessary to the due occupation of each office is concentered in one Person. Now he is discoursing most eloquently on the defects of the last law for mending the Highways or taking care of the Poor, and the great labor and anxiety of the magisterial office; and should the conversation turn that way, will inform you that 'His Majesty's Mails' go in the coach – and expatiate and enlarge on the trouble and responsibility of taking charge of the whole correspondence of a village, which, while it requires a man of superior abilities, gives him so paltry a pittance. But ask him the number of freeholders in his township, and straight he calls the roll, and gives you each man's name from 18 to 45, and enumerates the accidents and diseases of those who are exempt from drill – here you perceive his martial character bursting out – he is familiar with all works treating of the manual and platoon exercise – keeps an edition of the 'Martial Register' at home, and carries abroad with him a full account of all the great battles which have been fought for the last forty odd years, and can give you a running criticism on the errors committed on both sides – and, before he finishes, leads you to understand that he thinks, next to himself, the greatest military genius that ever drew a sword is the Inspecting Field Officer of his district.

A young lawyer, who has been down to town 'getting his licence to plunder', is also one of the party;[27] and perhaps entertains you with the three last legal jokes cracked at our Bar – two of which you perceive

27 Howe's facetious remark on the predatory inclinations of lawyers sounds like a well-worn quotation or proverb, but it does not appear in the standard reference works. The idea was common enough, having been expressed in various ways since the time of the Roman satirists. Howe may have given the commonplace his own turn of phrase, but it is more likely that he is repeating a common saying.

were stolen from Curran,[28] and the third from Joe Miller.[29] A Butcher in search of the flesh, and a Preacher full of the spirit, make up the melange, and add their mites to the dish of variety in which you mingle. The first thing that strikes the eye after leaving Fultz's is the alteration of the Road, by which so many hills are avoided, and so many houses left in the rear; and when you think of the pleasant views that you might have had from the tops of the hills, you are half inclined to regret the alteration – but so it is, utility and uniformity will triumph over nature, and the picturesque must suffer from the change.[30]

At the half way house we breakfast[31] – and you perceive that the varieties of appetite are as numerous as the varieties of character and countenance – the fat lady eats little – the consumptive girl more – and the man of office appears to eat three meals, in virtue of his three employments. Having mustered into the coach again, you drive on, past the Collector's and Attorney General's fine farms,[32] and meet but little remarkable for many miles, except a singular experiment in road making, by which Travellers are taught the advantage of going over a hill in order to get round it. The middle Stage to Windsor is the most

28 John Philpot Curran (1750-1817), the Irish parliamentarian, judge, and orator, was known as a witty and amusing conversationalist. His 'legal jokes' would have been available in reported anecdotes, in his published speeches, and in two memoirs published in 1817.

29 Joe Miller (1684-1738) was an English actor whose reputation was made for him after his death by John Mottley, who compiled in 1739 a collection of jests and entitled it *Joe Miller's Jests*. The volume ran through many editions and re-issues. By Howe's time, Miller's name was popularly associated with jests and witty anecdotes.

30 On this subject, Captain Moorsom observes 'It is not many years since the science of road-making in England was enlightened by the discovery, that it was better to go round a hill of spherical form, than to mount over it. The same discovery is now obtaining general attention in Nova Scotia' (*Letters from Nova Scotia* 243).

31 This was Hiltz's Inn, 21 1/2 miles from Halifax and 9 1/2 miles beyond Fultz's, therefore nearly halfway to Windsor. It was the end of the first stage from Halifax, at least during the early days of coaching, and stood about a mile beyond Lewis Lake. While the passengers ate breakfast the horses were changed. Apparently the original building was demolished or destroyed sometime in the later nineteenth century.

32 The Collector of Customs at Halifax was Thomas N. Jeffery (1782-1847). Before coming to Nova Scotia he had beeen a clerk in the Audit Office, Somerset House, London, from 1798 to 1803. He was appointed Collector in 1803 and retained the post until his death in the same year in which he was due to retire. His very large salary, which was frequently the target of indignant critics, enabled him to own a fine country estate known as Lakelands. The present small community derives its name from the old estate.

Terfry's Inn, Newport Corners
as it appeared before its demolition in 1917

monotonous and tiresome on the journey – much of the land is bad, and but poorly skirted with timber; and until within a few miles of Terfry's,[33] at whose door we are getting out, there is but little cultivation. From the hill above this House, however, a pretty scene may be viewed,

The Attorney-General was Richard John Uniacke (1753-1830), one of the most prominent men in the province, who held various public offices throughout a distinguished career. Besides being elected to the Assembly on three occasions (for Sackville Township, Halifax County, and Queens County) and acting as Speaker in two Assemblies, he was Solicitor General (1781–97), Attorney General (1797–1830), and a member of the Council (1808–30). In 1813–15 he built Uniacke House on his large estate at Mount Uniacke. The house is now restored and open to the public as a Provincial Museum.

33 Terfry's Inn was 35 miles from Halifax, and 10 miles from Windsor. As it marked the end of the second or middle stage to Windsor, Howe had time for a short stroll while the horses were being changed. The inn stood at Newport Corner, the junction of the Windsor road and the road to Newport Landing. It was built soon after 1820 and was run by Terfry (or Trefry) from 1825 to 1837. Other owners kept it as an inn until about 1864, several years after the railway had brought an end to the coach service on this route. The inn was a long, low structure of one and a half storeys, 45 feet by 35 feet, with dormer windows set in a pitched roof. It contained nineteen rooms. Photographs of this inn, which were taken before it was demolished in 1917, are in the Public Archives of Nova Scotia.

which will repay us for ascending – on the right we see cleared fields and a cottage or two – on the left the Windsor road meanders along, and opposite is the highway leading into Newport, bordered by some fine fields and snug looking farm houses; the hills, both before and behind, are finely wooded with stately trees, while a stream runs across the Windsor road, bubbling and sparkling in the sunbeams. There are, indeed, but few parts of Nova Scotia to which a man can travel, where his eye will not be refreshed by the sight of water. He either sees it rolling its calm and majestic wave upon the gravelly beach, and bursting into foam which the moonbeam changes to a silvery wreath – or beholds the stern heavings of Fundy Bay –

> That glorious mirror, where the Almighty's form
> Glasses itself in tempests.[34]

Or he finds it winding its silent course between two hills, kissing the wild flowers that spring up upon its margin, and roving along to mingle with some lake, or perhaps pay its tiny tribute to the mighty deep, adding its slender offering to swell the confines of Neptune's watery kingdom.

Although the view from Terfry's hill is far inferior to many that you will see, yet even here there is enough to make us

> Pause awhile – the world disown,
> And dwell with Nature's self alone.

Small hills and small vallies, crowded together, without much regard to formation, and here and there displaying the industry of the settler, but not exhibiting any continued line of cultivation, are all you can see till within a very few miles of Windsor – which you are momently expecting to open upon the eye. Of this beautiful little village you have doubtless heard much and read more; and mayhap you have seen a caricature thereof in a Magazine, which the Editor asserted the depraved taste of this illiterate Province suffered to perish;[35] a charge

34 Byron *Childe Harold's Pilgrimage* canto IV, clxxxiii

35 The reference is to the short-lived *Acadian Magazine; or Literary Mirror* (1826–8). Howe is probably referring to a long poem, 'Western Scenes,' which appeared in the magazine in January 1827. A long portion of the poem lavishly extols the charms

which would have made greatly against our literary character, if it had not been proved that a thing could not die that never had any life in it. 'But peace be to its manes' – for here is Windsor itself – with all its beautiful undulations of hill and dale – its upland fields

> Where the corn uprears,
> Like an Eastern army, its golden spears,

and its wide-spreading and verdant intervale, where the grass rises and falls before the western breeze, like the waves of the deep green sea. Around you the eternal hills are piled up, as though they were intended as a barrier to protect the fertility they enclose, and beyond the village is the Basin of Mines,[36] with its islands resting like ornaments on its bosom, and old Blomidon flinging his stern shadow upon its wave. It being high tide, you see none of the mud and much of the beauty of the Avon, as it steals along and branches off in different directions, gleaming and sparkling in the sun, and bearing with its rapid current a snug little topsail schooner, which has been discharging, I doubt not, a cargo of articles too numerous to mention, and which, if there be any Revenue Officers in the way, it would be very uncivil to name.

There stands the College on the hill,[37] and since it has been repaired, is a very decent-looking building; and now I might entertain you for hours, with the manners and peculiarities of the villagers – rehearsing all the civil and all the saucy things said of them – and amuse you with

of Windsor – so lavishly, Howe implies, that the passage is an unintended caricature. Howe was not the only critic of the *Acadian Magazine*, whose editor indeed showed little enterprise in seeking out local contributors but relied almost entirely on reprinted material from British and American periodicals and books. In the *Acadian Recorder* of 20 September 1827, 'Observator' writes a detailed analysis of the magazine's shortcomings. His criticism was not gratefully received, as he reveals two months later (24 November) in another letter on the subject.

36 Now known as Minas Basin, this body of water was called 'Les Mines' by the French because of copper deposits near Cap d'Or. Both Howe and Moorsom consistently write 'Basin of Mines,' but just a few years later, in *The Clockmaker*, 1st series, Haliburton has it as 'Basin of Minas.' Apparently the corruption to 'Minas' was gaining ground in the 1830s.

37 King's College, founded at Windsor in 1787. The Collegiate School still remains on the old site, but the College, now the University of King's College, was moved to Halifax in 1923.

sad stories of their inhospitality and pride; but the stage waits but an hour,[38] and far be it from me to paint people worse than we find them; and we have no time to form a better acquaintance. A traveller, who at the first inn where he stayed, found the landlady had a red head, wrote to his friends that carrotty locks were characteristic of the Russian females; and if we were to judge of the Windsor folks, after the same fashion, the good cheer and attention of the gentle widow Wilcox would persuade us they were a most endurable race.

IV

24 August 1828

Windsor has usually formed the ultima Thule of all peregrinating Tourists. In its beauties they have found sufficient to satisfy their disposition to see, and eke their propensity to describe. Its College – its Academy – its river – its rural and elegant seats, and the peculiarities of its society, are all fruitful subjects, and have yielded many a column to the groaning Press; and therefore, should we pass them by in something of a hurry, we have a fair excuse, because by lingering we would be apt to tread in earlier Travellers' footsteps. But the Muse forbid that we should pass from her native village without dropping a tear to the memory of Miss Tonge.[39] Goths or Boeotians should we be, if kindly

38 The stagecoach reached Windsor at 12:00 noon, and passengers bound for the Annapolis Valley were given an hour to enjoy their dinner at what T.C. Haliburton calls 'Mrs. Wilcox's comfortable inn.' At this time the Wilcox Inn was the principal hostelry of Windsor. It was called 'Wilcox's' from 1822 to 1826, and 'Mrs. Wilcox's' from 1827 to 1834. Captain Moorsom joins Howe and Haliburton in praising it for 'the comforts of solitude and gentle treatment' he found there, and also for its comfortable beds: 'I now revel in the luxury of a good hair-mattress, in place of the immense sacks of feathers under which, – spite of a thermometer at 80° – I have been buried alive in most of the country inns for the last fortnight' (p 283). The building is long gone, and no pictures of it are known to exist.

39 Grieselda Tonge, the daughter of William Cottnam Tonge (1764-182?), who was an outspoken MLA (1792-1808) and opponent of the authoritarian tactics of Governor Wentworth. Miss Tonge's local fame as a poet was based on verse contributed to

William H. Eager
View of Windsor, circa 1836

and sad thoughts did not come over our minds, at the recollection of her genius – her beauty – and her grave. For what are the delights of Windsorian scenery? what are her charms of water and land? and what are all her wealth and her pride, compared with the memory of that girl, which as long as the early breathings of our infant lyre are cherished and revered, will give to the scene of her childhood a hallowed and peculiar interest – will hang round it, as the spirits of the dead are thought to do round the objects they loved in life. Years after the present race of patricians and plebeians, and all their little jealousies and distinctions have faded away, the modest loveliness and

Halifax newspapers. She died at Demerara on 19 May 1825, only twenty days after she had arrived there on a visit to her brother, according to the death notice in the *Acadian Recorder* (16 July 1825). Apparently her father was also living in Demerara at the time, holding the post of Secretary. The sudden and unexpected death of this 'young lady' seems to have impressed several contributors to local periodicals and newspapers, although none quite equalled Howe's effusive tribute. According to one eulogist, Miss Tonge was 'the highly-gifted songstress of Acadia ... [who] has left behind her a few imperishable specimens of heaven-born genius ...' (*Acadian Magazine*, May 1827) unobtrusive talent of that gentle being will be fresh and blooming in the memory of her country. They will form a 'green spot of the soul' on which the eyes of our children's children will love to rest.

Methinks I can see her now, as the clover bends beneath her delicate foot, rambling along the fields, with the rosy hue of her cheek half hidden beneath her hat, while her glossy ringlets are flowing from under its rim to steal a kiss from the zephyr. In her hand she has flowers and strawberries, which she has been gathering as an offering to her

> Who rear'd her mind, even as an op'ning flower,
> Watching, with anxious love, each new expanding power.*

And then again

> I see her sit, in beauty's richest bloom,
> In youth's first budding spring – before me now,
> A shade of tenderest sadness, not of gloom,
> Tempering the brightness of her marble brow.
>
> Her dark hair clustering round her pensive face,
> Like shadowy clouds above a summer moon,
> Her fair hands folded with a queenly grace,
> Her soft cheek blushing like a rose in June.
>
> Her eyelid gently drooping o'er an eye
> Whose chasten'd light bespeaks the soul within,
> Lips full of sweetness – maiden modesty,
> That awes the bosom it hath deign'd to win.**

The billows are rolling around her, and the bark which bears her away from her sister blossoms is tossing amid their foam. The wearied mariners are slumbering -- and, in the solemn stillness of the midnight hour – in the lonely cabin, uncheer'd but by her lamp – unvisited, but by thoughts of her own dear land, and the loved ones it contained, she is pouring forth her feelings in tender and delicate strains, while the Muse bends over her favorite child, and yields a sweet solace to her

* Stanzas, addressed to her Grandmother, on her Birth Day [Howe's note]
** Verses, written at midnight, on her passage to the West Indies [Howe's note]

spirit amid the watery waste. Oh! God, that a thing so lovely and exquisite, so full of high and pure thoughts, so radiant with maidenly bloom and beauty, should be hurrying away to the grave. How surely doth the chilly hand of death gather the bright and talented of this earth into his gloomy garner; and how often the heart has to bleed over the fall of some sweet flower, whose bloom and fragrance, had it lived, would have cheered and brightened the age. Oh! that this daughter of our infant land could have been spared to us awhile; till the chords of her lyre had been more firmly strung, and her hand had learned to sweep over them with a less timid range, and her imagination had soared on a prouder wing, and her gentle heart had tasted of the admiration which a grateful country would have yielded to her genius; and then, when the measure of her fame was full – when her verse had been echoed on ev'ry hill, and her song had mingled with every breeze; she might, 'with all her budding honors thick upon her',[40] have calmly sunk into the bosom of the land which her genius had brightened and improved.

But, in the emphatic language of Uncle Toby,[41] *she shall not die,* while Acadia's lyre has a string – or a kindred spirit to mingle her memory with its silver tones. She shall live in our hearts, and we will think of her when the flowers are in bloom, when the stars are bright in the cloudless sky and the waves are sleeping 'neath Cynthia's smile; her memory shall come to us like music from a distant shore, soft and faint, but pleasant to our souls.

And now, my fair countrywomen, at the risk of some score of frowns, and mayhap some gentle visitations of your delicate fingers to the starboard side of my head, I cannot refrain from asking whether you think that nature intended you for nothing better than lacing your stays, and curling your hair – and leaving cards, and pricing ribbon, and gathering yourselves together in knots to discuss the faults of your friends and your servants? or did she intend that your lives should be passed in combing children's hair and making pies and pastry, and entertaining

40 Howe has combined parts of two phrases from Shakespeare: 'And bears his blushing honours thick upon him' (*Henry VIII* III.ii.354) and 'And all the budding honours on thy crest I'll crop' (*Henry IV, Part I* V.iv.72).

41 A principal character in Sterne's *Tristram Shandy*

your visitors with a long list of your domestic handicraft? Were your minds formed for nothing better than this? Can your intellects take no range beyond the kitchen, or your fancies soar no higher than the garret? and must your minds be forever employed in a perpetual round of gossip, ennui, and listlessness, when they might be more usefully and pleasingly engaged? Is there no elegant accomplishment that you might acquire, no feminine grace you might improve, no ornament that industry might lend to the mind? Is there no pleasing study, no literary or scientific pursuit, that without interfering with or weaning you from your domestic duties, might elevate and enlarge your understandings; might ennoble your nature, and strengthen your claims to man's homage and devotion? Then why are so many hours wasted and frittered away? why are the golden opportunities which youth affords, and which in every period of womanhood may be snatched as ye go, all lost and neglected? Were women made 'to suckle fools and chronicle small beer!'[42] or were they formed for higher and nobler purposes? To lure men by the gentle sway of reason, to win and keep them by the high cultivation and elegant blandishments of the mind, and to instruct and improve them by gentle and polished communion? Away with the old objection that intellectual pursuits interfere with domestic duties – dirty and slovenly women will be so to all eternity, whether learned and accomplished, or ignorant and stupid; but no inference can be gathered from this. Think you that the bright galaxy of peerless females who shed such radiance over the British Isles[43] are indifferent house-keepers, or careless of their personal appearance? no such thing – to them the duties and charities of life are matters of vital interest: but in their leisure hours – the odds and ends of existence – they give the reins to fancy, and enrich their literature and adorn their age; and why should not women on this side of the water 'go and do likewise.'[44] 'Tis for them to give society a useful and elevated tone; they are the

42 Shakespeare *Othello* II.i.161

43 Some of the 'peerless females' Howe had in mind, besides his favourite Mrs Hemans, may have been Letitia Elizabeth Landon or 'L.E.L.' (1802-38), Joanna Baillie (1762-1851), Mary Russell Mitford (1787-1855), Susan Edmonstone Ferrier (1782-1854), Maria Edgeworth (1767-1849), and Jane Porter (1776-1850).

44 Luke 10:37

Front Street, Windsor, circa 1829
(artist unidentified)

instructors of our youth, the companions of our manhood; they owe a large obligation to posterity; we may almost say the future destinies of Nova Scotia are in their hands; and in exact proportion as they are alive to the fact, the intellectual and moral character of the Province must be raised.

But a truce to moralizing and sermonizing, and farewell to Windsor; if we escape a few feminine lectures for the foregoing, we shall have more luck than we have had discretion. As we retrace a part of the road we came, we have an opportunity of surveying the College and Academy, and to mark more particularly the figure of the village, and the rural cottages by which it is surrounded; but we must restrain our amblings, and make more rapid progress, or the end of our journey will be like the end of Don Juan and Tristram Shandy, a pretty considerable distance off. 'Go a head you nasty ding', saith Peter, and away we roll through Falmouth; where a little Church overlooks some stretches of cultivation, and from which you see Windsor, and the water, from different points of view as you ride along. And now we ascend the Horton mountains, and having some feelings of compassion for the poor devils of horses, we get on our legs and show them the way up. On both sides the tall trees are towering over our heads, and, covered by rich and luxuriant foliage, nearly exclude the sun from the ferns and moss that creep around their roots. To plunge ten yards into the forest would as effectually shut us out from the world as if there was not one cultivated acre on this side of the Atlantic. Strange and undefined feelings alternately oppress and elevate the mind beneath these stately trees: truly saith the dazzling Hemans:

> The woods – oh! solemn are the mighty woods
> Of the great western world, when day declines.[45]

And had we leisure to ponder amid their stillness, we might be able to reconcile Colonel Boon's philosophy,[46] and vow vengeance on the first sinner who should break on our sylvan solitude. But we must get in again or we shall not reach the bottom of the hill so soon as Peter; for not faster down the steep did the devils send the swine, than our incarnate coachman drives his cattle. If I were a coach horse I would prefer the uphill work, however tedious and painful, to being hurried so rapidly down the descent; and until by a long course of practice the cattle have become thoroughly trained, this system will be always unsafe and uncomfortable to passengers. Nobody sets so much store by a man's neck as himself, and therefore every one is a most accurate calculator of the probable chances of its being broken – a hair will often decide; a fellow would as soon think of jumping into Vesuvius as a Stage, if he thinks there is one chance in the hundred of his getting upset – a quarter of an hour more of time, or a few extra cuts on the level road, would obviate the necessity for blowing the horses, and fidgeting the passengers by dashing so gallantly down hill, and by this

45 Felicia Hemans, 'Edith: A Tale of the Woods' ll.1–2

46 The adventures of Daniel Boone (1734-1820) had been well publicized by John Filson, the author of *Discovery, Settlement, and Present State of Kentucke* (1784), which included an alleged autobiography of Boone. The famous frontiersman was a suitable exemplar of romantic delight in the serenity to be found in deep forests far from settled communities. Boone moved westward as settlement spread over once-wild territory; he really preferred the privations of the frontier to the 'crowding,' as he called it, of the pioneer settlements.

arrangement the public would have nothing to desire at the hands of the proprietors, who have made their line most perfect, and they will find their advantage in it, by touching the fares of a score or two of timid gentlemen and ladies who desire to die in their beds.

Now, my gentle Traveller, mayhap you may think that I have yet shown you little and told you nothing, to reward you for leaving home; but open your eyes man, and look abroad, for as we emerge from the forest, the beautiful Valley of the Gaspereaux lies in all its luxuriant fertility before us. – In one minute your right arm is extended, the flush of pride is upon your brow, your foot is set more firmly upon the dickey,[47] a tear has started into your eyes, and dashing your clenched fist on the top of the coach, to the terror and amazement of the insiders, you unconsciously steal Haliburton's motto, and exclaim 'this is my own, my native land.'[48] Aye, and indulge the feeling, man, and don't be ashamed of it; for it is a tower of strength to the country; 'tis that must adorn and beautify its bosom – 'tis that must enrich its literature and preserve the purity of its institutions, and should the hour ever arrive, which God in his mercy keep from us, that our soil should be trodden by hostile feet, that feeling will sit on the peasant's sword, and flash from the peasant's eye, and the tide of invasion will roll back from the land that its children prize so dear.

But see where the meandering and beautiful little river winds along for many miles through an almost unbroken range of cultivation; its banks are formed by the base of two belts of mountains, and on the sides of which fields and farm houses are scattered farther than the eye can reach, while the hill tops are crowned with noble groves of timber. There waves the luxuriant clover and the heavy wheat, alternated with oats and maize, and wide spreading fields of potatoes; and a more gratifying and spirit stirring spectacle never presented itself to a Traveller's eye. You are almost tempted to scold yourself for never hav-

47 Here the 'dickey' is the coachman's seat. Howe later tells us that he had ridden outside on the top of the coach from Halifax to Kentville. This probably means that the coach was equipped with a seat on the coach roof immediately behind the coachman.

48 The line is from Sir Walter Scott's *Lay of the Last Minstrel* canto VI, st 1. T.C. Haliburton had placed it as a motto on the title page of his *Historical and Statistical Account of Nova Scotia*, which Howe was to publish the next year (1829).

ing seen it before, and to hug me round the middle for giving you a sight of it now; for as the rays of the declining sun are sleeping upon this delightful valley,

> There is a sweet accordant harmony
> In the fair scene;
> These sloping banks, with tree, and shrub and flower
> Bedeck'd; and these pure waters, where the sky
> In its deep blueness, shines so peacefully,

render the valley of the Gaspereaux one of the most delightful features of our Country.

V

20 August 1828

> *Puck* How now, Spirit, whither wander you?
> *Fairy* Over hill – over dale,
> Through bush – through briar,
> Over Park – over pale,
> Through flood – through fire,
> I do wander everywhere.[49]

I would we had leisure and fishing tackle to follow up the wanderings of the Gaspereaux, because, my fine fellow traveller, you would be delighted all the way. Verily, the eyes of Isaac Walton would glisten, as the leaping Trout broke the still water into a hundred circles, and showed his spots to the Sun; for never did the ancient angler cast a fly into a prettier River, or kill a fish surrounded by a pleasanter scene. But, the most striking feature of the Gaspereaux is its rapid and singular descent, for nearly a quarter of a mile, through a deep Ravine,

49 Shakespeare *A Midsummer Night's Dream* II.i.1-6

formed by two very high mountains, the sides of which are nearly perpendicular. It cannot be called a fall, as the descent is rather continuous than abrupt, but by many it is considered more curious and romantic; to approach the water from the summit of the natural walls which enclose it, is a work of some hazard and no little labor; as you have to cling to shrub and bough, to preserve yourself from performing a somerset, after a fashion that no rope dancer of the present day would feel disposed to imitate. Having reached the foot of the descent, you endeavour to collect your wind, and gaze around and above you, with feelings 'Which you can ne'er express, yet cannot all conceal.'[50] Above you the huge ramparts, which the hand of nature has reared, are towering away to the Heavens, and the forest trees are waving their leafy banners, as if proud of the giant battlements they adorn – the stream dashes past your feet as if anxious to hurry from a place so dark and wild, to steal along through the meadow flowers, and clothe them in a richer bloom. Now, mayhap, gentle Traveller – 'you are at ease in your possessions' and well-to-do in the world, and when surrounded by the luxuries and enjoyments of life, or while marking some successful turn of fortune's wheel, swellest thyself out with notions of thine own importance, and risest on tiptoe at the very idea of the commanding station you occupy in the world: but, standing in that deep ravine, surrounded by the awful handicraft of the Deity, the crest of your consequence falls; and you are content to believe that you are as a grain of sand, in comparison with the more glorious and wonderful creations of the Almighty hand. – You bethink you of all the sublime passages which you have heard or read, and pant for language to display the images which the wild sublimity of the scene has impressed upon your soul. You understand how the great I AM 'shut up the sea with doors, when it broke forth as if it issued out of the womb', and you feel the presence of him whose 'voice is like the sound of many waters.'[51]

But we must on, and trust all true lovers of the Picturesque – all who like to see nature, wild, unsophisticated and sublime, unprofaned by the hand of art, and untouched by the tiny labor of man's ingenuity,

50 Byron *Childe Harold's Pilgrimage* canto IV, clxxviii, l.9
51 Job 38:8; Revelation 1:15

will, as they range through the West, seek out the descent of the Gaspereaux, and strengthen the opinion we are anxious they should entertain, that there really is something in their own country worth going to see.

We ride on through Horton, and a prettier scene no man need desire – now you catch a glance at the Basin, and Blomidon and the Cornwallis River, to your right; and then in a moment more, some huge hill shuts out all these; and to your left, a stretch of Marsh, and a sweet little cottage, with patches of corn, and oats, and wheat, to say nothing of the garden and orchard, open upon your view, and make you sigh for the possession of the little Paradise, and almost forswear mingling in the City again. As you want to see the people as well as the country, have the kindness to blow a blast on Peter's horn whenever you approach a house, and every member of the family, man, woman and child, will either run out of the door or rush to the window. And a well favored population it is too – not an ugly female have I seen since I got over the mountain – and at this very minute there are four pair of as beautiful eyes stealing a peep at us from behind that garden wall, as ever looked through the cloudless Heaven of a Poet's dream. They have wreathed the sweet brier through their hair, and busked their bosoms with the roses, and – and – drive on Peter, or we shall lose the gentle Traveller, for there will be no keeping him out of that garden, so redolent of flowers, and enchanted by a

> Holy parcel of the fairest Dames,
> That ever turn'd their backs to mortal view.[52]

We could discourse for some hours on the beauty of the ride through Horton, for really the eye takes in at a glance more than a quire of paper would serve to display: but let our earnest advice ever be, when we cannot make a description to suit the original – go gentle reader and view the country yourself, and then you can fully understand how inadequate the language you speak is to paint the varying beauties of Horton scenery.[53]

52 Shakespeare *Love's Labours Lost* v.ii.160

53 Howe does not mention Wolfville because the settlement did not receive this name until 1829. By 'Horton' he meant the continuous line of settlement shown on the provincial map of 1829 from the Gaspereau River (near the present Melanson) to the

William H. Eager
View from the Horton Mountains, circa 1836

We are now approaching the sweet little village of Kentville, and a pleasanter place either to look at or be in, is not within the range of the North Mountain – it is seated in a valley, and contains about 30 houses; near its centre, the Horton and Cornwallis streets cross each other, and hence arose the old name of Horton Corner;[54] the rear is closed in by woods, which divide the village from the western parts of Cornwallis, and between the trees and houses the River winds along, and adds to the beauty and value of property in the neighbourhood, by some pretty strips of intervale, which invariably follow the course of the stream. On the south, a high mountain, which rises with a gentle inclination, helps to shelter the village, if shelter be needed from that quarter, and at the same time adds to its picturesqueness and beauty. And now let me warn you that you are getting into a bad neighbourhood, so remember it behoves you to beware, for 'hereabouts do

site of Wolfville and, more generally, the whole township from the Horton mountains to Kentville.

54 Kentville had been given its new name in 1826, just two years before Howe's first visit there on business for the *Novascotian*.

dwell' a set of fellows who are past all endurance: hardly do you get into the village, before some long-legged Merchant pops you into a gig and gallops you away to church – or some other sinner of the same stamp gets you into his house, from which it is no easy matter to escape. You may run about, like Blair's soul,[55] knocking at every outlet, but in vain – Port stands sentry in one place – Madeira in another, while Claret, at the head of Bacchus's light infantry, fairly cuts you off from every retreat; while the graceful restraint of a reiterated welcome from a youthful matron, and the childish prattle of sweet little Bess, make you almost forget your home, and swear that the village should have been called Hospitality instead of Horton Corner. There is also in the neighbourhood, what Shakespeare would call 'a good portly man, i'faith, and a corpulent; of a cheerful look, a pleasing eye, and a most noble carriage, and, as I think, his age, some fifty'[56] – and let him but get the flat of his generous palm upon your back, and may old Nick eat me for a sandwich if you get out of his clutches in a hurry – stories will he tell you and jokes will he crack, and if the bottle, when kept in motion by his good humour, does not travel as far or as fast as the sun (to which Sheridan once compared it)[57] it flies round its orbit much quicker.

It being in vain to think of going on in the Stage,[58] we must make ourselves comfortable for the night, and loiter a day or two away in a place where so much may be seen and enjoyed; but if you want to see

55 A reference to Robert Blair's poem *The Grave* (1743), ll.354–7:

In that dread moment how the frantic soul
Raves round the wall of her clay tenement,
Runs to each avenue, and shrieks for help,
But shrieks in vain!

56 The words of Falstaff, speaking of himself, in Shakespeare's *Henry IV, Part I* II.iv.463ff

57 Howe is thinking of these lines in act III, scene v of R.B. Sheridan's comic opera, *The Duenna* (1794):

This bottle's the sun of our Table,
His beams are rosy wine;
We, Planets that are not able,
Without his help to shine ...

58 Kentville was the overnight stop for the westbound stage, which reached the village at 6:00 PM and left for Bridgetown at 5:00 the next morning.

any thing but the inside of their houses, steer clear of the fellows I have named, and let me introduce you to my worthy friend Mrs. Fuller, who keeps the Kentville Inn, and who will make you as comfortable as heart can wish. Here you may enjoy either quiet or company as the case may be – a few steps up or down stairs will ensure either; and then there is none of the bustle and precision, and formality of an inn – an unobtrusive demeanor marks both the Landlady and her assistants, and without being eternally asked if you do not want something which they have not got, you are sure of getting what you do want; therefore, gentle Traveller, trust to the Widow Fuller to make you comfortable after your long day's ride, and as we are to go over to Cornwallis in the morning, get to bed by times.

'Night is the time for rest', sayeth Montgomery,[59] and you would not question even a less repectable authority, after riding on a Stage top from Halifax to Horton – 'My blessing on the man who first invented sleep' sayeth Sancho Panza, and you are ready to lend your aid to perpetuate the invention, not so much for the blessing as the health and vigor which a nap brings with it; and then such a nap – beyond the reach of trucks and carriages, of roaring sailors, and boxing labourers – so still – so noiseless, and so sound, that though the Boblincoln has been whistling under your window for an hour, and the morning sun is smiling on your cheek, you are still circled by its wreath of poppies. But away – away – away into the Township of Cornwallis, and feast your eyes with the riches of Nova Scotia's garden.

Leaving Kentville, we drive in the direction of Blomidon a matter of eight miles, and then, if you please, we can ride an equal distance, due north – and far as the eye can reach in every direction, you will see nothing but one wide scene of fertility and beauty. You know not on what to rest the attention, all is so rich and fruitful; yet a sameness rests on all, for you miss, except in one or two places, the gentle alternation of hill and dale – or the abrupt and bold scenery which may be often viewed, even in the centre of high cultivation. You have doubtless heard much of the beauty of this Township, and are now only surprised that you have not heard more; thousands of acres, almost as

59 James Montgomery, 'Night' l.1

level as the green cloth on your card table, are waving with grass and grain, while orchards, loaded with fruit, meet you at every step, and half shut from your view the neat little dwellings they surround. The Rivers which 'make up' from the Basin of Mines, pierce the bosom of this beautiful Township in every direction; and, as they are dyked and aboiteaued[60] to keep them from overflowing, they occupy no more of the land than is necessary to vary its aspect. The Cornwallis River takes its rise in the neighbourhood of the Carriboo Bog, and from thence to its confluence is about 30 miles; at the proper seasons, plenty of salmon and shad are taken in its waters, and the white sail of commerce not unfrequently rests upon its tide. Nothing can be more novel to the eyes of a person unaccustomed to this inland navigation, than seeing the hull and sails of a vessel, often before he can discover the water on which she reclines; it is a strange but not unpleasing commingling of Trade and Agriculture, and seems as if the great interests of the Country were on the best of terms.

Although Cornwallis Township reminds one of the fertile and rich monotony of a Dutch landscape, yet the scenery which surrounds it does not partake of its character; the high range of mountain which circles it on the north and east, and which terminates in the bold front of Blomidon, the hills beyond Kentville, and the view which you get of Lower Horton, all combine to form a most delightful panorama of natural beauty. Much do I fear, and more do I regret, that we cannot spend a day at the latter place, for the fame of its beauty has spread far and wide; it being formed by a great number of hills, and vallies, under high cultivation, where, at every step the Traveller takes, he observes a perpetual change of aspect.

But there is really so much that we have seen, so much that we would like to linger to gaze on with an eye of more strict enquiry, and so much that we shall not be able to see, that we must almost give up the task of description in despair, for truly enough saith the scripture 'the eye is not satisfied with seeing.'[61]

60 'Aboiteau' was the Acadian French term for a dam across a channel. It consisted of a double row of wooden piles driven into the mud, the space between being filled with tree trunks, stones, and earth; a floodgate controlled the level of the channel water. The term is still in common use.

61 Ecclesiastes 1:8

A full week might be spent to advantage in Cornwallis; indeed it would take a day to examine Mr. Prescott's beautiful and extensive gardens, where every variety of fruit which the country will produce is blended with every flower, and where the perfection of modern Horticulture may be viewed in successful operation.[62] But as

> Our legs can keep no pace with our desires,
> Here will we rest.[63]

VI

28 August 1828

The first reflection we make, after a full survey of Cornwallis, is, that the great mass of its population may live, and live well, by working three days a week. Some, of course, work more, but others do not even give this portion of their time to assiduous and persevering exertion. In all countries and all ages it has ever been recorded, that man has a natural antipathy to labor; it seems as if the few days of idleness which our first Parents spent in the Garden of Eden had so bewitched them – had hung round their memories so long, that at length their children, who heard of Paradise but never saw it, finding it difficult to fix any more definite idea in their minds, imagined that it was a place where plenty of comforts and luxuries were provided, and where *there was nothing*

62 Howe refers to the locally celebrated gardens of Charles Ramage Prescott (1772-1859). Prescott was born in Halifax, where he lived as a prosperous merchant until, some time between 1811 and 1814, poor health caused him to move to the country. On a tract of land in Cornwallis he built a fine house and took up horticulture. His gardens, greenhouses, and hothouses were the wonder of visitors. Although his success in such ventures as raising excellent grapes and peaches in the open air usually drew most attention, his best service was to the apple industry of the province, for he imported and developed many apple stocks and distributed free graftings to Valley farmers. He was MLA for Cornwallis Township, 1818-20, and a member of the Legislative Council from 1825 to 1838. His house at Starr's Point, Acacia Grove, still stands and in 1971 was made a Provincial Historic House and opened as a museum.

63 A slightly altered version of lines spoken by Hermia in Shakespeare's *A Midsummer Night's Dream* III.ii.445–6

to do. Hence, I believe, has arisen the disinclination of the bipeds to constant and unremitting industry. They have resolved the whole thing into a very consoling syllogism – 'Adam', say they, 'did not work in Eden – Adam was very happy while he staid there – ergo, if we do not work we shall be very happy too.' This kind of reasoning has at all times been more or less pernicious. When driven by stern necessity, Adam toiled; his children follow his footsteps, and taking them en masse, necessity is a task-master that gets more labor done than either Ambition or Industry. When overloaded by taxes, with a heavy rent to pay and few comforts to hope, the farmer works like a beaver – the early cock is disturbed by his footstep – night closes on him while his hand is still upon the plough, and his mind, quickened to a shrewd and constant activity, is employed during the evening in reflecting or resolving on something which can put one potatoe more into each hill, or hang an additional grain on every spire of wheat. Habit at length renders that a pleasure, which was at first a burthen; he soon finds that it is no great hardship to labour, and that thought, which at first seemed irksome, brings its own pleasures with it, and eke its profits too. But take the same man – give him 100 acres of soil which requires little or no manure, and for which he shall pay no rent – take from him no taxes, and give him a fair market for his produce, and I am not prepared to swear, but think I may venture to affirm, on a review of more than fifty cases in the Township of Cornwallis, that in a few years he will be just where he started; with this difference, that his house and barn will be getting older, while the stock of neither (children always excepted) will be much improved, nor the general appearance and intrinsic value of his farm heightened but in a very trifling degree. But happy is he if things are no worse than this; but there is too much reason to fear that his farm will be mortgaged to some griping old curmudgeon, who, if he does not foreclose, and arrest the indolent possessor, will sit on his future prospects with the specific gravity and cool taciturnity of an incubus. All this 'seems strange – seems passing strange',[64] and when assured of its truth, how sinks our estimate of the order to which we belong. The brutes labour while the rein is in their mouths, and the whip on their withers – and let but necessity slacken the ribbons, and

64 Shakespeare *Othello* I.iii.160

lay aside the scourge of poverty and want, and what becomes of man's superiority over the beast he drives?

But to leave general reasoning, and come to the practice rather than the theory of idleness, perhaps in no part of the province are its effects more injurious than in that Township which has been justly styled the garden of Nova Scotia. – More Mortgages are held on property in King's and Annapolis, than in any other counties of the Province, and the theory aforesaid is the only explanation I can give. The soil of both is highly fertile and productive – yielding, with less than ordinary labor, almost all of the necessaries of life in abundance; surrounded by water in every direction, export and import of bulky articles are easily made; and with regular habits of industry, frugal living, and common foresight, every farmer within their limits ought at least to be independent, and most of them comparatively rich. If this may be affirmed of the two Counties generally, it is applicable in a more especial manner to Cornwallis, where thousands of acres require no other labour than a little dyking, and the gathering of their bountiful and spontaneous crops; and where, with but few exceptions, every *necessary* article of use may be brought within the means, and created by the industry of a frugal family. But, unfortunately, the soil is too productive, and many, from finding that a living may be made with so little labor, think of course it can be made with less. And instead of running a race with fortune, trying by every effort of body and mind to tread upon its heels – what do they do? Run it with poverty, and so long as they can keep one length ahead, never think how close Sparebones is upon their rear. Nor is indolence the only evil – a cursed fondness for dress, and tea parties, and gossipings, which not only lead to the squandering of money, but to the squandering of time, which is the parent of wealth, all serve to make Mortgages grey headed, and if they do not saddle a farm with new incumbrances, are sure to perpetuate the old ones.

Musing on these things, as I gazed from an eminence down on this beautiful Township – the calm serenity of the view –

> The silent breathing of the flowers,
> The melting light that beamed above,[65]

65 Thomas Moore *The Loves of the Angels* ll.38–9

and the whispery waving of an oak that rose over my head, hushed me into a gentle slumber. God forbid that the noonday sun should ever again find my eyelids closed; and, were it not for the vision that blessed my sleep, and which I would fain describe, I should be ashamed to tell of my drowsiness, Methought that the Genius of Nova Scotia rose before my sight, as did the image of Coila to the inspired Burns.[66] – She was tall as the Pine, of a firm but not ungraceful frame; and though her features, on a first view, seemed rude and forbidding, yet when you gazed more intently upon them, new beauties struck the eye at every glance; her countenance was frank and open, and though its expression was various, there was a redeeming quality, even in the least benign. At one season she frowned, and a chill came over the plains, and the pleasant rivers were congealed, and rude blasts tore their verdure from the trees, and withered each blossom and flower; but the frost quickened the spirit and braced the nerves, and the germs of future plenty were scattered far and wide, beneath the white shroud in which the glories of spring and summer lay entombed. Then again she burst into tears, and her sighs stole on the ear with a sad sound, like the March wind – but anon, beautiful flowers sprung up where her tears fell, and the Forest was clothed with blossom and leaf, and a sweet smile mantled over her face, shedding life, and animation, and glory on every inanimate and every living thing. Her head was crowned with a sheaf of wheat – mingled with Barley, Oats and Rye, and round her neck was thrown a string of berries and Fruits; while a broad zone, in which many of the vegetable tribe were mingled, circled her waist, and sustained the dignity of her demeanour. Her right hand rested on the Plough, to which she seemed to look for a steady support – and in her left she held an Oar, which at times she waved around the coast, and the deep sent forth its treasures, and the white wings of commerce expanded to the gale. And, as she gazed around upon her offspring, she seemed to address them in the following words, to which her every feature lent force and expression. Children, I have spread before you all that your necessities require – Timber waves upon my hills – and

66 'Coila,' the Latin or Latinized name of Kyle, a district in Ayrshire, Scotland, is sometimes used by Robert Burns as a poetical synonym for Scotland.

fertility enriches my vallies, my coasts and rivers are swarming with fish, and minerals abound within my bosom, and all that I ask of you is active and persevering toil, industrious and frugal habits, untiring and diligent enquiry, and in return, you shall be rich, intelligent and happy.

I awoke, and the vision was gone – but there is many a drone in the Province, that I wish it would sometimes appear to, and rouse him from his lethargic slumber – and fright from his back and his board the miserable trappings which his pride substitutes for the lasting and substantial elements of independence. Idleness cannot be charged on our whole population – this would be unjust, but certain it is that in our western counties, it is by far too general. Men own farms – or at all events hold them, and expend a certain portion of labour on their cultivation, and gather a corresponding portion of increase – but few labour as assiduously as they could, or derive from their land as much as it might be made to yield. And then, with some few exceptions, almost all expend more for importations, either for personal and household decoration, or to administer to the profusion of their tables, than is consistent with the dignity and character of the Farmer. I say dignity – for of all employments on the face of the earth, there is none which lifts a man above the industrious and independent cultivator of the soil. There he is at his plough tail – turning up the earth which his own exertions have redeemed from the wilderness – his well-fed cattle repaying his care by steady and quiet toil, and the free air of Heaven fanning his cheek and the sun, smiling on his path. Only look at the brawny vigor of his limbs – the fearlessness of his stride, the elevated expansion of his brow – the whole man seems sentient with the feeling which Smollett so well expressed:

> Thy spirit, independence, let me share
> Lord of the lion heart and eagle eye.[67]

Let me see the Sheriff, or Sheriff's Deputy – or money lender, or lawyer's clerk, that would venture into that field, to profane the earth by his footstep. By the fist of a farmer, there is no merit in whip cord,

67 Tobias Smollett, 'Ode to Independence' (1773), ll.1–2

if he would not fly away from that fellow faster than he ever flew after one – why the very flash of the Ploughman's eye would wither him, as did the glance of Marius the murderous gladiator. With whom would he change situations? Can he envy the pale cheeks of Tinkers, Tailors, Lawyers, Parsons, Cordwainers and Editors – God forbid that he should – would he change the free air for some close cell, where sedentary labor might perhaps make him richer but could never make him so happy or healthy as he is now? which would cramp his free spirit, and change his firm stride into the mincing hobble of a rickety woman? No! he would not descend to be either.

But see where the sun sinks in the west – and the Ploughman unyokes his cattle, and returns to his home; and just for the sake of variety let us go with him, and partake of his evening meal. It is as it should be – simple but substantial, the produce of his own farm. Not one article of his food has helped to swell the Balance of Trade against the Province, or has paid a farthing of duty into the Provincial Chest. There, take a bowl, man, and help yourself to milk, warm and rich from the cow; none of your slops of Bohea and Hyson, – or if you must have tea, go and gather some leaves from the hill side and the good woman will make some for you; but as to bringing a weed from China to fatten a Ploughman in Nova Scotia, there never was a more confounded humbug. The Bread, Sir, was grown in that field, and ground in that mill, and though perhaps not so white as Howard Street, it is a great deal sweeter; and it is not saddled with half a dozen profits to Brother Jonathan for sowing, grinding, shipping, &c., nor has it paid a crown of British silver into the Custom House[68] – so fall to, man, and do it

68 Howe's exemplary farmer was the exception rather than the rule. Other travellers also noted how prevalent was the use of American white flour and lectured Nova Scotian farmers upon this evidence of foolish luxury. As Moorsom explains, 'Flour in barrels, and bread, is received in large quantities, from Boston, and all the more southern ports ... Of late years, the demand has been diminishing in inverse ratio to the provincial agriculture; and in order that this may be encouraged, a duty of five shillings sterling per barrel is imposed by Act of Parliament on all flour imported from the United States; but still a large balance remains in favour of the States, and bills on Boston or New York are always at a premium' (pp 58–9). Howe notes, quite accurately, that the bread eaten by Bostonians (Howard Street is in Boston) was much whiter than that made from local flour; provincial milling produced an inferior product.

justice, for when did such butter and cheese tickle your palate before, or a finer plate of raspberries gladden your epicurean spirit?

Only look at the fat and happy faces around you; Plenty has set its broad arrow on every member of the family; and why? Because Industry and Frugality preside over all – Because they scorn to be indebted to other lands for food and clothes that can be created at home. Think you the moulding of that Stripling's neck is not as well displayed in flax of his own growing, as though his shirt collar was bleached inn the Emerald Isle? Has not his breast as fair an expansion beneath that homespun jacket, as though it was cased in broad cloth? and take him altogether, with his keen eye and florid cheek, if you were a girl of 18, and wanted a fellow to cheer you by night and to toil for and guard you by day, would you not rather give your heart to his keeping than to any dandified imitator of city fashion and extravagance, who would range a black coat of the first cut along side of his home manufacture? If you would not, may you never have a sound nap on an honest bosom, nor march forth of a Sabbath, followed by your eighteen children.

The poisoned shirt of Dejanira was not more pernicious to Hercules, than are the frippery trappings of affected gentility to our Agricultural population; who, with a virtuous reliance on their own character and importance, should be too proud to wear them. Would they not laugh to see the Eagle, casting off the plumage on which he had cloven the air and gazed on the sun, to array himself in the gaudy feathers of the Peacock, when such a change would sink the brave Bird to earth, never again to rise? And how can they covet what lowers them from the elevation of independent yeomen to the galling servitude of country Traders, and the long train of legal cormorants, who live by the extravagance of the Farmer? But in this cottage there is none of it; the thrifty wife by whom we sit would not change the sweet scene before her – the sight of her own healthy and happy household collected round her evening meal, for the ominous gatherings of village gossips, with their ribbons, and caps, and tawdry ornaments; who ride five miles to waste five hours, and exhibit finery worth as many pounds, and for which their husbands' names are standing on the wrong side of some merchant's Ledger, who understands the whole mystery of cent per cent. What is it to her if Mrs. Turnip's cow has calved, or Mrs. Withrod has had twins, or Miss Broomstick has spoiled her new Bombazine with currant stains, and all the other items of important intelligence which take women away from their own firesides; which break in on these hours of sweet repose which labor claims for his reward, and wastes time which should be devoted to the cultivation and improvement of the adult and the infant mind, in the trivial idleness and dissipation which destroy them.

VII

11 September 1828

But, maugre the idleness of many, and the baneful extravagance of a great many more – there is a vast deal of real wealth in the western country. But mayhap, gentle Traveller, you have been bustling about the wharves and streets of Halifax for some thirty or forty years; and having gathered some cool thousands into your chest, have brought yourself gradually to the belief that there is no other kind of Property worth having but Stores, Wharves, Fish, Sugar and Molasses – and that the whole Province of Nova Scotia is bounded on the South by Miller's Wharf, North by the Dock Yard, East by the Harbour of Halifax, and West by the Town Clock; and that all the wealth, influence and intelligence of the Province aforesaid may be found every day, from one till two, in front of the Province Building. But look abroad, man, and let your mind take in other ideas of wealth – noble stretches of upland, waving with a plenteous crop, – groves of timber, every stick of which has its value – dyke and intervale – Orchard and Garden, which, if they cannot be barrelled up and sent to Jamaica, are nevertheless to be prized and toiled for, and make a man rich when acquired. Nor let it for a moment be supposed that if Mortgages exist in the country, they are all, as a matter of course, held in the Town – some are, no doubt, but the great body are not, for besides the property which the lawyers contrive to get into their hands, and which the Devil himself would not get out again, as you pass along through the Western Countries, the dwellings of the rich are pointed out to you at intervals of a few miles. Many, it must be confessed, are or have been Merchants, or Tavern Keepers, and this might lead us to believe that the only way to get wealth was to sell groceries and broad cloth, were it not for a goodly body of examples which you meet of men who, with industrious frugality and prudent management, have grown rich by farming alone; and who have lent the surplus profits of their industry on the lands of their more indolent and extravagant neighbours – these men may be met with in every direction, and are living examples of what may be done in a country where, unless reduced by some deplorable stroke of Providence, no man should be poor.

But, saith the gentle Traveller, we came here to spy out the beauties and not the nakedness of the land – to enjoy ourselves among the people, not to quarrel with them about their want of industry – to trace the loveliness of nature without seeking to dwell on the deformities which waste and indolence have scattered over the soil – and so we did, my worthy knight of the joyful countenance, and now I bethink me, we must quit preaching, although the text is fruitful, for a pleasant disciple of Esculapius[69] has promised to show us the Kentville Falls.

The 'dreadful accident maker' of a London newspaper, who has discovered a novel way of robbing a man or breaking his neck, which has never occurred to any of his brethren, is a wonderfully happy fellow for a day at least – the votaries of fashion who have invented a new waiste – or the Bard who has stumbled on an image unprofaned by the touch of former Poetasters, are joyous; but neither are as much delighted as the Traveller who pounces upon a scene which has escaped the searching eyes of earlier Tourists, nor has yet been forced to throw a dim image of its beautiful reality on the pages of the periodical Press. The Rocking stone[70] has been rolled over and over by pedes-

69 The legendary Greek physician and god of medicine, usually 'Aesculapius' in the Latin form.

70 A massive stone in Spryfield, near Halifax, often commented on by Howe's contemporaries as one of the natural wonders of the province. Moorsom estimated that it weighed nearly 200 tons, and a correspondent of the *Acadian Recorder* in 1823 worked out the figure of 162 tons. The stone still stands as it did in 1828, and can be set rocking without much difficulty.

trians and equestrians, who have speculated on its position, and favored the world with its dimension – The North River and Grand Lake Falls[71] have been exhibited to the wondering eyes of the multitude in a variety of ways; and we ourselves have already shewn forth the descent of the Gaspereaux. But the Kentville Falls have hitherto remained, like some of the rustic beauties around them, untouched by the hand of man – that is (mistake me not), they have never had prose or poetry written upon them. So let us mount and follow the Dr. up the hill, which overlooks the village. The distance is some three miles – and after riding as near to the scene as the New Canaan Road will take us, we dismount, tie our steeds to the first fence and turn off to the left, clambering over stumps and wind falls – plunging through wet grass, and shaking the dewy distillations from the birch leaves down on our heads and shoulders. Of all Pilots that chance may throw in a Traveller's way as he wends over this wild country of ours, commend me to a Village Doctor – he has the patience of Job, the perseverence of Sysiphus – the nerves of a Gladiator, and the good nature of Uncle Toby. If you roam over the high lands he knows the grandest views – if you wind along the vale, with the name and quality of every rivulet he is familiar – plunge into the forest, and in a twinkling he unfolds the mysteries of our indigenous plants – and get him on the sea shore, and he will discourse to you of geological and mineralogical formations as eloquently and intelligibly as Alger or Jackson.[72] – And then, as he

71 The North River is just north of Truro; Howe describes the area in chapter III of *Eastern Rambles*. Grand Lake or Shubenacadie Grand Lake, the largest of the Dartmouth chain of lakes, lies some twelve miles due north of Bedford.

72 Cyrus Alger (1781-1856) was an iron-master and industrialist of New England. In the late 1820s, with several Halifax business men, he built near Annapolis the first smelting furnace in the British provinces. Howe refers to these 'Iron Works' in chapter x when he is describing the countryside between Annapolis and Digby. According to Moorsom, the works were called the Clements Mining Company. Alger was also known as a metallurgist and had various inventions to his credit. Charles Thomas Jackson (1805–80) was a chemist and geologist who, with his friend Francis Alger, Cyrus Alger's son, twice visited Nova Scotia to collect minerals and study geology. He and Francis Alger published the results as a series of joint papers in the *American Journal of Science* for 1828. Howe reprinted extracts in a long article entitled 'Mineralogy and Geology of a part of Nova Scotia' in the *Novascotian* of 7 August 1828. The reference is probably to Francis Alger.

has the entree of every house for miles round, and has seen the inhabitants thereof in every variety of situation; having, as the marriage ceremony expresses it, visited them in 'sickness and in health', he has a fund of anecdote and odd stories with which to beguile the way. It would do a town physician good to see one of these men going his daily and nightly rounds – jumping off his horse six times in the course of a three mile ride to take down and replace the bars – now stopping to pick up his hat or umbrella, which some extending branch has struck from his head or dragged from under his arm – plunging up to his girths in a new road – or if it be winter, floundering on through the snow, to some log house, where a delicate operation awaits his frozen fingers and almost deadened faculties. This is bad enough, but to see him presenting his Bill is the most amusing scene of all – Harrow objects to the length of it first, and the Dr. has to recount his hairbreadth scapes, and run over the whole history of pill and potion; and having made out a very plain case, already feels the cash in the centre of his palm; but his countenance blanches as Harrow, in his turn, takes up the note of complaint, and as the Dr. has given him many good reasons to show that he has earned the money, gives him in turn as many more, equally good, to prove that he cannot pay it. His wheat crop has failed – his Potatoes run small – his cattle have died – his turnips have been devoured by the flies, and last, not least, the very brats which the Dr. brought into the world, are raised up against him as evidence of their parents' poverty. There are, perhaps, some setoffs that render a Doctor's life tolerable in the country, and were it not for these, it would be beyond endurance. If he happens to be old, he is an especial favorite at the gatherings of elderly Tabbies, has the softest seat on the sofa, is universal umpire in all disputes about etiquette, hard words and new dresses, and divides with the Preacher the best slice of the shad, or the kidney cut of the mutton; and then, if he be youthful, he is still more caressed – for the young ladies are as kind to him from anticipation of the future, as are the elderly ones from recollections of the past. He opens the Ball when Balls are given – and is sure to make one in every Picnic, or 'ride to the mountain', and in very desperate cases, where it is necessary to spend a whole night in a patient's house, a goodly portion of delicacies are laid out for his benefit, and a beautiful little nurse of 18 or 20 sits up with him, *waiting for a crisis*. But as Spenser has it,

> There leave we them, in pleasure and repast,
> Spending their joyous days and gladfull nights,
> And taking usurie of time forepast
> With all dear delices and rare delights,
> Fit for such ladies and such lovely knights,
> And turn we here,[73]

for the sound of the waterfall is in our ears, and the foam bells which have been created by its descent are gliding along on the breast of the stream that winds its way beneath the deep shade of the forest trees. About 30 yards below the principal fall is a small jet, or rather slide of water, 15 or 20 feet in length, which, if your guide be waggish, he may pretend is the sole object of your jaunt; and if there were nothing else, even this would be worth coming to see. But journeying higher up, as romantic and lovely a scene opens on your eye as ever gladdened the optics of a wayfarer: on both sides the hills rise nearly perpendicular, and the trees and shrubs, which spring from out their rifted rocks, serve to vary, if they cannot entirely conceal, the sternness of the mountain aspect. There is no great volume of water, but for several yards it is closely pent in a narrow channel, from which, as if glad of its freedom, it escapes with a hurried expansion over about 20 feet of inclined rock, and thence rushes into the gulf below, a distance of 30 feet more. When seen from the opposite bank, the slide and overshot seem blended together and have a very fine effect. Indeed there is a wildness and singularity in the whole scene that nothing can surpass; the mountain seems to have been divided to make way for the stream, and the stream to flow on to add to the fine effect of the features of the mountain, and you only regret that you cannot linger around it for hours, to give full current to the feelings which it engenders.

It is one misfortune of our Provincial infancy, that we cannot hang old traditions round a scene like this. What a spot for a Hermit's retreat where his evening hymn might mingle with the falling waters, and his knee bend in adoration of him whose power and beauty were ever

73 *The Faerie Queene* book v, canto III, xl, ll.1-6

before his eyes. Here would our Children of the Mist[74] have gathered, to brood over the story of their wrongs; and that jutting rock would form a befitting pedestal for Helen M'Gregor herself, while a score of highland gillies might defend the ascent against a whole company of red coats.[75] But these things are not for us – our wild and beautiful scenes cannot draw for enchantment on legendary lore, and like penniless maidens, must be loved for themselves alone.

VIII

18 September 1828

From the green fields – and good folks of the county of King's, in the language of the old hymn, 'the hour of our departure's come', for with spirits rather quickened than satiated by what we have seen, we must wend our way towards Annapolis, wondering in what consists the difference of general character between the two counties. Leaping, once more, on our old friend the Stage, we bid farewell to Kentville, and place our neck under the care of a steady and careful lad named Pat, who, for respectfulness of demeanour, and attention to his horses, is not excelled by any man on the road. There is nothing very striking to arrest the attention of the passenger, for many a long mile after leaving Kentville – much of the road is level and monotonous, and without stopping to enquire whether it be more tiresome for cattle than the hilly and irregular, which some assert, there can be no doubt that it is infinitely more wearisome to the traveller. On the right hand, a short distance from the village, a small lake is pointed out to you, half hidden

74 The 'Children of the Mist' were a particular branch of the MacGregor clan called MacEagh. See Scott's *A Legend of Montrose* chapter 22.

75 Helen MacGregor is the wife of Rob Roy MacGregor in Scott's *Rob Roy*. Howe alludes to a scene in chaper 30 of the novel in which Helen, dressed as a Highland warrior, appears on a rocky summit to confront a detachment of English soldiers searching for Rob Roy.

by the trees which surround it, and which presents as smooth and gloomy a surface as the Dead Sea. There are no fish in it – and it is said to be fathomless, but whether this be fact or fable, we must leave to future decision. Further on you pass over Carriboo Bog, in the neighbourhood of which the Cornwallis and Annapolis rivers take their rise. The bog itself is something of a curiosity, being a plane of miles in circumference, covered with wild laurel bushes and other low shrubs – there is nothing pleasing in its aspect, but the mind goes delving into the earth to find out how it got there; and although we might build up a theory as plausible and as perfect as our neighbours' to account, to the reader's satisfaction, for this singular morass, like many other Travellers, we are very glad to get over it.

As the Passenger sees so little of settlement and cultivation from the Post Road which passes through Aylesford and Wilmot, he is led to believe, that like Gregor M'Gregor's kingdom, they are townships only in name.[76] But let him take horse and strike into a cross road to the right, and ride a few miles in the direction of the north mountain, and he will soon discover his error; for all along under the high ground, there is as fine a range of farms as he would wish to behold; which, though hidden by the wood and wild land from the flying traveller, will amply repay a closer research. Indeed from Blomidon to Digby gut, there is an almost unbroken line of cultivation, embracing the base of the mountain, and more or less of the level land with which it is blended. In King's County it forms the north western part of Cornwallis and Aylesford – in Annapolis, Wilmot and Granville, and at the foot of the Handly mountain, where we are at this minute, it wears a most promising and delightful aspect. Indeed he must have a singular taste, who cannot find something here to engage his attention – if he is fond of rural pursuits, and has an eye for judging of fields and of stock, there

76 The MacGregor country was the mountainous area lying between Loch Lomond, Loch Katrine, and Loch Ard. Gregor MacGregor, the nephew of Rob Roy, was as a young man strongly influenced by his uncle and later supported him in many of his escapades. The country intermittently controlled by the MacGregors in the eighteenth century had been gradually taken from them by the political influence of powerful neighbours until, by the time of Rob Roy, it was indeed the kingdom of the clan in name only.

is no lack of employment, for there are abundance of both – if he be a mineralogist, he is at home in a twinkling; and if a Painter or a Poet, let him climb to the mountain top, from which he may see thousands of acres of land clothed with a fruitful harvest, on the one hand, and the Bay of Fundy rolling its angry billows on the other, with New Brunswick looming in the distance; while hundreds of objects are scattered in endless variety before him, out of which he may make as many pictures as would fill a wheelbarrow, or poems as would exhaust a Lady's Album.

In Wilmot, although there is in many instances the same lack of industry as in other parts of the country, yet here there are some fine and encouraging examples of persevering activity, rewarded by handsome and enviable independence. After walking over the grounds of a substantial farmer of the name of Elliot, and surveying their excellent condition – the smiling promise of his orchard – the neat and bountiful appearance of his garden, you are perhaps tempted to enquire with what stock in trade he began life, and, as the inventory is not very long, you may soon be satisfied. A wife and an axe were the sum total, and although, perhaps, the first years of his settlement were years of toil, and privation and anxiety, yet the fact that he now owns property worth some thousands is one of the many that might be named to show how handsome a competence our soil offers to the industrious. If you go into his house, the same frugal and active spirit which has cleared his fields pervades the interior of his dwelling – his cheerful helpmate is seated at her wheel, showing an example to her household; her daughters are engaged at the loom, or in the dairy, and from the oldest to the youngest member of the family, there is not a drone in the hive. A little further along you see Caleb Slocomb, hoeing potatoes in a large field, which belongs to himself; and adjoining it there are two extensive enclosures of upland, covered with grass and grain – in front there is a fine piece of intervale, and higher up on the mountain, he owns a large body of land, which is yet in a wilderness state. On the farm there is a good house, barn, smithy and other outhouses; and yet twelve years ago, Caleb was not worth a sixpence. But steady toil gained something, and an active mind made more of it; and now, with a fair chance of thirty years of life, he is not only surrounded by comfort, but with all that makes a man truly rich and independent. Now this is the class of men that I should like to see more numerous, because one of them is worth a dozen of your lazy, slow-going fellows, who care not how short the day is, if the task be short also; and who, while a heavy debt is hanging over their heads, will spend an afternoon at a tavern in harvest, or waste evenings which should be devoted to searching for information or making a close calculation of the interest of their mortgage, debating about a horse race, over a tumbler of brandy. Truly one's gall rises – Tush! saith the gentle traveller, if that be the case, let us back again to our seat on the stage.

And see where the Annapolis river winds along its sinuous and beautiful course, like Leviathan basking in the sun – now hidden from your view by a turn of the road – now half revealed through the long grass and the straggling elms which ornament its borders; and then shewing several of its glorious folds at once – a sight which to see is to be joyful. Nova Scotia has no proud Palaces to court the view – no Cathedral, nor Tower, to be gazed and wondered at – her attractions are those of nature – and she must trust to posterity for the adornments of art. It is a Spanish proverb, that he who has not seen Seville has seen nothing; and in like manner I would say, that he whose eye has never rested on the Annapolis River, as the mild rays of a Summer eve were reposing on its bosom, and the verdure of the season was scattered around it, is yet but a stranger to the beauty of our land.

I wish we had leisure to get into a Canoe, and explore it to its source, for I have been told by those who have done so, that there are many bewitching features that are only to be seen from the breast of the waters. These are not wide prospects of beauty – but sylvan nooks and dells, formed by the irregularities of the land through which it passes, and to which the ever-varying foliage of the forest trees, interspersed with wild shrubbery, and occasionally contrasted with an old pine rifted and riven by the storms of Winter, repay the voyageur with many a charm to render his passage delightful.

As we roll along the road, we pass through Laurence Town, of which a small cluster of houses on the wayside is the distinguishing feature. Here also are some fine fields and garden spots – a beautiful face, which you catch a glance of through that window – and on the opposite side of the river (that by the bye is viewed to great advantage from this spot)

– there is a Carding Machine, to which you may see all the old and young women in the neighbourhood going backwards and forwards, with their waggons loaded to overflowing with immense sacks of wool, and their lovely persons mounted on the topmost pinnacle of the fleecy pyramids, as gay if not as grand or as proud as any Duchess that drives through the Park with her coach and six.

And now we are approaching Bridgetown, at the news of which the gentle traveller starts – for many a time and oft has he seen the name thereof in print; sometimes leading a paragraph about building a Church or building a Ship, the like of which, as it was well set forth in the paragraph aforesaid, had never been built before; at others, appended to a copy of excellent verses, shewing the fruitfulness and energy, though at times the carelessness of genius; and until Homer and Barry fairly exhausted the subject of education,[77] Bridgetown was the birth place of many a long essay on the necessity of watering and cultivating the infant mind, which the gentle Traveller has read, like others of this thankless generation, remembering little but the place of their origin. But of this thriving village we must have a closer view, and after a night's repose, I doubt not we shall find something to amuse or instruct.

IX

25 September 1828

The Barony of Glasgow has its Bridgetown; Maine, Maryland and Jersey have theirs, and the delightful capital of Barbadoes bears the above appellation; but in christening our little Western Village, its

77 John Homer (1782–1836) was MLA for Barrington Township, 1826–36. John Alexander Barry (c 1790–1872) was MLA for Shelburne Township, 1827–30. Both men had delivered long speeches in the Assembly on the subject of education (see 'The Club' in the *Novascotian*, 28 May 1829, p 174), and Barry had taken up the same subject in the columns of the *Acadian Recorder*. Barry later became a controversial figure in provincial politics.

sponsors, in deference to Pope's advice, have 'made the sound an echo to the sense',[78] because its principal street runs across a bridge which has been thrown over the Annapolis River and conducts the Passenger from the right to the left bank of the stream, which here rushes along with considerable velocity and volume. Bridgetown is to Annapolis what Liverpool is to London – it is of comparatively recent origin – the whole Village having started into existence within the last ten or twelve years. Hence the dwellers in old Port Royal turn up their noses at the sound of its name, and pronounce its population a race of upstarts. The Bridgetownmen sneer at the torpor which pervades the capital – the stagnation of trade and the lack of enterprise and spirit; and again, their rivals console themselves with the reflection that if there is more business done up the river it is principally barter business; and add by way of corollary, that ready money is more plentiful in their ancient city than it is in the neighbourhood of the Bridge.

In Bridgetown the Traveller meets none of the starch and formality – the coyness and reserve – the ludicrous assumption of dignity and importance – which have been laid to the charge of some of our western villages. The fellows take you by the palm instead of the fore finger, and shake as if they were glad to see you; without trying to impress you with an idea that, though distant from the capital, they are versed in the chilliness of good breeding; there is no stateliness and humbug about them. The lines and distinctions of society are like the furrows on a man's brow, the effects of time; and thanks be to Providence on young men and young towns they are very faintly traced; and I never saw them less distinct than at this place. The population is insufficient for any but ridiculous classification; if parties were formed each would have but a solitary sojourn; of this the good folks seem to be aware, and the consequence is a hearty and useful amalgamation. There are, of course, the usual distinctions of religion, which divide the folks into Churchmen, Methodists, Baptists, &c. and, here as every where else, the ladies circulate their little items of gratuitous information, from which occasional coolness arises between the several members of the infant society; but notwithstanding all these, there is a freedom and cordiality of intercourse; and in undertakings for the general benefit,

78 Alexander Pope *An Essay on Criticism* part II, l.365

a unanimity, and disposition to pull together, from which Bridgetown has derived, and let us hope will still derive many advantages.

From the situation of this place it is well adapted for the business common to an inland town, as it is surrounded on all sides by a cultivated country, the increasing wants of whose population will cause it to advance with a steady and permanent growth. Besides this, it is also a seaport, and vessels of very heavy tonnage may come up the river, and discharge their cargoes into its bosom, an advantage which, notwithstanding the difficulties of the Bay and River navigation, is one of the first importance. Bridgetown, like other parts of the Province, received an impulse from the Timber Trade, which is now partially withdrawn.[79] Several very fine vessels have been built here, and above the Bridge; but those of more recent construction, like many others in the two Provinces, have not proved very lucrative speculations. Bridgetown would feel the present depression more if it was not sustained by the peculiarities of its situation.[80] But much as we may be disposed to

79 During the Napoleonic Wars, when the usual sources of lumber in Europe were closed to Britain, she imported large quantities from Nova Scotia. When, after 1815, the regular trade patterns were gradually resumed in Europe, the demands for Nova Scotian timber and lumber declined radically.

80 During the war years, the finances of Nova Scotia had been lavishly supplemented by British capital spent in the province. By 1814, for example, the provincial revenue had risen to slightly over £100,000. With the end of the wars, however, came the end of this artificial prosperity. By 1817 the revenue had dropped to less than half of the 1814 figure, and it continued on much the same disturbing course year after year. In 1821 it even fell to the alarming figure of £22,196. Sir James Kempt, the Lieutenant-Governor, had to refrain from repeating the usual optimistic platitudes as he addressed the Assembly in 1822, lamenting 'the great depreciation which property of all kinds has experienced within these two years,' the diminution of trade, and the low prices commanded by farm produce. Throughout the 1820s the province remained in economic jeopardy until finally, in 1834–5, the long-expected crash came. The causes of this state of affairs can hardly be surveyed in a mere note. Among them, and no doubt basic, was Nova Scotia's excessive dependence on British bounties and government contracts; office-seeking was a way of life for many people. Haliburton's Sam Slick, in spite of his hyperbole, was accurately assessing current ills when he criticized widespread place-hunting, lack of initiative in developing provincial resources, aversion to serious farming, and naive dependence upon government legislation to solve all problems. Likewise, Howe's not infrequent comments on 'the idleness of many, and the baneful extravagance of a great many more' are based upon actual conditions which disturbed him deeply. Some of the causes of the continuing depression were indeed economic and political forces beyond the reach of the average provincial citizen, but all too often, as Howe shows, he made no effort to offset them.

anticipate from the natural advantages of this village, there is a spirit of enterprise, emulation and improvement animating and exciting its inhabitants, in which the eye may discover the germs of future prosperity and advancement. There is an energy of character which, though it may sometimes be irregular, is often useful – a fondness for literary and general improvement, which makes the cultivation of the infant mind an object of primary importance. Parents, to whose early youth circumstances denied the blessings of instruction, are most anxious to give it to their children; and on these indications I would build with more certainty than even on the favorable features of its location. Rivers may dry up – a thousand circumstances may change the condition of a country – but, if the stream of mind flows through it, impregnate with the principle of improvement, it must flourish and progress. By far the most interesting feature of Bridgetown Society is its Sunday School, to the regulation and guardianship of which several gentlemen and ladies lend an active superintendence; and the success which has hitherto attended their efforts should prompt them to unremitting exertion, for the future.

I doubt not, my gentle Traveller, that many a time and oft you have seen our senators sawing the air, some with the right leg cocked up against the left, others with both legs forming a St. Andrew's cross, or both hands stuck into their pockets, or grasping a volume of the Province Laws, while their honors deliberately violated every rule of emphasis or action; and ye have listened to our Counsellors at Law, while they have raised their fore fingers and swung their bodies backwards and forwards, and drawled out sentiment and legal argument with precisely the same tone and gesticulation – and ye have also heard our Divines with their several professional twangs: and having heard all these, and wondered that men whose ambition led them to speak in public should not learn to pronounce their mother tongue with correctness and effect, you cannot fail to be delighted with the proficiency the Scholars at the Bridgetown Sunday School have made in this very necessary accomplishment. Youths from 8 to 12 years of age will repeat you page after page of prose or verse in better style than you would hear them read from half the pulpits in the Province. Little fellows that you would not suppose could repeat their A, B, C. will pour out one of

Milton's beautiful hymns with a correctness of emphasis and clearness of articulation which would almost impress you with an idea that the embryo orators of a future day were standing before you – that many of the ornaments of the Pulpit, the Bar and the Senate, who twenty years hence will appeal to the feelings and guide the destinies of their country, will have to trace the first dawning of their eloquence to this useful and very creditable School. There is also in this village an excellent day school, under the superintendence of Mr. Henderson, to whose care and attention both that and the Sunday School are much indebted.

I am sorry to be forced to add that here, as almost everywhere else through the Western Country, the ridiculous fondness for imported finery prevails, of which a friend furnished a characteristic instance – 'In one of our places of worship', said he, 'I lately counted 150 women, and admitting each woman to have 8 yards of ribbon, which is an under-calculation, and each yard to cost two shillings, which is also an under-calculation, for that one article of unnecessary finery, the expense must have been £120. Every thing of the same superfluous stamp, such as Leghorn bonnets, muslins, gauzes, laces, silks, bombazines, jewels, bracelets, &c, a list of which a sheet of foolscap would hardly contain, were seen about them in the same extravagant ratio.' Oh! that our fair countrywomen would learn that to build up a husband's or a parent's fortune by prudence is more praiseworthy than to scatter it by folly – that the loveliest attire is their own stainless beauty, the brightest ornament a meek and quiet spirit.

The Township of Granville, which extends from Wilmot down the right bank of the Annapolis River, and of which Bridgetown forms the capital, is one of the finest in the Province. Below the Village, the River, which is altogether free from even the partial shade that, higher up, the stately Elms afford, may be seen for miles winding through the township, and widening as it goes, until it empties itself into the Annapolis Basin. The Granville Marsh, of which there is abundance, is highly valuable and productive; and extending, as it does, all along the water side, adds at once to the beauty and real riches of the Township. Here there is a succession of fine farms, the owners of which are surrounded by every comfort, nay luxury that men need desire. Every cottage has its orchard; and in the spring, when the fruit trees are in blossom, the ride through Granville is indeed delightful. The bloom and fragrance are grateful to the eyes and the olfactories, and one might almost imagine themselves wandering through the groves of Araby the blest. This Township produces the best Apples that are raised in the country, and thousands of barrels are annually exported to other parts of this and the neighboring Province. For excellent Cider and admirable Cheese the character of Granville also stands deservedly high; and on this side of the River there is an excellent Pottery, in constant occupation, which supplies the surrounding country with all necessary articles of household ware, and from which a variety of domestic utensils are annually sent to St. John.

X

1 October 1828

The Township of Annapolis stretches along the left side of the beautiful River which bears its name; and with some features similar to those of Granville, differs from it in many of its characteristics. Granville is more uniformly level – stretches away from the water to the mountain with but little irregularity, and presents a more continuous line of cultivation. On the Annapolis side the table land is contracted in many places to a narrow strip, by the proximity of the South Mountain to the River; and hill and dale are met in gentle alternation, as the Traveller passes along. Although there is much wood and wild land between Bridgetown and Annapolis, there are some finely situated and tolerably cultivated farms. Some parts of the road are skirted to the left with huge masses of granite, piled above each other in wild and primitive singularity – here and there a little rivulet runs from the highland across the road, seeking its way to the general tide – rows of willows, which some ancient Settler's hand has reared, spread their umbrageous shade above the Passenger's head, as he glides by dwellings, the original founders of which have long since departed to another sphere. About three miles below Bridgetown, you pass over Bloody Creek, around which a tragic incident of our Provincial Annals has hung a singular interest. About the year seventeen hundred and twelve, Captain Pigeon and a party of men were sent up in boats from Annapolis, to cut wood; they had just reached the side of the Creek, and commenced their operations, when they were attacked by a party of Savages, who were lying in ambush, and who killed nearly the whole party, Captain Pigeon included; bones and other indications of the slain have frequently been found on the spot, and while passing along as evening closes around you, it requires no very vivid imagination to people the little glen with beings of another day. Indeed you can hardly persuade yourself that the dark eyes and scowling visages of the Indians are not hidden beneath the birch leaves; and as the stream rushes under the bridge on which you stand, a death groan will at times seem to mingle with the gurgling of its waters. Strange stories are of course told of sights seen and noises heard in the vicinity of the Bloody Creek; and I have little doubt that at some future day it will form a fruitful subject for a novel or a poem. One honest farmer will take his oath that as he was passing over the bridge, with his eyes wide open and his wits about him, he saw the flash and heard the report of a dozen muskets, accompanied by a mingled yell of triumph and defiance; and this story would pass for truth, if he had not been returning from the election, under the especial protection of Bacchus, who has been known occasionally to show strange sights to his votaries. Another lad is positive that he saw the soldiers passing up the stream, with Captain Pigeon at their head, but unfortunately for his veracity, it was recollected that the officer in command at Annapolis had alienated the affections of his sweetheart, after which the fellow saw a red coat on every object in nature.[81]

Annapolis, or old Port Royal, as it was called till the time of Queen Anne, has been the scene of more historical incidents, and is clothed with a garb of more interesting tradition, than any other part of the Province. Here it was that the earliest attempts at Settlement were

81 See D.C. Harvey, 'History in Stone and Bronze,' *Dalhousie Review* 12 (1932) 69–80.

made, both by the English and the French. From the first landing of Du Monts in 1604 down to 1713 it was continually changing hands. Like the Border Lands between England and Scotland it was desolated and disturbed by perpetual strife; and two of the most powerful nations of Europe seemed to have left the old world to decide their quarrel in a barren wilderness of the new. On the walls of a fort which at the present day seems hardly capable of offering a long resistance to any well directed attack, the banners of England and France alternately waved during a period of 100 years. Where stillness and peace now reign the battle shouts were mingled; and in the solitude, where the cattle's tinkling bell or the jocund song of some rustic beauty alone intrude – the fearful notes of war used to startle the echoes with a boding and ominous sound. Had I the happy faculty of Scott, and could evoke from the green sward the forms which once, in bravery and pride, trod where they now are lying, I could paint for the gentle traveller's eye many a singular and striking scene, and carry him away from the present, to behold the deeds and partake of the spirit of the past. The bloom of a thousand fields and the smoke of a thousand cottages should no longer delight his eye, the cattle should cease to low upon the mountain tops, and the flocks to crop the herbage by the river's brink. Where orchards are bending with the mellow fruit the Moose should rove in undisturbed possession; and, save where the vapour curling above the trees betrayed the Indian's tent, no indication of human existence should be traced on the wide and beautiful Vale of Annapolis, except in the immediate vicinity of Port Royal. From behind some rude breastworks, which they had hastily reared, and from the windows of the huts which formed the embryo town, the English soldiers under Philips[82] should fire on the fort, while their Gallic adversaries defended the works by every effort of valour. Now the Britons' war shout is raised, and they rush to the assault – the walls are mounted – the foe is subdued, and Nova Scotia for a time is an appendage of the British Crown. But a few months more and the French are the assailants, perhaps with similar success, and the white flag floats above the Fort, again to be torn down and trampled by the English.

82 Howe means 'Phipps.' Sir William Phipps captured Port Royal in 1690.

Such were the scenes which for many years were acted at Port Royal – which gave to the place an importance at the Courts of London and Versailles that it can never again acquire. In those days it was no uncommon sight to see men-of-war riding at anchor, or spreading their white sails on the Basin whose waters are now seldom disturbed but by the pacific votaries of commerce; and often when succour and supplies were expected by the beleaguered garrison, their arrival was hailed with shouts and tears of joy. But these matters are now the property of the Historian, and when time has thrown a deeper shade of obscurity around them they will furnish the *matériel* for poetry and romance. There is so much more of tradition mixed up with the early history of this part of the Province than with that of any other portion, not even excepting Louisburg, that Annapolis will always be an object of interest to Travellers.[83]

There is nothing very striking in its present appearance – the best view is from the Granville side, or from the high ground to the right of the road leading down to Bridgetown. There are, however, some beautiful gardens and gentlemen's seats on the outskirts of the Town, and a few well-built and handsome houses within it. On many of the buildings there are the signs of decay, and some appear to have been erected at a very early period. Business is rather dull, but the weekly visits of the Steam Boat,[84] and the passing and repassing of the Stages, serve to vary the monotony which pervades the society of Annapolis.

Midway between this town and Digby the Iron Works are to be seen. They are situated on the margin of Moose River, which runs down between two hills into the Annapolis Basin. As the works and the build-

83 Howe is right in predicting that Annapolis Royal will always be of interest to travellers, but could not foresee that the main attractions would be the preservations or reconstructions of the historic sites he mentions. The 28-acre Fort Anne Historic Park, within the present town, encloses old Fort Anne, where a garrison was maintained until 1854. The park contains the ramparts and bastions as they were at the time of surrender to British forces in 1710, and the museum, formerly the British officers' quarters, displays many relics of the fort and region. Across the river and about seven miles from the town is the meticulously reconstructed Port Royal Habitation, the original of which was built in 1605 by Champlain and his party.

84 The *Saint John*, a schooner-rigged steamboat, ran once a week between Saint John and Digby and Annapolis.

ings have already been exhibited to the public in such a variety of ways, I shall not weary the gentle traveller by attempting to describe them; but if he will climb to the brow of the hill on the Digby side he shall be repaid by a delightful view. The River is seen 'making up' till lost in the depths of the forest – on the left there is a noble grove of timber, divided from the eminence on which you stand by a deep ravine, along the side of which the road passes that leads to the Mines; beyond it the Basin 'rolls and shines' while the mountains of Granville bound the view. Immediately below you, on the River side, the several buildings which comprehend the works are grouped together; on the right, high land stretches along with the snug little Church on its Brow; while a cottage and orchard, with some cleared fields ornament the opposite bank of the stream; and away in the distance the Town and River of Annapolis may be seen, forming altogether a scene well worthy the pencil of genius.

XI

9 October 1828

The situation of Digby insensibly reminds one of Halifax – as it is built on the side of a hill, which slopes down gradually to the water. Here you again see wharves, running out into the sea, and stores and smoke houses upon them. As the tide falls a considerable distance, these, together with much of the flats, are left dry at the ebb. Digby, like Halifax, is seen to most advantage from the water, and is a very pretty little town. Its principal street winds along the shore, and contains some neat shops and private dwellings – from this, several others lead up through the town, in the direction of the Court House and Church, which are situated on the rise of the hill. On this eminence there is also a blockhouse, about the size of that which used to decorate the side of the Kempt Road;[85] but however formidable it may have been in the

85 The blockhouse on Kempt Road to which Howe refers was probably McAlpine's Blockhouse, built in 1808 during the Napoleonic wars.

ancient wars, it would not, at the present day, prove any very serious obstacle to the conquest of the country. On a little point which forms a curve at the lower extremity of the town, there are to be seen the remains of another small fortification; the breastwork, or embankments, have nearly sunk to a level with the surrounding soil – the guns are dismounted, and the barrack, a building some 20 feet by 10, has been turned into a private dwelling. A story is told of an American brig of war coming into the Bay, but taking alarm at the formidable appearance of this battery, she sailed off again without firing a gun. As Digby lies at the very entrance of the Bay of Fundy, and within gunshot of deep water, it is greatly exposed in time of war; and during the last struggle between England and America, the Inhabitants were continually called out either by real or false alarms; and for a considerable time performed regular duty, with great steadiness and determination. On one occasion the captain and one of the crew of a Privateer came into Digby in disguise, to reconnoitre; after their departure, suspicion was awakened and persons sent in pursuit of them: and young Morton,[86] then a lad in his teens, now a member of the Assembly, fell in with them, and though they were well armed, forced them both to surrender. There were other demonstrations of spirit at the time which showed that if it had been required the people would have defended their hearthstones. – To the eastward of Digby there are two indents, or narrow coves, which are styled the great and little Joggins, and to the westward there is another, along the side of which one of the cross streets of the town runs.

The good folks in Digby make sad complaints of the dullness of the times, and compared with the activity of former years, they certainly are dull. Before the depreciation in the value of shipping, it was no uncommon thing to see four or five vessels on the stocks in Digby or its immediate vicinity – and the necessary expenditure of Agents, Sailors, Artizans, &c. made, of course, a sensible impression on the affairs of the little seaport.[87] The scarcity of Herring, owing, as they

86 John Elkanah Morton (1793-1835), MLA for Digby Township, 1826–30, and a resident of Digby

87 Shipbuilding was another industry which slumped badly throughout the province after the abnormal demands of wartime disappeared. A few small vessels, mostly schooners and brigs, were built in the 1820s, but the industry did not pick up significantly until well into the 1830s.

state, to the noise the Indians make shooting Porpoises at the Gut, is another drawback on their commerce; and, as the fame of the Digbies has extended far and wide,[88] this is a matter that affects the whole Province; at least every man who likes a delicate relish for breakfast. From the proximity of Digby to the Bay of Fundy, and from its command of the fine Basin on which it is built, it must gradually rise into a place of some importance – the present depression may last for a time, but cannot have any very long duration. The view of the Valley and Basin of Annapolis is here most complete. From the Digby heights, of a clear sunny day, you can take in at a glance the whole extent of one of the finest sheets of water in the world; along both shores of which fields and farm houses are spread as far as the eye can reach; and, as if to prevent even a zephyr from curling the placid wave, the whole is enclosed by ranges of mountains, crowned by the forest groves. But, the gentle Traveller may exclaim, what is this to the Vale of Cashmere? where are the soft beauties of an Italian landscape or the glorious richness of an Italian sky? and he may have seen from the rocks of Cintra the Tagus rolling its sunny wave beneath its lovely city. Yet let him know that there is a moral as well as natural beauty at this moment before my eyes. Truly the waters are beaming and bright – the hills are stately, and the fields are green; but yet as I gaze on the Vale of Annapolis, to me it has a higher and holier charm. I feel that beneath the thousands of roofs which I see before me there are thousands of spirits as free as the air; who would unnerve the arm of faction by pointing to the blessings they enjoy, and who, if the minions of tyranny were to approach their dwellings, would drive them into the sea. I see them surrounded by the necessaries of life, while many of its luxuries are within their reach; and I see their offspring spreading over the land, adding daily to its strength and importance; and when I reflect what it was half a century ago, and think what it may be fifty years hence, I feel a glow that kindles my spirit and sets the blood dancing in my veins.

88 'Digbies' or 'Digby chickens' are small cured herring. Popular though they were at the time, they were not universally praised as a 'delicate relish.' To Moorsom a 'Digbie' was 'a favourite *morceau* for the breakfast-table of those who prefer a piece of leather well-dried and salted (which they greatly resemble) to a fresh-baked roll' (p 254).

The Digby Gut, which is the outlet from the Basin, forms about the same proportion to it that the neck does to the body of a jar; the tide, coming or going, rushes along with great rapidity and breaks into numberless eddies. On the farthest beach there are some thirty or forty Indians encamped, who subsist by catching fish and shooting porpoises. Charles Glower, who it may be recollected presented a petition to the House of Assembly last session, praying an Act to prohibit the selling of rum to Indians, is at the head of this party; and those who know him best represent him as a high minded gentlemanly fellow. Certes, he made but a short speech in the House, but he gave a better reason for it than many others who have made short speeches there. I could speak much in my own language, said Charley, but *you would not understand it.* Now as this was a good reason for making a short speech, it ought to be infinitely better to prevent the making of a long one. If Hon. Gentlemen would, like Glower, first calculate how much of an oration they could make us understand, but a very few would be spoken.

Coleridge's fine lines very prettily describe the broken mountains that form the Digby Gut:

> – They stood aloof,
> Like cliffs which had been rent asunder;
> A dreary sea now rolls between,
> But neither heat, nor frost, nor thunder,
> Shall wholly do away, I ween,
> The marks of that which once hath been[89]

(for there can be no doubt that in some awful convulsion of nature, the north and south mountains have here been rent asunder.) The fog, as it leaves the Basin, often hangs wreathes round their brows which make them resemble two hostile batteries enveloped in the smoke of their own destructive salutes.

The next place of importance below Digby is Sisciboo. It lies on the side of the St. Mary's Bay, which runs up to within a few miles of Digby; this Bay is formed by a long peninsula, called Digby Neck, which is a kind of continuation of the South Mountain, and runs for miles into

89 *Christabel* ll.421–6

the Bay of Fundy, at the termination of which lye Long Island and Brier Island. At these places the population do not prosecute agriculture any further than to the raising of cattle; they depend principally on the fishery, and such trade as they can carry on up the Bay, at Quoddy and other places at the lines.[90] On the Neck, although they fish and trade, they depend more on agriculture, and there are some extensive and excellent farms in that quarter, and the pasture is said to be particularly adapted for the raising of sheep.

Sisciboo takes its name from the River round which it is situated, and which runs into St. Mary's Bay about 14 miles from Digby.[91] The principal settlement is on a very pretty bend of the river, near its mouth; here there is a church, and something of a village, which was originally settled by old loyalists, and is now in a great measure peopled by their descendants. Here, from the lips of some surviving veteran, you may yet hear tales of '76, and the years of bloodshed and inquietude which immediately succeeded; while the names of Burgoyne, Washington, Howe, and Percy are as familiar in their mouths as those of

> Harry the King, Bedford and Exeter,
> Warwick and Talbot, Salisbury and Gloster,

were with the survivors of Agincourt on the festival of St. Crispian; and are often, in 'their flowing cups, freshly remembered.'[92] Sisciboo, though not densely settled, will, as the country around it becomes more generally and more highly cultivated, insensibly grow into a town. There are in its neighborhood many excellent and productive farms.

90 By 'the lines' Howe means the boundary between New Brunswick and Maine.

91 'Sisciboo' or 'Sissiboo' was by 1828 becoming known as Weymouth, but Howe's consistent use of the old name indicates how it persisted in spite of the official change. Several years later T.C. Haliburton has his character the Squire express disapproval of the change and refuse to recognize it: 'Scissiboo sounded too savage and uncouth in the ears of the inhabitants, and they changed it to Weymouth, but they must excuse me for adopting the old reading ... I am no democrat; I like old names and the tradition belonging to them' (*The Clockmaker* 2nd series, chapter 16). So apparently did the Assembly, for the old name appears in the 1835 Statutes of Nova Scotia. Haliburton regards the name as Indian in origin, but in C.B. Fergusson's *Place-Names and Places of Nova Scotia* Sissiboo is said to be an Anglicization of 'Six-hiboux' (French for 'Six owls').

92 Shakespeare *Henry V* IV.iii.53–5

As we ride farther down we cross a bridge, thrown over another bend of the river, which is of considerable depth even here. About 5 miles above this there is an interesting fall, of about 30 feet: the water, after a partial descent, is formed into a curve by the peculiar formation of the rocks, and again descends into the gulf below. The scenery around it is sylvan and wild; and although a man travelling in haste might not turn aside to view it, yet whoever wanders to the neighborhood to see the natural curiosities of the country should not fail to pay it a visit.

We are now in the settlement of Clare, which extends along the shores of St. Mary's and the Bay of Fundy, and has features so distinct and peculiar as to render it one of the most interesting in the Province. The whole population are French; they are the descendants of the old Acadians, and preserve to this day the language, customs, and manners of their ancestors, unchanged and uncorrupted. There are about 300 families of them in Clare, and about 200 more at Tusket. They do not intermarry with the English, and but few of them speak any other language than their own. They are a quiet and peaceful race, very industrious and very frugal, and are governed and controulled by their Priest, whom they regard with the highest veneration and respect. Doubtless, my gentle Traveller, you have ere now marked the pride, and ambition, the envy, hatred, and all uncharitableness, which too often fill the hearts and influence the actions of those who style themselves the ministers of God. Ye have listened to their dogmatism and framed excuses for their bigotry, and heard them denouncing each other as churchmen, schismatics and sectarians; and smiled at their little petty contentions for worldly influence and power, by which they disgraced the cause they professed to espouse; and having seen these things, ye cannot fail to contemplate with delight such a character as the venerable Abbé Segoigne.[93] He is a Frenchman of the old school, deeply learned, of polished manners, and with one of the very best hearts in the world. He left France during the revolutionary persecutions of the clergy, because he would not renounce the faith in which

93 Father Jean-Mandé Sigogne (1763–1844) in 1797 fled from revolutionary France to live in England and in 1799 came out to Nova Scotia as parish priest of the Acadians in the southern part of the province. Howe's praise of Father Sigogne as a remarkably dedicated priest is echoed by all travellers who met him.

he was bred, and forsake the ties that he had been taught to respect. He threw himself into this sequestered retreat, and during twenty years has seen the country improving around him, a simple and affectionate people rising up in usefulness and virtue, and looking to him with reverence and love, as a common parent and guide. In the hour of affliction he is their comforter and friend, the mediator in their disputes, the fearless reprover of their vices. He is, besides, the only lawyer in the settlement; and writes their deeds, notes, mortgages, and keeps a kind of registry of all matters in which their temporal as well as spiritual interests are concerned; and perhaps in no population of equal amount in the Province are there fewer quarrels or lawsuits than in the settlement of Clare. In 1823 this Township was nearly destroyed by fire, which consumed a number of houses and great quantities of grain, and other crops. The Chapel at this time was burned to the ground, and its worthy Pastor, in his anxiety to save some boxes which contained the title deeds of his flock, had one of his hands dreadfully burnt. The present Chapel is a wooden building something larger than St. Paul's,[94] but not quite finished inside. In a few years more it will hardly contain the people, as they obey the injunction to increase and multiply, as may be seen by a contrast between their Township and that of Wilmot, which has about an equal amount of population. In Clare there are 2038 souls, in Wilmot 2294; in 1827 there were 79 births, 22 marriages, and only 3 deaths in Clare; in Wilmot there were but 71 births and 15 marriages, while there were 15 deaths during the same period. Their mode of marrying is very peculiar – instead of a couple getting tied whenever it suits their inclination, they time matters so that in the spring and fall they are all married together, when anyone who brings a trifling contribution to assist the festivities may partake of their enjoyment. The only schism or distinction that exists in Clare is one of a peculiar kind. During the persecutions of the Acadians by the English and Provincials, some of the former were driven into the woods, and as death would have been the penalty for venturing to their settlements, they joined and intermarried with the Indians. The descen-

94 St Paul's Anglican Church in Halifax, which was built in 1749. Abbé Sigogne's chapel (St Mary's) at Church Point, Digby County, was first completed in 1808, destroyed in the great fire of 1820 (not 1823, as Howe says), and rebuilt by 1829.

dants of these people are now settled in Clare, and bear on their features the marks of the singular connexion from which they sprung. They live apart from the pure French, and are considered by them an inferior race, and even the strenuous efforts of their Pastor have never been able to conquer their repugnance, nor force them to intermarry, and extend to each other a cordial interchange of good offices. This is a subject of much regret to the worthy Abbé, whose whole soul is bound up in the happiness and contentment of his flock. The world has no allurements for him, no charm to wean him from the quiet tenor of his way; during the whole period that he has been settled at Clare he has only been two or three times to Digby, and but once to Halifax; he neither knows nor cares what changes convulse the political world, who is up or who is down, and perhaps the whole extent of his connexions with his own church amount to a letter of friendship now and then from the Bishops of Nova Scotia or Quebec. And who that has witnessed the happiness which he has diffused around him – who has marked the filial regard with which his name is mentioned, the blessings and devotion which follow his footsteps, would wish that life's bubbles were more intimate with his thoughts? May he long be spared to fill an office which he so highly honors; and when he departs for a better world, may the precepts he has taught and the example he has given live in the memories of those over whom he has so kindly ruled.

Here rest we, gentle Traveller; our rambles for a time are o'er; and if on the way we have seen aught that can endear to us our native land – if we have dropped one sentiment which has kindled an honest emotion, or prompted a thought that in its development may be useful, our travels are well repaid.

Eastern Rambles

I

17 December 1829

Peradventure the gentle Reader may bear it in remembrance, that on a sunny July morning we once invited him to a joyous ramble over the Western counties – among the verdant fields and pleasant scenery of which we had a merry sojourn. What with admiring the beauties of nature, laughing, crying and moralizing by turns, we passed our time pleasantly enough; and although we ran some risk of being 'burked' by the men for sundry hints about idleness, dissipation and mortgages, and was once or twice in danger of a scratch from the women for twitching their ribbons and flounces, and making fun of their tea parties, upon the whole we were civilly entertained, and came back perhaps a little wiser than we went. Not 'led by that damning restlessness of soul' of which some wandering Poet complains, but influenced by the laudable desire of knowing a little more of our own country than we have been able to glean from books, newspapers, and the conversational and epistolary communications of the Lord knows how many residents and wayfarers, we are half inclined at the present moment to take an EASTERN RAMBLE, and if we can prevail upon the gentle Reader to take the road, cheer us along by his company, and light up the dreary and barren places by his smile, we shall be 'over the hills and far away'[1] by the break of to-morrow morning.

The debilitated Beau makes it a matter of sad complaint against old Hardcastle, that he nearly broke his wind in trotting him over his grounds, shewing him his flowers and fish ponds, his parks and preserves, his flourishing orchards and dilapidated ruins,[2] and we believe it has ever been remarked as a distinguishing trait of the owners of fine estates that they think every living sinner is as much interested about them as they are themselves. Mercy preserve the unhappy wight who gets within their toils. He must trudge over hills and precipices, mount

1 John Gay *The Beggar's Opera* (1728), act I, sc. 13, air 16

2 Hardcastle is a character in Goldsmith's *She Stoops to Conquer*, but Howe confuses him with the *parvenu* Sterling, a character in another play. See note 4.

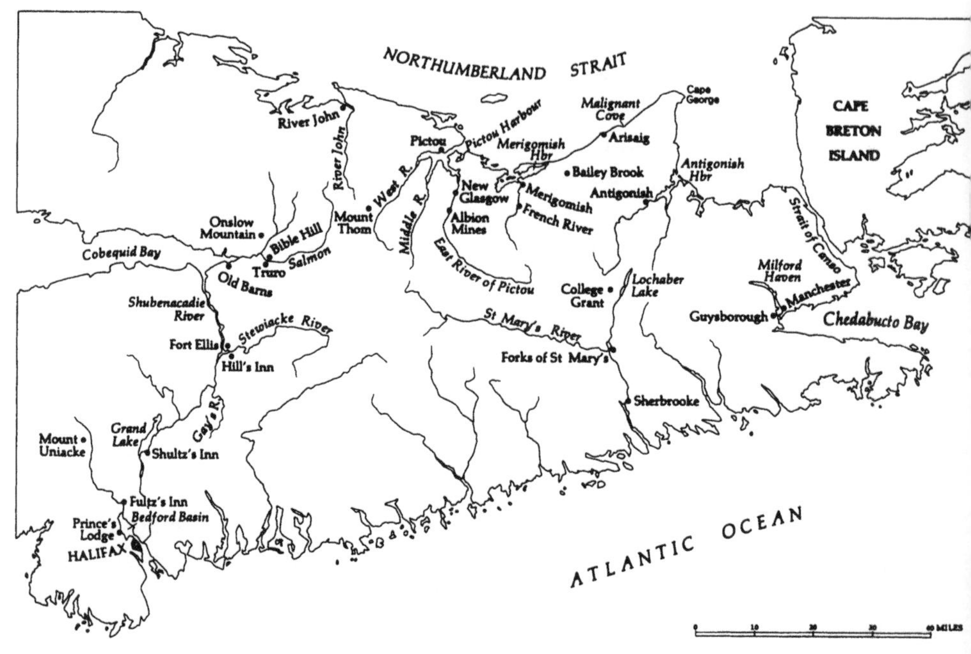

The eastern trip

styles and clear stone walls and hedges, think himself fortunate to get only knee deep in a quagmire, or to be hunted through ten acres of meadow with a mad bull in his rear. If he escape death from the horns of the monster, and does not die of fatigue, then is he fated to listen to a volume of details, compared with which the thousand and one scales and averages necessary to an examination of the Corn Laws,[3] or the endless variety of signs and symbols inflicted on a student of the Chinese language, are mere matters of mirth and amusement. Verily he must examine the shape and admire the beauty of every swimming, flying and creeping thing; he must taste every species of fruit and thrust his nose amidst the perfume of every flower, and charge his memory with the age and genealogy of every tree in the orchard, and every horse in the stud; while at each step of his progress he must be upon the lookout for latent beauties, and give his nod of assent and burst of extempore admiration to each learned commentary on a trifle, or communication of an unimportant fact. Were you, my gentle reader, a wanderer from another clime, were you a visitor instead of being as you are, an inhabitant, had you no tie to bind you to the soil we are about to tread but a desire to indulge a languid curiosity, you, like Ogleby,[4] would get tired of the excursion in an hour – would sicken at our enthusiasm and perhaps fall asleep by the way. But you are a joint owner of the estate, and have more than a life interest in the soil. To you there is or should be a glorious music in its running streams – a magic beauty in its tranquil waters, and while the turf should give

3 Corn Laws, regulations governing the import and export of grain in England, were enacted as early as the Middle Ages, but in the nineteenth century they became the subject of incessant conflict until repealed in 1846. In 1815, faced with the ruinous effects upon British farmers of low prices for continental grain, the British government passed a new Corn Law fixing the price at which grain imports were allowed duty free. Although the landed interests approved, all other classes of society strongly opposed this protectionist measure which forced up the price of bread and all other grain products. Attempts in 1821, 1827, and 1828 to create more generally acceptable legislation proved ineffective. Howe is referring to the intricacies of a sliding scale of import duties introduced in 1828, by which duties rose or fell according to the current price of European wheat and other grains.

4 Lord Ogleby is the 'debilitated Beau' in *The Clandestine Marriage* (1766), a play by George Colman, sr, and David Garrick. While Ogleby is a guest in Sterling's country house, his patience and rheumatism are sorely tried by his host's insistence upon showing off every foot of his large and lavishly 'improved' estate.

to your tread a buoyant elasticity, the air an hilarious energy to the spirit, the waving forests a majestic grandeur to the eye, every feature of this our common heritage should have a charm for you. Its barren wastes and culitvated fields – its sunny slopes, and deep and solemn shades – its buds of promise, natural, moral and intellectual, should awaken your attention and fill you with intense delight; as the lisped and simple words, the soft and placid smile, of her darling Babe gives to the mother's heart a joy no other heart can share, and which has its source in the holy and hallowed ties by which they are bound together.

But let it not be supposed, my gentle Reader, though we are going to 'the East', that we are a Russian General with a name full of consonants, and fifty thousand barbarians in our train, or that we are a pilgrim with pease in our shoes – or a Jew on a visit to the site of the Holy City, or an Irishman on a mission to the Hindoo widows to convince them that the arms of a second husband are more attractive and rational than the funeral pile of the first, or a tall thin lad 'frae Aberdeen' in search of a berth in the Honorable East India Company's service, with small fears of a liver complaint and great hopes of the gathering together of sundry lacs of rupees. Faith we are none of these, but plain, sober folks, who intend travelling no farther east than the distance of a hundred or perhaps a couple of hundred miles, and who have no other object than to see a little of the country, and pick up any thing odd, curious or useful on the way.

'Tis the first step that costs' says the French proverb, and in no part of the business or pleasures of this life is its truth more fully exemplified than in making an excursion from home. There are so many things to be thought of – so many that we have forgot, and so many more that we fear will be forgotten, that we appear to be beset with a legion of difficulties and obstructions that like the charmed spirits in Tasso's *Jerusalem*,[5] seem determined to obstruct our passage into the woods. We are inclined to the belief that many an intended expedition has been defeated by the annoyances of packing up and getting under way. That many a voyage that would have been made has never been attempted, and many a Book of Travels that would have been perpetrated upon the public has laid quiescent in the brains of the author,

5 A reference to canto XIII of Tasso's *Jerusalem Delivered*

merely because the first step of a journey was beset by doubts, difficulties and fears that engendered indecision and delay, and finally frighted the would-be Traveller from the erratic bent of his humour. But cost what it may, we have made the first step, and being snugly seated in the Eastern Stage, may be allowed to spend half an hour in grave and sober reflections on our 'locomotive engines', which if they do not convey folks thirty miles for a halfpenny, are, nevertheless, the means of easy and agreeable transportation.[6] In journeying West, we took occasion to express our gratification and delight at the accommodation afforded by the line of stages which then plied and still plies between Halifax and Annapolis. That line has been kept up with a spirit that does credit to those who have had the active management of the concern, and under whose auspices a large and commodious Hotel is now in a course of erection at Kentville.

During the summer a stage ran daily to Windsor, and notwithstanding a partial opposition was generally crowded.[7] The effects of increased facilities for communication with the capital are already apparent in the Western country, throughout every section of which shrewd and close observers profess to see the awakening impulses of a new spirit among the people; a spirit from whose further development the fairest and most beneficial results may be anticipated. In June last, as everybody knows, an Eastern Stage was established;[8] the shares

6 Railway passenger service in Britain was a favourite topic of speculation and argument in 1829. It was in the next year that the Liverpool and Manchester Railway, on a line thirty miles in length, ran the first passenger coaches drawn by a steam locomotive. Whatever extravagant claims had been made about the low fares to be charged, the actual fare for the thirty-mile journey was initially seven shillings. Though it was soon reduced to four shillings as the thrill of speeding through the countryside at thirty miles an hour attracted throngs of passengers, it certainly never dropped to the Utopian sum of a halfpenny.

7 In addition to its tri-weekly service from Halifax to Annapolis, the Western Stage Coach Company ran an extra coach as far as Windsor on the days not covered by the regular schedule. In 1829, the extra coach ran until 10 November. The competitors may have been Smith and Todd, whose coach lines had been in operation long before the Company began its service.

8 As Howe says, the Eastern Stage Coach Company began its operations in June 1829. Although the service was instituted as bi-weekly, it must have shortly become tri-weekly, at least for the summer months. The 1830 schedule as published in *Belcher's Almanac* states that the stage for Truro leaves Halifax on Monday, Wednesday, and Friday.

were purposely made very small, in order to make the interest in the concern more general, the loss trifling if it proved unsuccessful, and the profit too contemptible to allow private or party feeling any operation in the management of a concern intended for the general good. This line has been running all the summer three times a week to Pictou, and we are sorry to say, has not yet met with sufficient encouragement to keep it up, unless the Legislature steps forward to give it an ample aid. That they ought to do this we have not a doubt; that they will we have a well-grounded confidence, because we are persuaded that there is nothing to which money can be better applied, and because we are aware that the rapid increase of the population of the Eastern country will, before a great while, supersede the necessity for legislative grants beyond a very limited period.[9] Until the time arrives when the line can support itself, so long as the Legislature is convinced that the concerns of the company are economically managed,* and that the public money is not required to support any private job, so long should the Eastern Line of Stages receive such a liberal support as will enable the company to procure a better class of vehicles, and make such other arrangements as may be necessary to increase the facilities for travelling over this very important road. But it may be asked, how comes it that there should be such a difference in the number of travellers on the Eastern and Western roads? and thus we answer – the great point of advantage which the latter has over the former is in being the medium of communication with the Province of New Brunswick, by means of sloop and schooner navigation from Windsor, and the Steam Boat from Annapolis. In the continual locomotion induced by the Collegiate and Academical Institutions at Windsor, to and from which some forty or

9 In spite of Howe's 'well-grounded confidence,' the 'ample aid' was not forthcoming from the Legislature. The annual grant it had passed in the session of 1829 (£275, to run for five years) kept the line in operation but did not provide for significant improvements. The finances of the Company were somewhat improved in 1831, however, when it received the mail contract for the route.

* That they are we believe can be satisfactorily proved. The Agent in Town gets a mere trifle for his services, the Agent at Pictou nothing; and the Agent at Truro, who in addition to the general superintendance of his part of the line, keeps the accounts and transacts the general business of the company, gives his time and attention gratis. [Howe's note]

fifty students are passing and repassing during certain seasons of the year, to say nothing of the frequent visitations of fathers, mothers, aunts, uncles, cousins, sweethearts and youthful cronies, by which the seats of the stage are not unfrequently occupied; while its top is continually loaded with bundles of boots, breeches, hats, shirts, pound cake, and other things needful and necessary to a due discussion of classical lore, and the accommodation and comfort of the youngsters. Then again, the western country has been settled longer, and there is, perhaps, a greater number of independent and wealthy farmers, who can afford to take a ride in the coach and who think nothing of trundling down to the races, the regatta, the theatre, or the Assembly, sometimes with one or more of the feminine members of their establishments, who, perhaps, succeed in killing one of our Town lads by the beams of a sparkling eye, or in whisking them off in their train, to negotiate for another ride to the city under a different title, and by the leave and consent of the parish parson. These are some of the advantages, which, to our simple apprehensions, the Western enjoys over the Eastern Line – and it is for the Legislature to take these things into consideration, and 'govern themselves accordingly.'

II

31 December 1829

We linger not to expatiate on the beauties of the Basin, nor the excellence of a Breakfast at Fultz's;[10] for are not the former written on the memories of every way-farer, and is it not as much a matter of course to get well fed at Fultz's, as to have a good appetite when you get there? But who have we for our fellow Travellers? for nothing gives a better idea of the nature of the relations between Town and Country than an

10 The stagecoach would have reached Fultz's Inn at about 8:00 AM, two hours after it had left Halifax. It will be recalled that the Western stage made its breakfast stop at Hiltz's Inn, nine miles farther from Halifax.

enumeration of the passengers in a Stage. First, then, we have a Merchant from Pictou, who, having been down to the capital on business, is on his return home – then we have a Trader from Richibucto – and an Agent of a Timber House in Miramichi; with a young Orangeman, fresh from the Emerald Isle, who, fearing that since the passing of the Emancipation Bill,[11] the Protestants would all be devoured by the hungry followers of the Pope, has wisely sought safety in emigration, and is on his way to seek a quiet and pleasant asylum on the fertile bosom of Prince Edward Island.

The road to Truro, like the road to Windsor, is, generally speaking, dull, dreary and monotonous; and it requires no ordinary stretch of credulity to believe, as you are passing along, that there is either rural beauty or extensive cultivation at the end of it. Near Fletcher's[12] you pass over the ground intended for the site of one of the locks of the Canal,[13] and during the rest of the route you leave the Shubenacadie and its lakes on the left. At Shultz's[14] you make a short stay, and from the neat and tasty appearance of the house, and every thing about it,

11 The bill for the emancipation of Roman Catholics was passed by the British parliament in 1829.

12 Fletcher's Inn, eighteen miles from Halifax on what is now the Old Cobequid Road, stood on the northern side of the road at Fletcher's Bridge, now Fletcher's Locks, at the entrance to Fletcher's Lake.

13 The Shubenacadie Canal was planned to provide water communication from Halifax Harbour to the Minas Basin by following the chain of lakes and rivers that had once been used as a canoe route by the Micmacs. Several surveys of the route were made (in 1797, 1814, and 1815), a joint stock company was formed early in 1826, and by the first of March the legislature had voted £15,000 to the Shubenacadie Canal Company for the construction of the waterway. The work began on 24 July 1826. It was envisaged that the canal (by means of fourteen granite-encased locks between Dartmouth and Shubenacadie, and a tidal lock at Fort Ellis) would enable heavy freight to be carried quickly and cheaply across the province. All went well at first, and considerable work was completed on the system, but the project collapsed in 1832. Sporadic attempts were made later to have construction resumed, and parts of the existing system were actually used in 1861. Indeed a little steamboat, the *Avery*, passed through the entire watercourse from Dartmouth to Fort Ellis. By 1870, however, the company then owning the canal closed its books and ceased operations. Even by mid-century, the coming of the railroad had made such a canal obsolete.

14 Shultz's Inn, where Howe's coachman stopped to change horses, was twenty-three miles from Halifax. As the coach left Halifax at 6:00 AM, it would have reached Shultz's about 10:30 AM. The inn was on the eastern side of Shubenacadie Grand Lake at what is now the village of Grand Lake.

William H. Eager
View of Halifax, circa 1836

you regret that you cannot stay longer. You catch a view of some pleasant fields in passing over Gay's River; and as you go by the dwelling of the Rev. Mr. Blackwood, are not ill pleased to find, that while laboring in his spiritual vocation to improve the morals of his flock, he does not disdain to attend to the cultivation of the soil.[15] At Hill's,[16] near the

15 The Reverend Robert Blackwood (1785-1857) was a Scottish Presbyterian minister who landed in Halifax in 1816 and was given the pastoral charge of Gay's River-Shubenacadie-Nine Mile River in the same year. He remained there for twenty-four years, moving in 1840 to Tatamagouche. His manse was at Coldstream, twenty-one miles from Truro and two miles north of Gay's River. As he had some medical knowledge, he was often called upon to attend to the physical as well as spiritual ailments of his parishioners. Apparently he also turned his hand to the plough.

16 Hill's Inn was eighteen miles from Truro, near the present village of Stewiacke. If the coach was running on time, it would have reached Hill's at about 3:15 in the afternoon. As Howe's breakfast would have been at 8:00, his rhapsodies over the meal at Hill's were naturally heartfelt. Presumably he appeased his appetite more regularly on his actual journeys.

Stewiacke, the prospect is rather more extensive, and the cleared fields along the River's banks, on both sides of the Bridge, contrasting with the wilderness land in the rear, make quite a pleasant scene; and when wearied with gazing at the natural beauty on the outside of the house, what think you they have prepared within for the appeasement of your hunger? You are an old Traveller through the interior, and exclaim, with a knowing shrug of the shoulders, Ham and eggs, of course – No such thing, Sir, no such thing – try another guess – broiled fowl – No! Veal cutlet – No – but what think you of a fine fresh salmon, that but two hours ago was flashing about through the clear waters of the River, and dashing aside the long spires of grass with a switch of his vigorous tail. How would the heart of a Wilson[17] bound within his bosom were he to find himself opposite your plate at the present moment; the sight of that fish – so welcome, and yet so unexpected at this distance into the interior, would make North forget his gout, and the eyes of the Ettrick Shepherd[18] flash with a lustre, that like the blaze from the burning mount, would bespeak the emotion within. Verily it is a delicate morsel at this season, and in this place, and to a Townsman, who never sees a salmon after July, it is a perfect oasis in the epicurean wilderness.

The fine River in which it was caught is one of those meandering and tranquil streams which pierce our country in every direction, fertilizing and beautifying as they flow along; and as the land partakes of the same alluvial character which distinguishes the borders of nearly all those streams, it is in many places highly cultivated and extremely productive – sending forth to the capital fine quarters of beef, very superior mutton, and lots of pigs and poultry. There are about 1300 inhabitants contained within this settlement, who have cleared over 6000 acres of land, and who are remarkable for their persevering and active industry. The Stewiacke empties into the Shubenacadie, just above Fort Ellis, and from what we remember of the impressions made by a former visit to that quarter, adds very materially to the beauty of the view from the elevated ground upon that fine farm. On the right the Main River is

17 John Wilson (1785-1854), the 'Christopher North' of *Blackwood's Magazine*, was best known for his authorship of much of 'Noctes Ambrosianae,' a popular series of sketches in *Blackwood's* involving 'North' as one of several leading characters.

18 James Hogg (1770-1835) was the 'Ettrick Shepherd' in 'Noctes Ambrosianae.'

sweeping along, and is visible for a considerable distance above and below the Fort; and on the left the Stewiacke is seen spreading its broad bosom to the sun, until its folds are lost behind the foliage of the trees, and the shade of the irregular landscape. Extensive upland fields relieve the eye, as it moves along the left bank of the Shubenacadie, and a hill of considerable elevation, which slopes down to the water side, forms, as it were, a dividing point just above the junction of the two Rivers. Upon its brows the hand of the husbandman has been active; and mayhap you may find a herd of cattle, or a numerous flock of sheep, cropping from its fertility their nutritious evening meal.

Pass we over the remainder of the road, for save and except some recent improvements upon it, there is but little to attract attention – and now as the shades of evening are deepening around us, and the stars are beginning to peep from their azure chambers in the sky, we approach the little village; but ere we enter its borders, the night is too far advanced to admit of our seeing more than the straggling lights, which, beaming out from both sides of the road, seem to tantalize us by their indications of settlement which we cannot see – and a collective population, of whose doings we can form but a vague and indistinct idea.[19] Perchance it was kindly done of the goddess of darkness and gloom, to throw her mantle over the object of our fond anticipation – our hourly hope – that we might, for twelve hours more, be kept in doubt and uncertainty as to the features of 'Truro the beautiful', whose praises have come to us in sonnet and song – in ode and pastoral – in toddling octave and stately hexameter, until we have learned to think of nothing but rural loveliness at the very mention of its name. But there is no alternative – the tide will not roll back at our bidding, the moments will neither flee faster nor close their buoyant wings to suit our pleasure – nor will the shades of night yield to our wish of beholding the undiscovered loveliness of nature, until their appointed time. So that we must even content ourselves with the comforts which are to be found in Squire Blanchard's Dwelling, which we cannot but acknowledge might console a man under many a more serious depriva-

19 The Eastern coach schedule gives 7:00 PM as the time of arrival in Truro. As this was summertime, however, and as darkness was falling when Howe's coach entered the village, it must have been as much as an hour behind schedule.

tion. A bounteous board, handsome accommodation, and a pleasant Veranda to protect a fellow's head from the evening dews while he puffs his quiet cigar are a combination of comforts that are devoutly to be wished, but are not always to be expected in travelling in the interior of a new country like this.

Here for the first half hour all is bustle inside the house, and out. Yourself and your fellow passengers are busy securing your baggage, and ascertaining the latitude and longitude of your bed rooms. The Richibucto man's voice is heard, in anxious inquiry as to the hour at which the Cumberland Courier starts in the morning;[20] the Pictou gentleman is as solicitous to procure sundry items of knowledge about the probable movements of the Stageman, while some half dozen men and boys, who have gathered round the door from the houses in the immediate neighborhood, are just as anxious to gain accurate intelligence as to the names, appearance and destination of the whole cargo.

How sweet is the balmy slumber that refreshes our weary spirits, after riding some sixty miles in the wind – we lay our heads upon the pillow, and it 'overcomes us like a summer cloud',[21] and then our dreams! oh! for pencil and brush to give the hues and coloring of our dreams, for we have sunk to sleep with the consciousness that the morning sun will make for us a glorious revelation of rural beauty, and like the Persian on the eve of his nuptials with some maid he has never seen, we revel in imagination on the charms which will be ours with the coming day. We remember hearing of a youth, who in times gone by, hired a man to lead him blindfold from the centre of our good town of Halifax, to the neighborhood of the Dock-Yard, that he might, on a Valentine's morning, see the fair features of his well beloved, ere any other piece of womanhood had crossed his path, or given rise to ominous presage; and if the traveller can get any body to bind up his optics,

20 The Cumberland mail was carried by horse and waggon, there being no stagecoach service on the Northern road to Amherst until the 1840s. The bad section of road over the Cobequid Mountains made the route unsuitable for a coach-and-four. The service was advertised as a 'weekly stage,' however, and there was sometimes room in the waggon for hardy passengers. The mail courier left Truro at 7:00 AM on Thursdays and was supposed to reach Amherst at 11:00 PM on the same day.

21 Shakespeare *Macbeth* III.iv.111

lead him to the top of Chipman's hill, turn him to the right about, and then tear off the shade, he will be amply repaid for his trouble, for from that spot the full, unbroken loveliness of Truro is spread out before the eye, and makes one distinct and perfect impression upon the mind. It is a striking characteristic of Windsor, that you can examine it from twenty various points, and find each view materially different from the others; every one beautiful, but every one having some leading feature, or agreeable combination, peculiarly its own. While there is hardly any one point from which the eye can take in all the elements that make up its general aspect; and we never looked on any place of which we found it so difficult to carry off a correct impression, as this little village of the west. With Truro this is not the case – it is one sweet and placid scene, that, from Chipman's hill, lies full before the eye, which may traverse from one extremity to the other, while the heart prompts, and the tongue exclaims, as did the Deity when the fresh world sprung into being, 'it is good – it is good.'

III

6 January 1830

Though the entire character of the scenery of Truro is not changed by the locomotive propensities of the Tourist, still a change of position furnishes sufficient variety to compensate for sundry rides and rambles to different parts of the Township; and truth to say, there are lots of good fellows in the village, who, with a fine frank cordiality that is widely distinguished from obtrusive ostentation, are ready at a word to mount a stranger on a piece of horseflesh, and shew off the lions to the best advantage. One of the most agreeable excursions is a ride to the North Mountain. The road turns off from the highway leading to Onslow, and you pass through some finely tilled intervale land that stretches away from the back lots of the village, and which is very rich and fertile. As you recede from the village, the North River appears on the left, flowing onwards through low and cultivated soil, the distant border of which rests on the unfelled wilderness. Turning to the right you ascend the mountain, by a woody and steep road, which runs up a little in the rear of the highest part of it, and tying your steeds, scale the fence which encloses the pasture land that extends over its brow. From this spot the prospect is uncommonly fine, – and a traveller who has an eye for the soft and luxuriant in rural scenery cannot look upon it without an involuntary burst of admiration, and ever and anon, as his eye roves over the features of the extended landscape, he lisps forth his broken and unconnected praises of the scene, and his gratitude to the jolly companions who have galloped him over to the 'North Mountain.'

On the right, the Onslow mountains bound the view and from their base to the Northern bank of the Salmon River, which, winding up from the Cobequid Bay, passes directly through the Town, there is a fine stretch of extended cultivation, that reaches from the spot on which you stand as far as the eye can see; taking in the finer parts of Onslow, beyond which you catch a glimpse of some of the more prominent points of the Township of Londonderry, while, of a clear day you may distinguish the bald front of Cape Blomidon, at the further extremity of the Basin of Mines. Perhaps there is not to be found in the Province a finer Agricultural district than that included within these bounds – nor one, which, for natural fertility, high cultivation – and industrious and systematic tillage, could be offered with more pride to the notice of a stranger, as a specimen of our eastern country. On the left, a range of upland, which is a continuation of the line of hills that stretches from Mount Tom in a westerly direction, passes down in the rear of the village, and flanks, as it were, the fine intervale land that is spread along the banks of the River and Bay to the mouth of the Shubenacadie. Immediately below you is that portion of the Town which lies on the right of the river, and which, from its gentle elevation above the other, is known as 'the Hill.' It is a fine piece of Table Land, and the descent from it to the river side is in many places steep and precipitous. Some of the finest fields and gardens, and some of the most tasty and neatly built houses are scattered over this division of the Village; and from the corner where the principal Inns are situated, the Cumberland road sweeps on through Onslow and Londonderry, and the Pictou road passes over the rising ground on which you stand. Beyond 'the Hill', to which it is connected by a handsome new Bridge that is not the least picturesque piece of architecture in the village, lies the denser portion of the settltlement – or rather the collection of buildings which make up the little town. The Episcopal church is the most prominent object, and around and beyond it are scattered some sixty or seventy houses, of various size and structure, to the most of which are connected small fields and gardens – some enclosed very tastefully by little white rails.

It is the misfortune of the Tourist, that, in his efforts to transfer them to paper, he is forced to mangle many a pleasant scene; and tired of our efforts to convey to the gentle reader an adequate idea of the leading features of Truro, we are disposed to give up the task. For what pen can do justice, by a tedious enumeration of the various parts that make up this pleasant scene, to the still life, the rural loveliness, the apparent fertility of the whole. To those who have ever stood upon Chipman's hill we have said enough; and to those who have not, the best advice we can give is to wait till the approach of spring; and then, when the earth is clad in green, and the woods are covered with foliage, and the flowers are sprinkled upon the ground, let them step into the Eastern Stage, and away! away! away!

The spot is a favorite location for a picnic, and the lads and lasses of the village not unfrequently hold their merry-makings here, and while regaling on the cold contents of their well-furnished baskets, turn from admiring and complimenting the scene, to admiring and complimenting each other. The distinguishing features of the village itself are not seen so distinctly from the brow of the North Mountain as they are from Chipman's Hill, but the great outlines of Colchester are more strongly impressed upon the mind by the extensive survey which it affords; – and after satisfying your optics with the scenery, should you turn into the hospitable cottage of Mrs. Miller, who lives in the rear of the road, she will regale you with a cheerful smile, a slice of excellent bread and butter, and a glass or two of delicious strawberry wine.

Making a circle round the side of the mountain, you return to the village by a different road from that on which you departed; and as you ride along your attention is attracted to some mills, that are situated at the lower extremity of a small lake and are well worthy the passing notice of all who take an interest in the progress of our domestic industry. The establishment embraces a Grist, Fulling, Saw, and Oat Mill, and it is a gratifying sight to see the whole in operation. Indeed the mills of Colchester are worthy of especial notice and commendation, as they are perhaps more numerous and efficient than those of any other portion of the Province, and afford very many facilities to the population of the district. The Oat Mills supply a great abundance of meal, which, much to the credit of the people, has for some time been in very general use; and, aided by the other coarse bread stuffs, amply makes up any deficiency that a failure of crops may occasion in the supply of wheaten flour. The Grist mills are more than equal to the manufacture of all the wheat, and the fulling mills are kept in pretty constant motion by the labors of the worthy maids and matrons of the 'country round.' Long may the whir of their wheels be heard by their happy firesides; long may the clatter of feminine tongues be drowned by the rattling of their looms, and the labor of man in the field, and woman within the precincts of her quiet home, keep the mills of Truro in 'perpetual motion.'

There is another pleasant ride down the south side of the River and Bay, through what is called the Lower Village, or Old Barns; and he who takes his departure without seeing this part of the Township has but half performed his errand. There are perhaps no farmers in the District who are more wealthy and independent than those who occupy this fine tract of country, and certainly if they were not, the fault would be more in themselves than in the character of the soil. The upland is not inferior, and the dyke is extremely productive and valuable, extending, with irregular breadth, all the way from the mouth of the Shubenacadie to the immediate neighborhood of the upper village. The lower village can scarcely boast of any collection of houses that can entitle it to the name, or that can be fairly grouped in a bird's-eye view; but these extend all along, at irregular intervals on both sides of the road, which sometimes passes over the rising ground and at others pursues its quiet way over the dead level of the Dyke. From the hills on this side of the Bay a very agreeable prospect is afforded of the

Townships of Onslow and Londonderry, which stretch along the opposite shore, and partake essentially of the same fine agricultural character.

The 'old Barns' which gave its name to the Lower village have only been torn down within a very few years. They were built by the French settlers, previous to 1701, and were retained with a kind of rustic reverence until the progress of decay rendered them no longer worthy or capable of preservation. The Acadians seldom, if ever, made permanent settlements on the upland, but wherever a fine stretch of rich intervale was to be found there they were sure to gather together, and verily they showed their taste and discernment in selecting the spot which we have attempted to describe, for nowhere, within the circle of the Province, is labor better rewarded, or a smaller amount of physical exertion required to supply the necessaries of life. There is no very marked division between the upper and lower villages, but a small creek which puts up from the Bay in a southerly direction is generally recognized as the dividing line; near this spot, a little to the right of the road, stands the Presbyterian Meeting House, a plain wooden building, dedicated by the early settlers to the humble worship of the Deity. The graveyard lies immediately in the rear – and see, my gentle Traveller, the gate is half unclosed – as though it would invite us to pass through, and linger a moment among the lowly beds of those whose spirits have departed to a better world. He must have a dull and sluggish soul, who can look without emotion on the quiet graves of the early settlers of his country; who can tread upon their mouldering bones without a thought of their privations and their toils – who can, from their tombs, look out upon the rural loveliness – the fruitfulness and peace, by which he is surrounded, nor drop a tear to the memories of the dead; who won, by the stoutness of their hearts, and the sweat of their brows, the blessings their children have only to cherish and enjoy. Who plunged into the forest, not as we do now, for a summer day's ramble or an hour of tranquil musing, but to win a home from the ruggedness of uncultivated nature, and in despite of the dusky savage, thirsting for their blood. Oh! for the muse of Gray to pour out a befitting tribute to the dead. He caught, from the sanctity and softened associations of an English Churchyard, an inspiration that rendered him immortal;

but the graves among which he stood were the resting places of men whose lives had been tranquil and undisturbed; who had grown up amidst the fruitfulness of a civilized and cultivated country, and had enjoyed the protection of Institutions long firmly established, and the security and cheering influence of ancient usage. How much deeper would have been the tones of his Harp, had he stood where we now stand – had he been surrounded by the graves of those who found his country a wilderness, and left it a garden – who pitched their tents amid the solitude of nature, and left to their children her fairest charms heightened by the softening touch of art; who had to build up Institutions as they built up their lowly dwellings, but nevertheless bequeathed to their descendants the security of settled government – the advantages of political freedom, the means of moral and religious improvement, which they labored to secure, but never lived to enjoy. We have no Abbeys or Cathedrals where our warriors and statesmen are preserved – we have no monumental piles, fraught with the deeds of other days, to claim a tribute from the passer-by; the lapse of ages, political vicissitudes, violent struggles, and accumulated wealth are necessary to the possession of these; but in every village of our infant country we have the quiet graves of those who subdued the wilderness – who beautified the land by their toils – and left not only the fruits of their labors, but the thoughts and feelings which cheered them in their solitude, to cheer and stimulate us amidst the inferior trials and multiplied enjoyments of a more advanced state of society. May we, while contrasting the present with the past, never forget the debt of gratitude we owe; and while standing beside the humble graves of our early settlers, may we ever feel our spirits awakened by the recollection of their lives, our thoughts ennobled by the remembrance of their trials, and our holiest and best resolves strengthened with a portion of their strength.

IV

13 January 1830

Our province has no Niagara to lure to its bosom the countless swarms of peregrinators, that year after year wend their way to the Canadas, to be delighted with the majestic sublimity of falling waters, or deafened with their roar. Perhaps we have hardly a waterfall that would prove of itself a sufficient inducement for a man beyond our own border lines to take up his stick and walk, or mount his nag and ride; but, nevertheless we have sundry miniature cataracts, and less pretending *jets d'eau*, that if they do not withdraw attention from everything else, materially add to the pleasures of a country ramble, by giving to the scenery a varied and often a very picturesque and romantic character. We have nothing in Nova Scotia that can be called a mountain – and, therefore, if we had all the water in the universe, we should never be able to get up a cataract, for want of a sufficient acclivity to roll it over. But we have innumerable lakes, rivers, and streams; and, as many of the former are pent up between ridges of elevated land, and many of the latter have to wind their devious way to the ocean, through the narrow gorges or openings formed between the rocky acclivities, or hilly ranges, which they meet in their onward course, it is not strange that there should be, in very many parts of the Province, Falls of comparatively trifling magnitude but of surpassing beauty.

We noticed one of these in the neighborhood of Kentville – and there is another of the same general character, but differing in its particular features, close on the borders of Truro. Following up a small stream which runs along a narrow strip of meadow that extends to the rear of the fields on the southern side of the village, as you recede from the cultivation and improvements of man, and approach the wildness and primitive negligence of nature, a sudden turn to the left shuts you out from the softened and beautiful scene of mingled meadow and woodland, and encloses you between two high ranges of land, that rise up on each side of you as abrupt and precipitous as the waves of the Red Sea are said to have towered above the host of Pharaoh. The small stream is still murmuring at your feet, and pursuing its way sometimes over and occasionally under a luckless windfall that the violence of some borean gust has stretched across its current. For the distance of 100, perhaps 150 yards, this ravine is highly picturesque and attractive. It keeps narrowing as you go on; its sides, which are in most places crowned with trees and shrubbery to the very edge, offer more singular and attractive combinations, and you find your progress in some places nearly impeded by the lower steps, so to speak, by which the waters descend from the highland to the quiet vale below. After clambering up sundry ledges, and rural staircases, formed by the projecting points of rock, old stumps and bending saplings; and after stopping a dozen times to gather breath, or admire the minor beauties which claim a portion of your notice ere you arrive at the chief attraction, you come in sight of a steep rock, which, having been thrown across the ravine, has for ages withstood the efforts of the falling waters to push it from its place or wear it away. From the level of the clear pool at its base to the summit over which a narrow and beautiful stream descends may be about 50 feet. We do not pretend to speak accurately as to distance – leaving errors in length, breadth and extension – the movements of the weathercock, and the variation of the compass, to those jotting and dotting travellers, who care not if they get one distinct idea into their heads, or one beautiful and touching impression upon their hearts, so that they get all they see and hear carefully written down upon their Note Books. Out upon such violators of nature's chosen sanctuaries, who lose half the pleasure which her charms would convey to them in their over-anxiety to convey them to others – who cannot surrender their souls to the magic of a scene, for fear some of its details should be lost in their pitiful enumerations; whose vitality would be utterly destroyed, and their enthusiasm turned into despair, even at the brink of Niagara itself, by the breaking of the point of a pencil. We prefer letting nature do her own work for us and with us – and have never a fear that when she has impressed a beautiful picture upon our souls, we shall be able to recall it at the distance of half a century, with a memory tenacious of its very charm.

Lay thee down upon that rock, my gentle traveller, which the heat of the noon-day sun has warmed, despite the coolness of the neighboring waters – and there, with thy senses half lulled to forgetfulness by the murmurs of the falling stream – thy eyes half closed – and thy spirit all unconscious of earthly turmoils and care – give thyself up to musing, for never was there a more appropriate spot than the Truro Falls for our old men to see visions, and our young men to dream dreams. You are as effectually shut out from the world as though, like Colonel Boon, you were at least a hundred miles from a human being; and if you are poetical you may weave rhymes, if you are romantic you may build castles in the air, and if you be a plain matter-of-fact man you may pursue your calculations by the side of the Truro Falls, without the slightest danger of interruption. Should you be advanced in years, my gentle Traveller, how must you sigh that Time will not allow you a discount of twenty summers; and place by your side, within the quiet shelter of this beautiful ravine, the chosen deity of your youthful adoration. Oh! would not her accents of acknowledged affection mingle delightfully with the falling waters? and would not every vow you uttered catch a solemnity and power from the retired holiness of the scene? Perhaps on that very rock where you recline many an expression of pure and sinless regard has burst from lips that, after long refusal, at length played the unconscious interpreters to the heart – many a chaste and yet impassioned embrace has made eloquent acknowledgement of all that the young heart has dared to hope; and perhaps we err not when we say that there are, among our numerous readers, many a happy couple, who, while tasting the pleasures of the domestic circle, bless the balmy summer eve when they first strayed to the Truro Falls.[22]

There is fine fishing and abundance of game in the vicinity of this pleasant village; and if you be an angler or are fond of the gun, you may find almost constant employment. There are plenty of partridges, woodcocks and snipe; and in the proper season, lots of pigeons, plover and curlieu; and what with the sports of the field, the examination of the scenery, and the attendance on rural parties and merry-makings among the hospitable and light-hearted inhabitants, the time of a sojourner is pretty well employed.

22 The secluded retreat Howe describes is now Victoria Park in Truro. There are two waterfalls in the park, one of them named after Howe.

Extending due east from the principal Inns, and forming the southern termination of what is called 'the hill', is a very steep bank of red clay, which the action of the elements keeps continually wearing away – and threatening, as it were, to convert the upland of the worthy proprietors into very excellent intervale. Along the sides and part of the brow of this bank are a range of Trees, and beneath their shade, in times gone by, as the village Tradition goes, there stood a rural bower. The Deity to whom it was dedicated we could not with accuracy ascertain, but certain it is, that it used to be the scene of singular cantrips[23] and orgies. The peasantry who thereabouts do dwell are bold to declare that of a summer evening as they passed along, a volume of smoke would be seen bursting from its leafy sides, and ascending in varied curls upon the balmy air; but whether it smelt of brimstone or tobacco has to this day remained a point of doubtful settlement, and given rise to much rural and 'nice argument.' True it is that voices used to be heard, and sometimes a ringing and tinkling sound, like the meeting of friendly glasses, and ever and anon there would break forth from that mystical bower the sounds of song, sometimes accompanied by instrumental music, which the credulous passer-by took for some fiendish scraping, but which the less timorous believe to have been the notes of a violin.

There were many things to strengthen the belief that hereabouts did dwell the very spirit of mischief; for it was no uncommon thing for marvellous accounts of slaughtered Bears and chivalrous captains to be sent to the Halifax newspapers, bearing date at Truro, and purporting to be accurate and faithful narratives of heroic and daring exploits; and on connubial occasions a troop of cavalry would sometimes wheel up in front of the bridal chamber, and discharging a volley of fire arms in at the window, gallop off in the twinkling of a bedpost; or mayhap, a large standard would be found waving from some chimney top, like the banner of a feudal chieftain from the loftiest battlement of his castle, spreading terror and anxiety around. But these days are past – the mad spirits who used to play such pranks are either caught in traps matrimonial, and, like the gentle Ariel, confined to the clefts of their

23 'Cantrip' is a Scottish word for 'trick' or 'piece of mischief.'

domestic hollow trees, or are scattered to other portions of the Provinces, where, from the want of countenance and example, they are forced to restrain the bent of their humour, and conform to the even tenor of a more matter-of-fact existence.

The Bower has fallen to earth; its branches are scattered along the side of the bank, and its leaves are dancing on the breath of many a breeze, but from its site there is decidedly one of the prettiest views of the course of the Salmon River that are to be found in the neighbourhood of Truro.

V

4 February 1830

Although we should be well pleased to dwell *in* Truro all the days of our life, perhaps we may weary the gentle Reader if we attempt to dwell *on* it much longer; so, bidding farewell to its smiling scenery and hospitable Inhabitants, we once more consign ourselves to the care of the stageman, and turn our faces to the East.

He must be a most ungracious Traveller, who, having spent three or four summer days in Truro, should, in that time, have discovered anything to find fault with – there is so much to admire and to amuse, that for the souls of us we could not discover a single blemish; and having got quietly seated in the stage, were not a little astonished to hear our laudatory remarks on the village and villagers treated with the most sovereign contempt by a crusty old curmudgeon of a fellow passenger; who, whenever we broke out in a cheerful and complimentary strain, was sure to interrupt us by whistling, or by trundling from the fertile store house of his imagination, some crying sin or ungracious feature, to set in opposition to our praises. At last he got so eloquent that we were constrained to hold our tongue, and listen to something like a regular summing up of all the abominations he could group together, and of which the following may be taken as what Hume would call the 'tottle of the whole.'[24]

'If all the people were assembled round the base of Bible Hill (said he), and I were on the top of it, let me tell you, sir, I would soon give them a piece of my mind. Talk of the beauty of the prospect, – to be sure it would be beautiful if it were not deformed by the dozens of dirty gables, that, turn where you will, are presented to the eye. Much use it was for Stepsure to hold them up to ridicule – I believe, instead of giving the people a hint, if he had given them whitewash, it would have had as little effect.[25] And as to the high cultivation you talk of, with the exception of Blanchard's and Whitter's diked fields, and a few others within the village, there is scarcely any thing like regular and systematic farming to be found. – Rob. Dickson's Oatland farm is certainly an honor to Onslow; and he and some of his neighbours set praiseworthy examples to the country, but too many adhere to their old slovenly habits – and though they are eternally talking about the march of intellect, and political reformations, they take good care to have no reformations in agriculture, nor ever to let intellect march over their fields, side by side with industry. – Sir, if I had the People within the compass of my lungs, I would tell them that their Masonic Lodge looks more like the Temple of Cloacina[26] than of Solomon; that they half starve their minister and ill treat their horses; that the capital wasting in Harness and Gigs, in meagre and inefficient Horse flesh, cannot be less than £3,200 per annum; and that the needless gossiping and neglect

24 Presumably Howe means David Hume (1711-76), the renowned Scottish philosopher and man of letters, 'tottle' for 'total' being the way Hume would have spoken the word. Though a polished stylist of written English, Hume always spoke with a very marked Lowland accent and manner of expression.

25 Stepsure is the fictitious narrator of Thomas McCulloch's sketches, *The Letters of Mephibosheth Stepsure*, which were first published serially in the *Acadian Recorder* in 1822-3. The following passage from the *Letters* clarifies the remarks of Howe's fellow passenger: '... the house could no longer be known by its fine white clapboards and its green corners and facings. Time had swept away all the paint, and the only contrast to its general weather-beaten appearance was a strip of white, reaching from the garret window to the ground, occasioned by certain nocturnal distillations, which, on a cold winter's night, it is not always convenient to carry to the door' (*Stepsure Letters*, New Canadian Library edition, p 24).

26 Apparently Howe's coinage from 'cloaca,' so in effect, 'the temple of the goddess of sewage'

of domestic concerns induced by those wretched conveyances certainly amounts to £9,600 – that early rising would materially improve their appetites and constitutions, and that a habit of prompt payment would save time, trouble and lawsuits. I would tell them (continued the old fellow, gasping for breath), to leave off smuggling and ship building; or, if they must build, to erect a Temple in the shape of a ship, and dedicate it to the Jack Ass. I would tell them to walk to meeting instead of riding, like a parcel of devils to a carnival; I would tell them, that though they have a creditable Library, a debating Club, and one of the most talented men in the Province for a Teacher, that they must either be deficient in intellect or spirit, to allow Truro to be turned into a rotten borough.'[27]

Here the old fellow's voice broke down, and fearing that he might resume the thread of his declamation, on the recovery of his vocal powers, we followed his example, and began to whistle; taking care that a gentle reproof should be conveyed by our choice of an air – which was the familiar ditty of 'the lord forgive us for lying, for lying, the lord forgive us for lying'; and as by this time we had left the village far behind us, our fellow traveller appeared to forget his bad humour, and, save and except an occasional ejaculation, when the inequalities of the road would, by a trying bend of his spine, remind him that there was no back to the front seat of the waggon, he did not, on the whole, make a bad travelling companion.

The Eastern Drivers are both experienced men: Lynds has been riding or driving post for a great number of years,[28] and the other, whose name we forget, is a very careful steady sort of fellow, who seldom trou-

27 The system of representation in the House of Assembly had by this time become seriously marred by inconsistencies and anomalies, many of which were caused by the joint existence of township and county representation. The worst example was Colchester, which had not only three townships enjoying representation (Truro, Onslow, and Londonderry) but, as part of Halifax County, could elect a county representative as well. Howe's crusty informant calls Truro a rotten borough because this generous representation occurred in one of the most sparsely populated electoral divisions of the province (Colchester) and because, in practice, Truro could easily gain (and often did) two representatives in an election, one for the township and one for the county. He could have added, perhaps with some plausibility, that Truro was a pocket-borough as well, for the Assembly lists show that two related families held the Truro seats for decades.

28 Jacob Lynds had driven the Truro-Pictou section of Witter's line from 1816 to 1828.

bles you with more conversation than he can help – unless when you are about descending a steep hill, or have got safe and snug at the bottom, when he never fails to exclaim against the 'bad broos', and to expatiate on his own skill, and the excellent training of his horses; and feeling that your bones are all whole, you cannot find in your heart to gainsay his harmless self-commendation.

While struggling up the side of Mount Tom, the attention is turned to a fine alteration of the road, which is now nearly completed, and by the aid of which the Traveller will, in future, be able to avoid the tiresome ascent and descent. On the very summit of the Mount there lives a man, who, more perhaps than any other in the country, is calculated to bring to the mind of a sojourner a conviction of the rapid increase of population, and commercial and agricultural improvement, of the eastern section of Nova Scotia. This is no other than – Stewart, who was the first Postman on the eastern road. Previous to 1805 the settlement at Pictou Town was very insignificant, but about that time Mr. Mortimer began to ship immense quantities of timber,[29] and it became an object to have a regular communication with Halifax; Stewart was accordingly employed by the Post Office Department, and the road being impassable by wheel carriages, and almost too bad for a horse, he used to trudge on foot to and from the capital, generally carrying the whole mail *in his waistcoat pocket*; and there being but poor accommodation on the road, a small wallet of oatmeal was always slung over his shoulder, which, when moistened by some of the numerous streams that he had to pass, served to sustain both the frame and the spirit of the hardy and frugal Postman. Scarcely 25 years have passed away, and the Eastern Mail now forms a load for a horse and gig; and so great is the accumulation of letters and papers on some occasions, that when the body of the vehicle is removed, and the bags and packages are piled

29 Edward Mortimer (c 1767-1819) had been the most prominent business man in the eastern part of the province during the first two decades of the century, when he carried on a thriving timber trade. He was an influential member of the Assembly (Halifax County, 1799-1819), a judge of the Inferior Court of Common Pleas, and a chief magistrate of Pictou. His wealth, his prominence in business and politics, and his skill at playing the role of magnate and squire earned for him the waggish title of 'King of Pictou.'

up on the framework, and secured by cords, a stout horse is scarcely equal to the task of transporting them through the country. Since that period towns and villages have risen, where then roamed the moose and the bear, and a numerous population have scattered the blessings of cultivation over a wide extent of country that was then little better than a howling wilderness. Nor has Stewart failed to improve his own situation, as the country around him improved. He has a snug house, and a nice little farm in the rear of it, and having long since retired from his erratic occupation, he can now look out and see his overloaded successors passing by his door, with the accumulated correspondence of thousands, who were perhaps unborn at the period of his weekly peregrinations.

There is not a vast deal of cultivation visible from the road in the immediate neighborhood of Mount Tom, but there are several settlers upon it remarkable for their great age; and you may perhaps see an old fellow of ninety, looking over a fence, or a woman of 95 or 100 sunning herself by a cottage door. The view from Mount Tom is very extensive, but the widespreading and still unfelled forest, notwithstanding all the improvements that have been made in the East, occupies the largest portion of it. However, reasoning from what has already been done to what may shortly be accomplished – there can be little doubt that before the passage of many years, the Traveller will forsake the level road along the vale, and, clambering up the side of the Mountain, look abroad on an unbroken prospect of smiling and peaceful cultivation.

After leaving the Mount, the road continues rather monotonous and tiresome, but although still surrounded on all sides by the woods, you begin to perceive unequivocal indications of a speedy approach to more extended and continuous settlement; and at length emerge from the wilderness, and find yourself by the side of the West River of Pictou. This delightful stream, though in point of depth and volume it is not to be compared to the East River, which also empties into the Harbor, is, nevertheless, of surpassing beauty, and, favored by the contrast afforded in the sudden transition from a forest to a cultivated scene, has a singularly agreeable effect on the feelings of the wayfarer. The river steals away with a tranquil and placid current, through a fine strip of rich, productive intervale, along the Eastern extremity of which extends a range of upland, that in some places rises rather abruptly, and in others slopes down more gently to the level of the western border of the stream which is less elevated and pretending.

Verily we have been in raptures too often already since we set out on our journey, or we might be forgiven for breaking forth in terms of gratification and delight at the numberless beauties which are presented to the eye while riding along the West River. There is a peculiar character about nearly all our Rivers – none of which come tumbling, roaring, and bellowing down the hills, threatening, like great bullies, to carry all before them – on the contrary, they are in general modest, douce and gentlemanly streams, that move on with little noise, distinguished by the grace of their curvatures, and the rural elegance of their attire – if in a state of nature, they are fringed to the very edge by our forest trees and shrubbery, but if flowing through a cultivated country, they are sure to have their strip of intervale, decorated here and there by the tall and graceful Elm. The one before us may be taken as a fine specimen of our River scenery, and cannot be seen to more advantage, than from the window of Archibald's Inn, where we stop to change horses, and which is fitted up in such a tasty style, and supplied with such a bountiful store of comforts, that there is no need of the pleasures of the mind or the imagination being disturbed by a vacuum in the stomach.

VI

25 February 1830

Lightly bounds the Traveller's heart, when he heaves in sight of the Harbor of Pictou. There is a magic about salt water that never fails to infect those who have been accustomed to see it making a portion of almost every prospect, from boyhood upwards – and who having,

R. Carpenter
View of Pictou, circa 1841

perhaps for the first time in their lives, been surrounded by land for several hours, again catch a glimpse of the blue waves, as they ripple in the breeze or glow in the sunshine. Truro is essentially an inland scene, although the Rivers wind along through the Township, and the Basin of Mines is seen in the distance; but Pictou stands on the water – its wharves stretch into the Harbor, and the presence of the salt sea is immediately felt by the Traveller, although the extent of its surface may be comparatively insignificant, when compared with the wide and almost oceanic scene of which Blomidon forms the western boundary.

The ride round the Harbor of Pictou is very pleasant; the Town is situated on the side of a Hill, and reminds the Traveller of Halifax in this respect. – The best view of it is, perhaps, from the high land on the eastern side, or from the bosom of the Harbor; and we have seen an oil painting, from a sketch taken on the latter, which exhibited its characteristic features with considerable effect. But mercy preserve us, we are riding into Pictou with as much ease and as little ceremony as we would into Chezetcook, or the Dutch Village.[30] Into Pictou! that seat of disaffection and bad government – that abode of patriots and den of radicalism – that nook where the spirit of party sits, nursing her wrath to keep it warm, during ten months of the year, in order to disturb the Legislature all the other two.[31] Into Pictou, that cradle of liberty – from whence, after strangling the serpents that would have crushed her, she is to walk abroad over the four quarters of the globe, regenerating and disenthralling mankind. Into Pictou, where it is a mortal offence to one man to take a pinch out of another's mull – and where, as the Yankees have it, it is impossible to live upon the fence; or in fact to live at all, without 'going the whole Hog' with one of the parties into which its society is divided. The Lord only knows whether we may ever live to come out, but here we go merrily in – we may be burned by the Antiburghers, or eaten without salt by the Highlanders, but our 'foot is in our native soil, and our name is —'[32] no matter what; having got to the threshold of Pictou, we are not to be frightened out of a peep, by all the hobgoblins that the diseased imaginations of the timid and uproarious have conjured upon our path.

The most prominent object that presents itself to the eye, in an approach to the town, is Mortimer's Point, and the buildings by which it is crowned; this is a long and very beautiful tongue of land which stretches out into the Harbor. It is regularly formed, and is laid out in

30 Chezetcook or Chezzetcook is a coastal village a few miles east of Dartmouth, Nova Scotia. The Dutch Village was originally a settlement of German immigrants on the isthmus of the Halifax peninsula; in 1830 it was still about two miles west of the town proper.

31 At the time, Pictou was notorious in the province for the conflict there between the two branches of the Presbyterian Church – the Church of Scotland or Kirk party and the dissenters or Seceders (Antiburghers). Most of the earlier Protestant settlers of Pictou were Seceders but, as the Church of Scotland soon sent out ministers of the Kirk, the religious disputes of the homeland were reproduced in Nova Scotia. The Kirk party opposed the Pictou Academy, regarding it as a seed-bed of the dissenting ministry. For several years after 1826, supporters of the Kirk tried to undermine or gain control of the Academy, petitioning the Legislature and pressing their views in the newspapers.

32 A paraphrase of Rob Roy MacGregor's declaration in chapter 34 of Scott's *Rob Roy* – 'My foot is on my native heath, and my name is MacGregor!'

fields and gardens; and near the extremity stands the largest and most extensive private establishment that Pictou contains.[33] It was built by the late Edward Mortimer, Esq., who was for a great many years the most affluent and enterprising mercantile man in Pictou, and an influential and independent Representative of the County, in General Assembly. It is now occupied by his widow, and though the place seems to lack the superintendence of a master's mind, it is still a very handsome and valuable seat. As you pass along, the residence of Dr. McCulloch is pointed out to you, and from the celebrity which its owner has acquired in our Provincial doings, it is well worthy of a passing notice.[34] It is a small, plain-looking stone house, with a few flowers in front, and has a most unpretending aspect. A little further on, you perceive the Academy, which is a very modest, two-story wooden structure, with a small tower or steeple rising above it; the Meeting House appears at a small distance from it, but both buildings belong essentially to the northern division of the town; while, as if the two contending parties were determined to preach and pray as far from each other as they possibly can, the Kirk and Episcopalian Church are situated at the southern extremity. They are all neat wooden buildings, and their spires serve to give variety and expression to the general aspect of Pictou.

The principal street of the Town runs along the water side, and may be about half a mile from end to end, allowing for variations and irregularities; for, be it known to the gentle Reader that in the early settlement of Pictou there was no regular plan laid out for a Town – every man built his house just where he pleased, and as the streets had to be formed after many of the Houses were built, they are now blessed with their due proportion of sinuosities; and, as if by common consent, every Building has its own particular frontal line, that very seldom

33 This was Norway House, still standing as the Oddfellows' Home.

34 Thomas McCulloch (1777-1843) was a Secessionist minister at Pictou and the founder (in 1816) and first principal of Pictou Academy. Later, in 1838, he became the first president of Dalhousie College in Halifax. His 'celebrity' in the province was well deserved: not only was he remarkably well-versed in the humanities, medicine, and theology, and very successful in teaching all the courses in Greek, Hebrew, Logic, Moral Philosophy, Theology, and Natural Philosophy at the Academy; he was also a writer of considerable talent, a powerful preacher, and the indefatigable champion of the Academy and of humane education generally.

agrees with that of its next door neighbour; and in one instance a fine large freestone house extends about a dozen feet further into the Highway than is at all consistent with uniformity.

Another street, cut along the side of the Hill, runs from end to end of the Town. This is of more recent and more regular formation, and is intersected by five or six crossroads, running upwards from the Harbor. It has long been the custom of wayfarers to anathemise the Streets of Pictou, and verily in bad weather they support but an indifferent reputation; but summer – balmy and genial summer, that clothes the fields with flowers, dries up the vapours that moisten and mistify the Highways; and as they are dry and passable enough at the present moment, we see no reason for joining in the general outcry. They have of late years been very much improved, and we have little doubt, that under the influence of the Highway Act,[35] they will, ere long, undergo a thorough change.

The first House built in Pictou was reared in 1790, so that the place is only about 40 years old; and, as 40 years are no great matter, it has certainly progressed in a manner very creditable to the zeal and perseverance of the original settlers and their descendants. It has now a population of about 1500 souls, and contains from 150 to 200 buildings, of different descriptions, including some very handsome private dwelling Houses, and some large and commodious stores.

Above the Town, on the side and brow of the Hill, are numerous cleared fields, gardens and pasture lots, which add to the beauty of the water view of Pictou; but hie we out of the streets and lanes of the village; let us get up upon the Hill aforesaid, and seek a more expansive view of wood and wave, and try to form some definite notion of the general outline, not only of the Town, but the Township. Slowly sinks the great orb of day into the bosom of the dewy west – the waters of

35 The Act to which Howe refers was passed during the 1827 session of the Legislature. It was concerned mainly with new roads and alterations to old roads. The preamble states that the previous method whereby road commissioners laid out new roads and valued the land through which the roads ran 'has been found tedious and expensive.' The new legislation authorized justices in General Sessions to administer statute labour and to regulate gates and bars on roads, and established a system by which government appraisers would take over the laying out of new roads and the evaluation of the land required.

the broad Harbor are spread out like a mighty mirror before the eye; bounded on the left by the high land which stretches away towards M'Lellan's Mount, Merrigomish, &c. and on the right by the woodland that lies between Pictou and the River John; while the East, West, and Middle Rivers, the folds of which are lost in the foliage of the trees and the undulations and irregularities of the land through which they flow, seem, as they wind away from the opposite shore of the Harbor, like vast and beautiful veins, passing through the very heart of the country – the happy medium of circulation for the animating and sustaining tributes of Agriculture, Manufactures, and Commerce.

Faith, there is something agreeably disappointing in the view from this pleasant highland. To those who have heard nothing of Pictou, but that its streets were miry and its politics barbarous – who have been used to associate with its name any but the most agreeable impressions – who have had their very dreams of it disturbed by dirty-phiz'd radicals and red-headed Highlanders – there is something delightfully enchanting in this pleasing and panoramic scene; and, as the eye roves over its placid and softened features, one is almost tempted to believe, that if the population of the Town were scattered along this upland range, and would look on the rich and mellow landscape in a cordial and proper spirit, they would never allow the gorgeous sun to go down upon their degrading and paltry bickers.

VII

30 June 1830

Perhaps the gentle Reader may remember that some four or five months ago,[36] he was standing beside us upon the hills of Pictou, gazing

36 Chapter VI of *Eastern Rambles* appeared in the *Novascotian* on 25 February 1830. His letters indicate that Howe had made his first journey into eastern Nova Scotia in the summer of 1829, as he writes of seeing Pictou for the first time in a letter written in August of that year. What he calls a few lines further 'the immediate pressure of domestic politics' – his extensive reporting and discussion in the *Novascotian* of the issues raised in the annual sittings of the Legislative Assembly – probably left him no time to turn out further numbers of the *Rambles*.

upon the setting sun, and moralizing upon the unkindly bickers of the Kirkmen and Antiburghers. It is well for us both that we have not been standing there ever since, for many a chilly blast has blown over the highland since that day – many a torrent has rushed down its gullies, and many a snow bank sat, like a crystal diadem, upon its brow. But these having passed away, and the immediate pressure of domestic politics having passed away with them, what say you, my gentle Reader, if we commence our journey again? what say you, if we re-ascend the steep, and seat ourselves upon the very stone where we last gave utterance to our mutual cogitations. It is no uncommon thing for the second volume of a Book of Voyages and Travels to make its appearance a couple of years after the first – and why should not our Rambles, though sent forth through a more humble medium, be allowed the same indulgence? The features of this young country of ours, moral, social, physical and political, are essentially the same in 1830 that they were in 1829 – the passage of a few months may have added some trifling grace, some slight amelioration, and, if so, our onward journey will not be the worse for the change.

See you that long line of coast stretching away to the left, or rather in a northerly direction from the spot on which we stand? That is what is usually called the Gulf Shore, part of which is included within the district of Pictou, and the remainder belongs to the County of Sydney[37] – we shall have more to say about that Section of the Eastern Country, when we come to travel through it; – in the meantime we cannot do less than bestow upon it a passing notice, as it forms one of the finest features of the beautiful prospect from the hills in the rear of Pictou. A continuation of the elevated range, of which Mount Tom forms a part, runs in an easterly direction for many miles in the rear of the road, and the shore settlements, upon this tract of the country, and is divided by the East River at no great distance above the Albion Mines. The McLellan's Mount settlement is formed upon this range, which gives

37 In 1830 the County of Sydney took in the whole eastern part of the mainland of Nova Scotia, what is now Antigonish County and the eastern two-thirds of Guysborough County. Cape Breton Island comprised an entirely separate county called Cape Breton County.

a bold outline to a great part of the panoramic scene which is spread out before the view.

We might be excused for indulging in some speculations upon the gradual growth and future prosperity of Pictou, while gazing from a height that exhibits to the best advantage the distinguishing characteristics from which its prosperity must flow. It is utterly impossible for the Tourist to throw off the sober reflections that throng upon the mind, almost insensibly changing the current of his thoughts from poetry to political science – from the beauties of the landscape to the natural capabilities it displays, and, in short from the present to the exciting prospects of the future. Its safe and capacious harbor, its noble rivers, its mines, its agricultural and maritime capabilities, and above all the industry, frugality and intelligence of its growing population, claim from the Traveller a high and more enduring interest than is to be created by the mere effect of its scenery upon the eye. Its local contention and party feelings will inevitably pass away as its valuable resources become more fully developed, as the circle of its society widens, and wealth becomes more generally diffused. They are blots upon the moral aspect it at present exhibits – but blots that cannot fail to be effaced, as the great elements of its physical character are wrought by the hand of time. As it grows in population and importance, the memory of the present contentions will be like the tales of hardship, privation and danger, which many of its fathers and grandfathers recant to the happy households that crowd round the winter fireside.

For many years past, with the exception of 1829, Pictou has raised bread enough for its own population, and has had some to spare; the general use of oats enables the farmers, particularly the Highlanders, to offer their wheat for sale, when the folks in other parts of the Province, who like good living and mortgages, eat all they raise, and send to Halifax or St. John for more. Mills are gradually increasing in the District – either for the manufacture of flour and oatmeal, or for carding wool and sawing lumber; and in a few years there cannot be a doubt that a large quantity of flour will be furnished by the population of this district to other parts of the Province, where industry is less common or worse rewarded. The Timber Trade which was once carried on to an immense extent from this Harbor has now dwindled into comparative insignificance, from the operation of two causes – the scarcity of the article, and the decline of prices. About twenty vessels have arrived at Pictou, during the present season, but as many of them are loading at the outports, there are only some half dozen in the Harbor at the present time.

Besides the direct trade with the mother country, Pictou has several small vessels which run to Prince Edward's – the New Brunswick ports on the Gulf of St. Lawrence, Cape Breton, or Sir Isaac Coffin's estates – the Magdalen Islands,[38] to which goods and produce are taken, in exchange for fish and oil; and sometimes, a handsome speculation is made by the purchase of wrecked goods, which, by a pretty summary process, are often curiously disposed of, within the dominions of Sir Isaac. The trade from Pictou to the West Indies is necessarily circuitous, and generally passes through the port of Halifax. Of the coal trade, we shall have to speak by and by, and shall pass it over for the present – only observing that it gives additional life and energy to nearly every other business carried on upon 'the Harbour', as the people along the back settlements say. There are some good wharves, and extensive wooden stores in Pictou, offering facilities for a greater amount of business than is at present transacting – the shops, if not very capacious, are well filled, and some of them very neatly arranged – indeed the demand for various kinds of goods increases as rapidly as do the heads and heels in the district, and a continual influx of agriculturists keeps the dry good and hardware men on the alert.

A curious feature in the character of the Highland population, spread over the eastern parts of the Province, is the extravagant desire they cherish to purchase large quantities of land. Indeed, this is a propensity which in a greater or less degree influences almost every person who emigrates to this Province from the mother country. There the possession of the smallest patch of land ensures an independence, a few acres make a man rich – and a few hundreds raise him to the first circle of rank and influence in the kingdom. The habits of thought and

38 The Magdalen Islands in the Gulf of St Lawrence became the property of Sir Isaac Coffin (1759-1839) in 1787.

reflection created by such a state of things are not to be shaken off when the emigrant arrives in a country where land is of comparatively trifling importance; we have known many instances of serious embarrassment on the part of those who once possessed a handsome capital, and many of the poorer settlers seriously injure their prospects, by curtailing the means necessary to the successful cultivation of the land they have, in their over-anxiety to make a further purchase.

They will toil night and day – spend as little as possible – and live upon the commonest fare, until a sum of money is saved, either sufficient to buy an adjoining tract, or to pay the fees required to get a grant from the Crown. But a faint idea can be formed of the amount of population, or of the extent of settlement in Pictou, from riding along the main roads or from looking upon the surrounding country from the height on which we stood. Some of the finest and most populous settlements are either scattered along the banks of the rivers, or are hidden behind the wide ranges of forest, which appear to overshadow the land. But plunge into yon grove of birches, which spread out their broad branches to the morning sun and rustle their leaves in the gentle breeze – seeming to shut out the busy, bustling, artificial world, to which, gentle reader, both you and I belong, from the deep solitudes, the unbroken wilds of nature, which your imagination may people with the moose and the bear. Plunge in without fear of sacrilege; you are not the first to disturb the presiding genius of the place, for just as your eye is roving from stem to stem , or following the tops of the trees into the heavens – just as you are repeating – 'Oh solemn are the mighty woods'[39] – and admiring the taste of the ancient sages who taught philosophy in the groves, where every object could furnish them with a pleasing illustration, your reveries are disturbed by the stroke of an axe, the bark of a dog, the bell of a cow, or some other equally significant hint of neighbouring cultivation; and as you proceed, you find a clearing occupied by one, two, or a dozen settlers, as the case may be, who perhaps steal a moment from their vigorous toil to bid you good morning, or make a tender of some rude hospitality in a dialect you cannot understand.

39 Felicia Hemans, 'Edith: A Tale of the Woods,' ll.1–2

VIII

7 July 1830

Here we are, gentle Reader, right opposite the door of the Pictou Academy, and what say you – shall we take a peep in? After all the hot blood it has created, and all the hot words it has occasioned, a man might well be excused for pausing upon the threshold of the place – for who knows but the very air of it may be impregnated with the spirit of discord – and what douce sober body can be certain that he will issue from its walls the same happy wight that he entered? Who knows but we may come out a fierce and uncompromising seceder, ready to quarrel with our best friend, should he venture to hint that the institution is susceptible of any improvement, and to maintain that the cause of civil liberty, all the world over, is deeply involved in the perpetual grant;[40] who knows that we may not come forth an obstinate and stiff-necked kirkman – seeing danger, disaffection and disloyalty in the face of every Antiburgher we meet – holding the perils of the Lion's den as matters of light consideration, when compared with the danger of sending a boy to the College, and ready to maintain that, because his Majesty's Council have opposed the perpetual grant, they never can do any thing wrong, impolitic, or absurd. With something like the feelings with which the knights of old knocked at the portals of enchanted castles, where ghosts and hobgoblins were known to abound, or which prompted the 'Open Sesame' of the honest woodcutter, whose curiosity to see the inside of the Robber's cave was not to be o'ermastered by the danger, do we make our entrance into an institution, which, next to the old fort at Annapolis, has caused more battles than any building in the country, and has been assailed with a perseverance and address only equalled by the vigor and ability with which it has been defended.

We mentioned, elsewhere, that it was a plain wooden building – two

40 Pictou Academy had for years petitioned the provincial government for a perpetual grant. Its petitions, though supported by the Assembly, were invariably turned down by the Legislative Council; it had to be content with an annual grant.

stories high, with a small tower or belfry on the top of it, and surrounded by some poplar trees. It is divided into four large apartments, having the Laboratory and class room upon the ground floor, the Museum and the Library in the upper story. On entering the Laboratory you find yourself surrounded by philosophical apparatus[41] – some of it showing an orderly arrangement, and some, perhaps, unscrewed for the purposes of purification and repair. Bottles containing chemical compounds are ranged along on shelves, and perhaps you may find the Doctor, in his shirt sleeves, stooping before the fire, boiling a skillet, in which is contained the ingredients for a further experiment, another inroad upon the wide dominions of nature. Finding that the worthy Doctor makes no attempt to scalp or to bite you, that he merely gives you a kindly welcome, and a pinch of snuff, without blowing you up with a charge of electricity, or assailing your lungs with his air pump, you begin to be re-assured, to take courage, and to look about you, without any serious apprehensions of danger. There is nothing particularly attractive in the class room; the library is rather extensive and well chosen; but the Museum offers the richest treat that can be had within the Province – containing, as it does, an ornithological collection embracing nearly all the birds of the country, from the stately loon to the beautiful chick-a-dee. Here you may stand, face to face, with the mottled owl, the flap of whose wing struck terror into your heart as you roamed through the forest, on some nocturnal excursion – mayhap to see the fair-haired daughter of your next-door neighbor, or to plunder the orchard of some miserly curmudgeon, whose fruit was not quite so sour as his visage. There sits the partridge, the print of whose delicate foot upon the snow has given you many an hour's anxiety – many a winter day's sport, as you stole along through the woodland, with your piece upon the cock, ready to fire, when she should rise from the butt of an Alder at your feet, with a whir like the spinner's wheel. Often have you heard her, too, in the balmy mornings of spring, as sitting upon some fallen pine, the drumming of her wings sounds like some distant waterfall, or broken peal of thunder, calling her mate to

41 Howe uses 'philosophical' in the old sense as pertaining to *natural* philosophy (physical science).

the banquet of love, for every year is leap year with partridges. Here we have the beautiful blue-winged duck, choice object of epicurean care, and provincial legislation – and tell me, thou horrible gourmand, wouldst thou not rather gaze upon its compact but delicate plumage, than thrust thy unsparing fork into its breast, while thy nostrils take in the savory steam that arise from the dish on which it lies? wouldst thou not rather mark its strong wing, battling with the tempest and the storm – cleaving the dense air, and flushing along the troubled wave, than sit at thy luxurious board, with the wing aforesaid stuck between thy teeth? Oh! thou saucy sea pigeon, how dost thou remind us of the days, when, like the prophets of old, or the Cameronians of more modern times,[42] we have hidden us in the clefts of the rock, and, despite the sleet and the rain, have watched for thy approach, as sailing about upon creek and inlet, you sought your daily food. Many a cold foot and frozen finger hast thou cost us – and many a shilling of our boyish savings has been fired at your head, in the matter of powder and shot, for thou wert a very devil for diving at the flash. Hail to thee, Robin Red Breast, the pleasant harbinger of spring – and thou little Grey Linnet – though thy plumage be modest and quaker-like, and thy body no bigger than the hand of a newborn babe, the richest treasures of memory are thine – for, on those happy evenings of our youth, when we sat on the sloping bank, overlooking the tranquil waters – when the blissful placidity of the scene made more happy the young hearts, over which sorrow had thrown no shade, thou nestled in the leaves of the beech that fluttered above our heads, and joined thy note of joy to the simple songs our fair companion warbled. Oh! gentle reader, but that we fear thy patience might be exhausted by our rapturous recollections, gladly would we allow each bird in this beautiful collection to lend its wing to our spirit, and carry it back to some happy hour of our bygone days – some of the green spots of the soul, watered and refreshed by the sacred springs of uncorrupted feeling.

42 The Cameronians were the Scottish Covenanters who followed Richard Cameron in holding to the covenants of 1638 and 1643. In the eighteenth century they were known as the 'Reformed Presbyterians.' As a persecuted sect, they were often driven to take refuge in caves and other wild retreats. Howe would have encountered them in his reading of Scott's novels, especially *Old Mortality* (1816) and *The Heart of Midlothian* (1818).

We think the greatest enemy to this Institution – the warmest opposer of Doctor McCulloch, must allow that his Museum is not only highly creditable to his perseverance and industry, but honorable to the Academy and the Province. We believe that the primary object which the Natural History Society of Canada has in view is to make similar collections, but we doubt whether, with more enlarged means and the conjoined efforts of a numerous body, they have made a more respectable progress. With a few foreign exceptions, the collection is made up of the Birds of the country, and although some additions are still necessary to render it complete, it is a matter of astonishment to the casual observer, whose habits of thought have seldom induced him to reflect upon such subjects, that it should be so extensive; it is no easy matter to persuade him that there are so many Birds in the Province. These specimens are very handsomely prepared, and are ranged round the room in glass cases, and if there were no other inducement to lure a man into the interior, the high gratification they afford would reward him for a journey to Pictou. We stay not to enlighten the reader with grave disquisitions upon the merits or defects of this institution; we are not going to bother our heads or the heads of our readers with any sober argument about it – for as to the views of its assailants and the determinations of its Trustees, the pros and cons, the whys and the wherefores – are they not written on the Journals of the Assembly for the last ten or a dozen years, and on the pages of all the Newspapers that have been sent forth within the same compass of time, for the instruction and guidance of the Province? where those who have not had enough of the dispute may turn and refresh their memories, while we proceed across the ferry, on our way to the Albion Mines.[43] – But stay we a moment to return our thanks to the Pictonians for the kindness and hospitality which, in common with almost every other part of Nova Scotia, they invariably extend to strangers. From the divided state of the district, a Traveller might reasonably expect but little civility from either party, and while he rambled towards it for the mere purposes of business, or the gratification of his curiosity, might be excused

43 The name 'Albion Mines' was given by the General Mining Association to their collieries in 1827. It remained the name of the town which grew up around the mines until 1870, when the town was renamed Stellarton.

if the kindly courtesies of life made up but a very limited share of his pleasurable anticipations. An agreeable disappointment awaits him, and if he be disposed to accept the civilities of the people in the same spirit of frankness in which they are proffered, he may spend his leisure hours in a round of social intercourse that charms away the 'chimeras dire'[44] which beset his path when he made his entrance into Pictou.

You pay a couple of shillings for getting yourself and your pony ferried across to Fisher's Grant, which forms the eastern side of the Harbor, and there are then about eight miles of tolerable road – (one long bad bridge over a creek or inlet always excepted) between the country and New Glasgow. As you ride along the Town, Harbor, and surrounding country are seen from different parts of view, and from the more elevated parts of the Road, some of the best proportions of the East River are spread out before the eye, exhibiting the finer features of our river scenery to very great advantage. Here we have the level, rich and highly productive intervale, from which the sloping upland rises, until it is hidden under the broad belt of forest, still waving in its ancient glory – majestic and unsubdued. In some places where a clearing has been commenced, but not completed, or where the fire has run through the woods, the scenery is injured by the unsightly stumps, or an army of scathed and blackened trees, that look like the unfortunate objects of some electric visitation.

New Glasgow is a thriving little village upon the eastern side of the River, but connected with the opposite bank by a substantial wooden bridge. Judging from the fresh or new appearance of the buildings, it is of very recent erection;[45] the operations at the Albion Mines have, within a year or two past, given it quite a start, and several houses and shops are either in progress or appear to have been very recently completed. There is one handsome house in the centre of the village built of the freestone of the district, and another of the same material upon the outskirts; all the others are built of wood. This village has been

44 Milton *Paradise Lost* II, l.628

45 New Glasgow was settled in the two decades before Howe's visit. The first settler established himself there not long before 1809, and by 1828 the population was only 200.

called into existence by the increasing population of the East River, the settlements at McLellan's Mount, and other places in its neighbourhood – and as these become more extensive, populous and independent, it must rise in wealth and importance. Pictou Town will always command the general trade of the district, but New Glasgow, which is some eight miles nearer, to say nothing of the ferry, will always supply the population of the East River and the mountain settlements, so long as its Traders are able to find a vent for their produce. Small as this place is, it is not free from the party spirit to which we have so often been forced to allude since we came into this district; here, too, are Kirkmen and seceders, and their hundred and one little jealousies, hard thoughts and local contests; in spite of which, however, the place is growing; and our worst wish is that its progress on the high road to prosperity may be so rapid that the spirit of party may be left a league behind. Two miles more on the back of a horse, and we are snug and safe at Mount Rundle, looking out at the Albion Mines, over which, when the gentle reader shall have rested and reposed, we will give him a curious ramble.

IX

21 July 1830

Be it known to the gentle Reader, whose love of locomotion has never led him so far, that Mount Rundle is a pleasant little seat, overlooking the Albion Mines, where the superintendent resides.[46] It has arisen upon the borders of the forest within a few years past, and although the grounds around it are not yet brought into high order and cultivation, they already exhibit evidences of good taste and liberal expendi-

46 In 1827 the General Mining Association bought property at this site and built on it a mansion, Mount Rundell, as the residence of their agent, Richard Smith, an English mining and metallurgical engineer who came out to Nova Scotia in 1827 and returned to England in 1834.

ture. The best view of the whole mining Establishment is to be had from the windows of Mount Rundle. It is situated on the west side of the River, which is hereabouts divided into two channels by a strip of intervale, each being crossed by a wooden bridge. Near the edge of the western channel stands a large building, comprising an extensive store, cellar, counting House, &c., in which are kept a more various and extensive stock of goods than is to be found in any mercantile Establishment in the country. This Store is intended for the supply of the persons more immediately engaged about the mines, and is also a great convenience to the population on the East River, who resort to it for supplies; which, from the facilities for purchase and importation the company possess, they are enabled to furnish upon the most advantageous terms.

Some 40 yards in the rear of this Building the Pits are situated, and you may see 10,000 chaldrons of coal lying in one body on the surface around them.[47] – The steam machinery by which it is raised is contained in a small brick building, devoted exclusively to the purpose; from its top rises a lofty chimney, through which a stream of smoke is continually rushing, and gives notice to the Traveller of his near approach to the seat of industry and art, before he catches a view of the Mines. From the Engine House long chains and bands of rope pass upon wooden frames or scaffolds, over the shafts, and descend to the depths below. One of the most important and expensive operations carried on by the Company, near the Albion Mines, is a Rail Road, which is to extend from the pits about a mile and a half to the spot where the coal is taken in the Boats, which carry it down to the place of shipment.[48] Nearly the whole of this Railway has been already completed, all the iron materials for it having been cast at the Establishment. It is intended to run stout wooden cars upon it, which hold just a chaldron, and are constructed so as to empty their lading immediately into the Boats. As the freight of the coal from the Boat landing to the vessels is the most expensive part of the business of transportation, it

47 A chaldron is a coal measure of 36 bushels.

48 This short line was one of the earliest railways in North America. It was built by the General Mining Association and was opened in September 1839, between Albion Mines and the coal-loading area below New Glasgow.

is supposed that if the Company would go to the expense of continuing the Rail Road to New Glasgow, and clearing away some of the Oyster Banks which obstruct the navigation so that the vessels might come up and take in the coal without the agency of Boats, it would ultimately repay them amply.

About half way between the Pits and the Foundry is a low range of brick work, in which there are six large ovens or furnaces, employed in the manufacture of coke. This, as the scientific Reader knows, is an article made from the fine or slack coal that will not sell, and which, after being about half burnt out, forms into large lumps or cakes, which are drawn out of the furnace, and cooled by throwing water upon them. The coke is used in various kinds of Black-smith work, and for such purposes is held in high estimation. The coal is emptied into the tops of the furnaces, each holding about three chaldrons – and, after burning for two or three days, it is broken into flakes, and drawn out with a long iron hook, when it is thrown into heaps to be cooled – The loss in burning is about ten per cent. A large quantity of the article has been prepared, and is now on hand. It sells for about 26s. the chaldron. This employment, as it may be well supposed, is not very agreeable to those engaged in it; with a hot fire in front, they are not protected by any covering from the weather, and may be occasionally half roasted and half frozen at the same time.

The Foundry is also a brick Building, calculated for carrying on the smelting and manufacture of iron on a very large scale. It is formed into three divisions – in one of which the casting is carried on, the machinery works in the centre, and the other contains a workshop, where moulds and woodwork are prepared, and where the castings are finished off after coming out of the furnace. The smelting and manufacture of iron was always intended to form a very important feature of the company's operations at the Albion Mines; but, from various causes, a great deal has not yet been done in this department. Except the bars for the Railway, some plates for Brewery-kilns, castings for Mill machinery, and a few articles of hollow ware, but little else has been furnished by the Establishment. These have been principally cast of pig iron, imported from England; from which also a considerable quantity of chain cable has been wrought at the smithey, an old wooden building situated between Mount Rundle and the Pits. These have not yet been offered for sale, nor will they be, until a proving machine is erected by which their strength can be ascertained. They are considered, however, to be of a superior quality; and should the gentle Traveller desire to have an idea of Vulcan's workshop, let him pop his head into the building where the swarthy artizans are busied adding link to link, and fashioning, by the cunning of their hands and the sweat of their brows, those mighty chains to which the ship of some 'great admiral' may be indebted for her safety, during those awful tempests which sweep over the wide wilderness of rolling waves.

A gentleman of the name of Davis has lately arrived from England to take charge of the Iron Department, in all its branches, and has taken a lease of the Foundry.[49] The only thing which is required to ensure his success, and to lead to the almost indefinite extension of this branch of manufacture, is an abundant supply of the Ore. The experiments which have been made prove the ore to be excellent, and should it be forthcoming in sufficient quantities to supply the furnaces, there is not a doubt that the business may be carried on to very great advantage. We are doubtful, if, even with the facility afforded by having coal upon the spot, the manufacture of iron could be carried on by importing the raw material from Europe; but there cannot be a doubt, that if the ore be abundant in the very neighborhood of fuel, the Province will, ere long, be supplied by domestic manufactures. Mr. Davis has, we understand, had great experience in the branch of business he has undertaken, and possesses an excellent knowledge of machinery, so that should he succeed in obtaining Ore, his Foundry cannot fail to be of essential service to the Province. There are a great many articles of iron manufacture required for Saw and Grist Mills, Kilns, Breweries, carding Machines, and for multifarious objects connected with our domestic industry, that cannot now be obtained within the Province; and consequently, those by whom they are required are subjected to the delay and uncertainty of a correspondence with Great Britain or the United

49 W.H. Davies took over the supervision of the iron foundry at the Albion Mines in 1830. He was still living there in 1852, when he was appointed as one of the two churchwardens of Christ Church.

States, and to the additional expense of transportation; whereas, had we a well-organized Foundry within the Province, a person might send his pattern, and receive his article, within the compass of a week or a fortnight; or if it were necessary, the work might be done under his own eye. Mr. Davis has, we believe, superintended the erection of several Steam Engines in Europe, and will be able to supply such as may be required, either in this, or the adjoining Provinces. We shall take some other opportunity of informing our readers of his progress, and of calling attention to such further encouragement as we think it might be prudent to afford to our Iron Establishments, east and west, as the Province cannot fail to be essentially benefitted by the successful prosecution of the trade.

It would be of service to those who carp and cavil at this valuable and highly respectable company, to pay a visit to their establishments, and see how much has already been done for the credit and the improvement of the Province, and how little it has yet derived from its liberal outlays. A sum equal to £70,000 has been spent already upon the Albion Mines, either in the purchase of Land (of which the company own about 1500 acres at the mines, and about as much more in other situations) – or in the erection of buildings, the importation of machinery, the construction of a Steam Boat, &c., &c. The latter will be completed in about a week, and is intended to ply upon the East River, for the purpose of towing the coals down from New Glasgow. The returns of the company have hitherto borne no proportion to their liberal outlay, and therefore, instead of venting upon them a superabundance of spleen on every petty occasion, we ought to cheer them on in a frank and liberal spirit, to the more successful prosecution of an enterprize that has already done much, and promises to do more for Nova Scotia. The annual importations of goods, &c., from Great Britain, and of West India Produce, &c., received through the Port of Halifax, amounts to a very large sum, besides the horses' provender, boards, timber and produce purchased from the farmers of the District. There are 50 men and 7 horses kept constantly employed in the Pits – 80 men and fourteen horses on the surface, besides the employment given to Tradesmen and Mechanics, and to the country people round, who, with horses and boats, are engaged in the carriage of the coal. Some idea may be formed of the extent of excavation, when we say that there are about fourteen boards, or openings, made in different directions, 17 feet high, and 18 wide, at a depth of from 200 to 240 feet under the surface – one of these extends for a distance of 250 yards. Besides the buildings we have mentioned – there are upon the surface, a range of Brick and a number of wooden tenements, where the Miners and their families reside.

We cry thee mercy, oh! gentle and imaginative reader, for this dry and dull detail of sober serious fact. Were we like Syntax,[50] in search of the picturesque only, we should pass over such matters, as unworthy a moment's consideration; but, you must remember that we made no promise at the outset to banish all serious thought and grave and sober cogitation; and therefore we hold ourselves at liberty, to see whatever may come in our way and utter our wise saws – economical, moral or political, as often as it suits the bent of our humour. But come, take heart, our fine fellow, for verily, you shall have food enough for your fancy before long. We have had you into the clouds some dozen of times at least since we left home, and now we intend to give you a plunge into the bowels of the earth. But, first lay aside your coat, and envelope your shoulders in this pea jacket, draw over your inexpressibles this pair of fearnought trowsers, and a Kilmarnock cap may be no bad exchange for your Beaver; for depend upon it, the niceties of dress are but little regarded in a Coal Mine. Jump upon that sled, seize hold of the chain, and you shall presently have as beautiful a representation of the infernal regions as is to be found in any Poet from Dante to Milton. Up we go for a foot or two – away slides the scaffold – and now, my gentle Traveller, you are suspended over the mouth of the pit, and should any part of the tackle give way, you will have just about thirty seconds to say your prayers, before you are dashed to the consistence of a jelly, at the distance of 240 yards from where you at present hang. This, you will say, is no very pleasant reflection; however, you have the satisfaction of finding, as you slowly descend, that the probability of

50 'Dr. Syntax' was the pseudonym of William Combe (1741-1823), the author of a long humorous poem, *A Tour in Search of the Picturesque* (1812).

breaking your neck is not so great as it was – that with every revolution of the Engine it is becoming 'beautifully less',[51] as the Poet hath it. All uncertainties are disagreeable – should we, for instance, have popped a question to some delicate sprig of womanhood, how painful it is to 'pause for a reply',[52] to linger upon her faltering accents, to learn from her ruby lips whether we are to be quietly lowered into the delights of matrimony, or dashed to pieces against the rocks of despair. Then, should we be next of kin to some rich old uncle or superannuated cousin german, whose goods and chattels are to be gathered to ourselves when he is gathered to his fathers, how annoying is the reflection that the cord of the old fellow's existence may last till we are lowered so far into the grave – that we shall not be able to enjoy what he has been kind enough to accumulate. The sensations attending our first descent into a coal pit may not be so intensely painful, as it is certain they do not continue so long as any of these, but there is a sort of inexpressible something that gives the spirits at least a momentary flutter as we descend, and gives a buoyancy and lightness to the mind when we find ourselves again restored to firm footing upon the surface. The imaginative Traveller, as he descends through the circular shaft, which for a considerable distance down is cased with brickwork, may fancy that he is Captain Symmes travelling through the opening at the Poles, to pay a visit to the earth's centre[53] – or as he takes a last look of the light of Heaven, that he is descending with some political offence upon his head into the bowels of Siberia, or going into the silver mines of Brazil, to expiate, by a life of subterranean toil, the horrible crime of smug-

51 Matthew Prior, 'Henry and Emma' l.430

52 A phrase from Brutus' address to the plebeians in Shakespeare's *Julius Caesar* III.ii.35

53 In 1818 Captain John Cleves Symmes (not to be confused with the Revolutionary leader and western colonizer of the same name, who presumably was his father) sent a circular to institutions of learning in Europe and America outlining his theory that the earth is hollow and open at the poles. In 1823 he petitioned Congress to send out an exploring expedition to test his theory and, though the petition was turned down, it received twenty-five affirmative votes. With James McBride as collaborator, Symmes published *Symmes Theory of Concentric Spheres* in 1826. His theory first appeared in fiction in *Symzonia* (1820) by a Captain Adam Seaborn, possibly a pseudonym for Symmes.

gling. Now we look up, as though we were gazing upon the sky through Herschell's forty-foot telescope;[54] now we look downwards, to see how far we have yet to go, or to discover the origin of the strange sounds which begin to strike upon the ear, and increase in number and distinctness as we descend.

At length the sled on which you stand reaches the bottom, and before you are aware, a few links of the chain may be coiling on top of your head; but be in no hurry to leap off – wait until the guide, who has accompanied you in your passage, trims his lamp, and takes the lead, or mayhap you may bump your shins against a block of coal, or measure your length upon the bottom of the pit. For the first five minutes you can discover nothing; then you begin to see, as 'through a cloud, darkly',[55] and at length, by the aid of the lamps carried about in different directions, you can find your way along without much risk of losing your foothold. And now you discern a lot of Beings, looking more like Demons than men, with their loose trowsers tucked up to their knees, their bodies only protected by a flannel shirt, the sleeves of which are gathered up to the elbow – the neck and breast being generally open – their heads are covered by a close cap, something like a Welsh wig, and what adds to the singularity of their appearance, each has a small lamp suspended by a wire to the front of his cap – making them look like the Cyclops, who had but one glaring eye in his forehead. From head to heel these people are covered with the coal dust, which mixing with the perspiration drawn out by their hardy toils, gives to their features a singular, and rather a melodramatic expression. They look like neither blacks, whites, nor mulattoes, but have an appearance peculiarly their own; their white teeth contrasting curiously with their sooty faces, as they crack their jokes, or carry on their desultory conversations. These people are variously employed – some are digging away with their pick axes into the coal measures, or boring holes for blasting; while others are loading the sleds, or driving the

54 Sir William Herschel (1738-1822), the famous astronomer, completed in 1789 a large reflecting telescope forty feet in length and with a four-foot aperture.

55 A paraphrase of 1 Corinthians 13:12

horses back and forwards from the place of excavation to the bottom of the shaft. These sleds run on a moveable railway extended along the level of the pit – a broad iron hoop is laid upon the surface, and as the coal is filled in, another and then another is added, until the load is completed, when the traces are unhitched from the empty sled and attached to the full one, which is presently sent up to the surface by the agency of steam. The incessant clatter of the Miners' picks – the rattling of the coal as it is filled into the sleds – the rapid passage of the horses to and fro – and the circulation of two or three dozen lamps, altogether make up as singular a combination of sights and sounds as the greatest lover of medleys might require.

There is also heard a strange noise, as of the gurgling and rushing of waters, which for a moment would make a visitor think he had got into the Tunnel under the Thames, and that the King of European Rivers was bursting through his bed to punish him for his intrusion; but there is no such risk, for the streams we hear are used to preserve and not to destroy life. A large pump, which is sunk in one of the shafts and worked by the Steam Engine, draws up a great quantity of water, which it deposits in a hogshead, bored with holes – from thence it again descends into the pit, carrying with it a large quantity of air, by which the boards are ventilated, and all dangerous vapours carried off. As the coal is dug out, the roof of the pit is supported by logs, which are stood on end and wedged with plank, whenever the nature of the strata may seem to require them; large bodies of coal are left at certain distances for a similar purpose, and thus there is but little risk of any danger from the falling in of the ceiling. 'But, Heaven preserve us, what was that? Are we blown into a thousand atoms? Are we suffocated by sulphur and fire damp? Are we not lying, like an Egyptian Mummy, beneath a ponderous pyramid of ruins?' Nothing of the kind, my gentle Traveller, it is only a blast which you might have seen two stout fellows preparing, and which has upturned as much coal as would serve to keep an old maid and her cat warm and comfortable, during the approaching winter. But, if you get so nervous upon our hands, seize hold of the chain again, and let us proceed on our journey.

X

4 August 1830

Having escaped out of the Coal Pits, and taken in a draught of the pure air that without the aid of forcing pumps refreshes the surface of the earth, we may now, like the wise men of old, set our faces towards the east, and journey onward. Fain would we explore this fine river to its source, and examine for ourselves the improvements which the hand of industry has made upon its borders, even for fifteen or twenty miles above the mines; but for the present we must be content with such description as we can glean from those to whom each winding is familiar. How often has the heart of the pale and weary student sank within him, as gazing around the shelves of the rich repositories of learning, the sad reflection came upon his mind, that even the efforts of a long and laborious life would be insufficient for a full fruition of their treasures – a complete examination of each valuable page. And, in like manner, one of the first lessons which a Traveller has to learn is that it is morally impossible to see with his own eyes every thing that is worth seeing, or to bring within the compass of a journey the whole 'broad surface of old mother earth.' He must make up his mind to forego the pleasures of many a scene, to tear himself away from many a spot which rumour and hearsay would lead him to approach – and, indeed to use the language of Eloise, if he be a reasonable Traveller, he must see all he can, and be contented to 'dream the rest.'[56] – The East River is divided into two branches – the east and the west branch, and from the Mines upward the settlements run all along their borders, taking in the finest parts, if not nearly all the intervale, and running back some distance upon the upland. To give an idea of the extent of population in this direction it may be only necessary to mention that the Census gives to the East River nearly as great an amount as is given to the West and Middle Rivers, together with the Town of Pictou; and although the population is divided by the two Presbyterian churches, each of which has its followers in all parts of the District, we have been told that four

56 A phrase from Alexander Pope's poem 'Eloisa to Abelard,' l.124

thousand people (nearly double the number that recently assembled at Pictou) have been seen at a Sacrament, held about a year ago, upon the hills in the rear of New Glasgow.

Before he quits this neighbourhood, a scientific Traveller may amuse himself, if he pleases, by trying experiments with the gas that may be seen bubbling up from the River as it flows along over the coal measures. By taking an empty cask, boring a hole in the end, and placing the other over the bubbles, any quantity of gas may be detained; and, if a light be applied to the hole, it will burn with a steady and brilliant flame. The River side, until recently, boasted of another curiosity, which, through the ignorance or stupidity of some fellow who did not know its value, has lately been removed. This was an Ash and an Elm, about fifty feet high, growing from the same stump, and so intimately associated and bound together, that few persons would have been able to discover the union; and hundreds have passed and repassed, supposing them to be a single Tree. When the attention was called to the phenomenon, a slight division line was discovered upon the Bark, and where the stem was parted the branches from each portion bore its appropriate leaf. Upon the grounds of Mr. Dennison, at Kentville, there is a curiosity of a similar character[57] – Nature, in one of her vagaries, having united an immense Beech to a very tall Pine. Of course the bark and the colour of the Trees do not harmonize so well, as do those of which we have spoken, and therefore the deception is not so complete – but still there is the same intimate union of the stems, and the lower branches are twined together with a grasp of singular tenacity and strength. We saw them in June, when the luxuriant foliage of the Beech formed a wide circle round the otherwise unprotected stem of the Pine; while, at a distance of 15 or 20 feet above the top of the former, the small fringed branches of the latter were formed into a head. – A Disciple of Darwin might be disposed to speculate on these phenomena, and giving the reins to his fancy, might find in the 'Loves of the Trees' ample materials for poetry;[58] but as we have other matters

57 This was probably Colonel Sherman Denison (1769-1853), MLA for Horton Township, 1821-6, and a colonel in the militia.

58 Erasmus Darwin (1731-1802) was the author of several long poems in which he naively attempted to make poetry of the discoveries of natural science. Howe refers to *The Loves of the Plants* (1789), which describes in heroic couplets an Ovidian metamorphosis of the flowers, with stamens and pistils figuring as beaux and belles.

on hand, we shall leave him to account for what we have only attempted to describe.

From the mines we retrace our steps to New Glasgow, from whence the road to the French River runs nearly due East. There are a few fine farms along its course, and among the most extensive and best cultivated is one on the left, owned by Mr. McKay, overlooking the little village; but a large break is made in the line of cultivation by one of those immense grants, which retard the settlement of the country wherever they are found. For many miles, through a fine body of land, there is not a single clearing, and settlers have been forced to go in upon rear lots, often of an inferior quality, shut out from the main road by this unwieldy and burthensome grant.[59]

Those who pass over a new country must be prepared for many a long forest ride, where the tall trees shut out the scenery from the eye, and force the mind back upon its own resources for its recreation. When thrown into one of these solitudes, it is useless to spend the time calculating the distance, or to whip and spur, if the stately children of the forest should seem more numerous than the Ghosts which appeared to Banquo, and the overshadowed highway to lengthen before you, until you almost dream that you are wandering in the Cretan's labyrinth. Never fret or fidget, gentle Traveller, nor weary yourself and your beast, but recollect how Trenck amused himself in his prison with a Spider,[60] and how Bloomfield lacked not sources of

59 In the last decades of the eighteenth century, and even later, various land grants of huge extent were made to individuals, often to land speculators. The 'Governor's Grant' to which Howe refers was that of Governor Wentworth. It fronted on the western part of Merigomish Harbour, extended about eight miles inland, and was about five miles wide on its inner side. Wentworth, unlike some grantees, did made efforts to settle his grant, but failed to attract the substantial numbers of settlers from Connecticut (120 families) he had envisaged. The conditions of granting were that grantees were to pay a quit rent of one farthing per acre for one half of the property within five years and for the whole in ten years, and were to place settlers (one person to every 200 acres) upon it within ten years from the date of the grant. As these conditions were not fulfilled, thousands of acres lay unsettled for decades after the time of the original grants.

60 Frederick von der Trenck (1726-94) was an adventurer and soldier-of-fortune whose autobiography (published in German in 1787) related, among many other experiences, details of his years in prison, to one of which Howe refers. The book would have been available to Howe in the English translation of Thomas Holcroft, which was first published in 1788 and several times reprinted.

delight in the confinement of a cobbler's garret.[61] If you be a philosopher you ought never to be lonesome – if a Botanist jump off and gather a plant – if addicted to ornithology, there are birds on every bough – and should you be a devoted follower of the muse, heaven save the mark, are not the woods all poetry? But, luckily for us, who are neither, we are gaining fast upon the heels of a Pedlar – one of that numerous class of indefatigable pedestrians, who are scattered over every section of the Province, and who may be seen upon almost every road, bending beneath their packs, with a stoop like that of Atlas, when he took the world upon his shoulders. In the mother Country, pedlars may have a distinct character, but they are in general either English, Irish, or Scotch, according to the country in which they follow their avocation – but, here they are as various in dress, dialect and feature, as the mixed population upon whose necessities they live. In former years, the great majority of them were Scotch – now it is remarked that the Irish preponderate; but, whether such is or is not the fact, we leave to those who are more deep in the statistics of such matters than we pretend to be. As far as our own observation goes, we think the *profession* can boast of having within its circle the representatives of half the Tribes of Europe. It is rare to meet an Englishman, but they are sometimes found. Scotchmen and their descendents are much oftener met with – the 'guid mornin' of the one, or the 'Mathin ma ' of the other, being the shibboleth by which you discover whether they are of highland or lowland extraction. There is a certain flush of the cheek – a roguish roll of the eye – or an oblique cock of the beaver, that immediately betrays the Paddy, meet him where you will; and bad indeed must be the road, and wet and cold the day, when his buoyant spirit and native humour are entirely weighed down by his pack. The great end and aim of these people is to get money, and not a few of them follow the advice – 'get it honestly if you can – but, at all hazards, get it.' The first object to be attained is to visit Halifax, Pictou, or some of the country Towns, and purchase, upon credit if they can, or for

61 Robert Bloomfield (1766–1823) was the author of *The Farmer's Boy* (1800), a long poem popular in its day. As his family was very poor, Bloomfield grew up with little schooling and was apprenticed to his brother George, a cobbler. Living in a garret with his brother and four other cobblers, Bloomfield practised reading by studying newspapers with the aid of a dictionary.

cash if they have it, a full pack of such articles as are most likely to meet a ready sale in the interior. Some of those who are forehanded, as the phrase goes, can afford to take a waggon; but the great majority of them travel on foot; some east, some west, and some north, until their stock is exhausted, and their pockets filled, when they return to town to seek for a fresh supply. Sometimes you may see them, down on their knees upon the floor of a loghouse, a cottage, or a country Tavern, unfolding the green baize which usually envelopes the pack, and displaying their wares to the best advantage before the eyes of the wondering household; and it is very rarely that they unfold it in vain. Some article is sure to strike the eye of the auld man, or the guid wife, or one of the growing youngsters. Barren indeed must be the pack that has not something suited to a family of sixteen or eighteen, with an old man and woman at its head, and a little suckling bairn forming the extreme point of a finely graduated scale of existence. There is tobacco and pipes, and jack-knives for the father; and knitting needles, and spoons, and 'sneeshin'[62] for the mother; while the hoarded pence of the boys and girls are insensibly attracted towards the Pedlar's pocket, by sundry little articles that experience has shown him are almost irresistible. Many of these people, after accumulating a little money, either buy a house, or a Town lot, and set themselves down as stationary Country Merchants; and from their very general acquaintance with the characters and circumstances of the people, are well calculated for carrying on the business. There is a sad sin laid by the scandalous upon the packs of the Pedlars, particularly that portion who come from the Emerald Isle – and which is always taken into account when the country merchants are urging the Assembly to tax them heavily; this charge is neither more nor less than that they are strongly inclined towards the recreation of bundling, and to convincing the country girls of the ridiculous nature of the Malthusian theory of population. But, without pretending to decide how far they deserve such a reputation, we may turn to less unlovely traits in the general character; and were we to consult the interests of the corps editorial, we would be almost inclined to

62 A dialect word (of Gaelic origin) for 'snuff'

join the country merchants in a system of persecution, for verily, the pedlars are the greatest newsmongers in existence. They generally carry in their heads as large an amount of intelligence as of goods in their pack, and may be said to be the only *periodicals* which the remoter settlements can boast. Like other men of genius, too, they scorn to be tied down to mere matters of fact – and often deliver to their customers curious medleys of things which really have happened with others that owe their origin to a ready tongue and fertile imagination. You can always tell when you are on the track of a pedlar, by the strange questions that are put to you, by every one you meet. Fearful tales of 'battle, murder, and sudden death' – of wars and rumours of wars[63] – of mysterious plots and political convulsions, are as certain indications of a pedlar, as are the cropped branches and delicate footprints of the recent passage of a moose. Some of these men are close, mercenary, suspicious rascals, who take every stranger they meet in a lonesome place for a highwayman, and measure him from the head to the heel. From these you can only get monosyllables, or the most laconic answers to every question you put; and they seem glad when you ride on, and leave them to a solitude which is preferable to any society, alloyed by the fear of being robbed. Others, again, of a less suspicious and churlish temper, will quicken their pace for miles, in order to keep up with an equestrian – that they may learn his name, character, and business – and while imparting to him such information as he may want, never fail to glean something of the passing occurrences of the day, wherewith to increase their store of general intelligence. A few are men of information and observation – some of them are humourists, if not philosophers, and throw over the evils and hardships of their occupation the hues of a cheerful and contented spirit. Such was the creature we overtook on our road through the Governor's grant, and may we never spend an hour with less profit and pleasure, than that which was enlivened by the cheerful tone of that light-hearted and intelligent pedlar.

63 'From battle and murder, and from sudden death ... Good Lord, deliver us': The Litany, *The Book of Common Prayer*; 'Wars and rumours of wars,' Matthew 24:6

XI

18 August 1830

Having arrived at the margin of the French River, a stream which comes down from the south and falls into the Harbour of Merrigomish, you are not much gratified at finding the Bridge in such a state of delapidation, that you can neither pass it on foot or on horseback; and while waiting till the scow is brought over, you have ample leisure to reflect upon the probable consequences to the country of a continuation of our legislative difficulties and discords.[64] The River, at the ferry, is some fifty yards wide, and every horseman, besides paying a shilling for his passage, must lay his account to wait some twenty minutes or half an hour; which, if the weather is bad, cannot be very agreeable. How long such a state of things is to last our wise ones alone can determine, but we think, if they were occasionally to cool their heels upon the margin of the French River, it would quicken their understandings as to the importance of roads and bridges. At Copeland's, about a hundred yards from the River, there is very good accommodation – that is, all that a traveller who is not fastidious can possibly require, viz. – a clean bed, a good cup of tea, a hot johnny cake, and excellent butter, with perhaps a saucer of preserves.

Merrigomish, which is the principal settlement of the Township of Maxwelton, the most eastern Township of the District of Pictou,

64 Howe is referring generally to growing conflict between the Assembly and the Council, and specifically to the system of apportioning the annual grants for roads and bridges. Local interests among members of the Assembly, the body which allotted the grants, indeed led to wrangling, and the most heavily represented areas of the province naturally fared best in the competition. It could easily happen that not a penny would be assigned to the repair of a particular bridge. Howe's remarks also imply that the Council, which fixed the total annual amount to be made available for roads, was acting in ignorance and did not realize that larger grants were badly needed. The state of the bridge over the French River probably was closely connected with the hard facts of politics: Maxwelton Township did not elect a representative to the Assembly. Moreover, the two MLA's for the County of Sydney (in which the township lay) may not have been much aware of its needs: Thomas Dickson was a lawyer living in the town of Pictou, and John Young was a busy merchant of Halifax.

extends along the post road for several miles, and although it contains a good number of houses and barns, and a large body of cleared land, the settlement is scarcely dense enough to entitle it to the name of a village. About two miles beyond Copeland's there is the nearest approach to a cluster; and you can tell by the scattered logs, and other indications of such manufacture, that ship building was formerly carried on to some extent. Here, as elsewhere, it has been for sometime upon the decline – a large part of the timber which clears from the port of Pictou is, however, still shipped at Merrigomish. The village itself is a fine little agricultural settlement – almost every building being surrounded by a farm – some of them stretching away south upon the upland, and others extending to the water's edge. The chief attraction of the place is the Harbour, which is one of rather a singular character; and of a fine calm sunny forenoon, offers to the eye a very delightful scene. It is four times as broad as it is long, extending from east to west some ten or a dozen miles. From the Eastern extremity a long low beach, called Cumberland Beach, runs about west north-west, and terminates in a stripe of excellent but uncleared land, which forms one side of the passage leading from the harbor to the Gulf of St. Lawrence. The other side is formed by a similar peninsula, stretching out from the westward, and both together furnish a fine shelter for vessels, in the whole extent of this fine harbour, in which there are several valuable islands. These, as well as the stretches of fertile land by which they are enclosed, are unfortunately included in another enormous grant; and consequently, with the exception of a few settlers who have neither leases nor legal titles, are destitute of population and improvement; but such spots as have been cleared, very favorably exhibit the qualities and capabilities of the soil. We should like to ask those whose business it is to attend to such matters, whether any, and what conditions, are attached to those formidable grants which are scattered over the country. Are there any obligations to clear and cultivate certain quantities, or to keep stock in proportion to the number of hundred acres? would not such matters be worthy the serious attention of the Legislature? and might not some plan be adopted to render these nuisances less intolerable than they are?

Merrigomish, like all other places which depended upon the sale of

Vessels and Timber, has sensibly felt the depression of prices at home, and has scarcely recovered from the change which has been wrought within a few past years. Though the Trade in Timber, as carried on in these Provinces, was in a great degree unsubstantial and injurious – luring the people from more useful occupations, breaking the constitutions, and injuring the morals of the population;[65] still it created a certain bustle and animation, drew people to some common centre, and kept money in constant circulation; and now that the bubble has burst, even though the people are betaking themselves to more substantial and less hazardous occupations, yet there is about all the Timber districts a certain appearance of depression – as though the tide of prosperity was upon the ebb; and the people seem as though they were scarcely reconciled to the altered state of affairs. There is something of this air about Merrigomish; but we believe those who know this part of the country well are of opinion that it has gained more than it has lost by the change; and that though money is scarce, the want of it is more than compensated by extended agricultural improvement, and the change of those desultory habits, and the absence of that dissipation, which are consequent upon the business of lumbering. There

65 Large-scale lumbering was commonly criticized as being of questionable value in a province which would presumably benefit much more by agricultural development. Howe, though critical of its effects, is somewhat more moderate in his assessment than is Captain Moorsom, who speaks as a thorough-going agrarian: 'That trade [the timber trade] may rather be termed a necessary evil than a benefit to a young country. The settler who arrives in summer from Europe without a shilling in his pocket, finds he is too late to raise any crop, and that he can only provide for the winter by constructing his log-hut, and cutting a few staves and shingles, which meet with an immediate sale: so far, so good: if he then devote himself steadily to agriculture, he will, in all human probability, become eventually independent; but he is more frequently tempted by his first little gains to engage in "lumbering", or cutting timber. He lives a severe and laborious life in the forests; he flatters himself with the prospect of realizing a considerable sum in a very few years; the timber-market falls in England; he finds himself overwhelmed with debt, and has to work his way again from his first potatoe plot ... The late depression of the timber-market, although a severe loss to many individuals, I am inclined to consider a decided gain to the country' (pp 51–3). The ruinous collapse of lumbering in the period is forcefully illustrated by a remark in one of Howe's letters from Miramichi: 'There is scarcely a man in business here with whom I would like to exchange – of some hundreds of persons who have dealt largely in timber here, there is scarcely six who have not been ruined, and I would give but little for the chances of those who remain' (letter to his wife, 1834).

are several other streams besides the French River which empty into the Harbor of Merrigomish, and a certain quantity of lumber is still floated down, but the business upon them all is visibly on the decline. The people of this settlement are principally Presbyterians – the Secession Church overlooks the village, and some miles further on there is a new building, recently erected by the Kirk party, who now have a resident minister. From Copeland's to Murray's is about six miles, and here we would advise a Traveller to lay in a hearty meal, in case of the worst, for go which road he pleases, as there are no decent Houses of Entertainment, he may stand a chance to dine with Duke Humphrey.[66]

If the gentle Traveller be an angler, and has had the precaution to carry his gear on the journey, he need not desire a prettier place to cast a fly than Barney's River, which flows along through a little intervale, about a hundred yards beyond Murray's. A skilful handler of the 'Rod and the Line' will, at the proper season, take a good fare of Trout, or perhaps a brace of Salmon, while Mrs. Murray is preparing his dinner. As we ascend the bank which rises up from the intervale, we have our choice of two Roads to Antigonish. That which branches off to the right, and is called the Mountain Road, is the shortest by about ten miles: after you pass over some three miles, it dwindles into a mere path, or bridle road, very tolerable for a horseman, but too narrow for a wheel carriage. It is aptly named, for through the whole extent 'hills peep o'er hills',[67] and you descend into a valley, only to struggle up the steep beyond. A noble growth of wood covers these mountains – and, after a spell of wet weather, numerous streams, of no great magnitude, run along in different directions; and often their murmurs break upon the ear, while they are withheld from the eye by the depth and luxuriance of the foliage. The land on these mountains is excellent, and although there is no continuous line of cultivation on this road, it is dotted with new farms, which are fast improving; and ever and anon as you pass onwards, a field of fragrant clover, or luxuriant grain,

66 'To dine with Duke Humphrey' is a proverbial saying which originally meant dining at another man's table, for Humphrey, Duke of Gloucester (an open-handed son of Henry IV), was noted for his generosity as a host. After his death, the phrase came to mean 'to go dinnerless.'

67 Alexander Pope *Essay on Criticism* II, l.232

relieves the monotony of the greenwood, and affords a peg on which to hang a calculation of probable increase and improvement. Baily's Brook is a thriving and very pretty Highland settlement, extending along between the Mountain and the shore Roads, upon the borders of a small stream, from which it takes its name. Its scenic character may be given in a few words – a winding brook – a narrow stretch of intervale, flanked by upland fields, bearing various crops, and exhibiting various signs of good or bad husbandry, according to the taste or information of their possessors. Here you may go into a dozen of houses without finding as much English as will suffice to tell you the Road; but you will find lots of genuine Highland hospitality, and before you have taken a seat a bannock of oaten meal will be thrust into your pocket, or a bowl of unskimmed milk presented to your lip; for the Highland dames reason right shrewdly, that, when on the road, hunger and thirst are as apt to overtake the Saxon as the Gael. And now it is in your power to return this civility at least tenfold, if you have been so fortunate as to provide yourself with a snuff box, well stored with Scotch or Maccabau; for there is no compliment you can pay, no kindness you can offer, to a Highland woman in the wilds of Nova Scotia, that equals in her estimation a pinch of excellent snuff; and if you but empty the contents of your own box into hers, you confer an obligation which she will never forget as long as there is a nose on her face.

But leaving the mountain road and mountain settlements, we must return to that which passes along the Gulf shore. This road, for some eighteen or twenty miles beyond Barney's River, is of a very different character from the other, being about as straight and as level as we can expect our Highways to be. On the left you have the broad bosom of the Gulf of St. Lawrence, breaking, by its gentle motion, the bright beams of the noonday sun into a myriad of sparkling combinations. Prince Edward's may be seen, like a streak on the verge of the horizon, while Pictou Island, the centre of which has considerable elevation, does not look unlike some monster of the deep, enjoying his slumbers in the sun. The white sail of a Timber Ship, pursuing her course to Richibucto, or an American, going to Pictou for a load of coal, serve to give variety and animation to the scene.

The range of high land, which we sometime since informed the gentle reader stretched away east from McLellan's Mount, on this side the

Albion Mines, and which passes in the rear of Merrigomish, extends along the whole line of the Gulf shore, until it terminates in the promontory of Cape George. The table land that lies between this range and the waters of the Gulf, and of which the finest farms are formed, narrows as we proceed onwards, until, as it approaches the Cape, it is lost in the upland range which swells out abruptly to the sea. The finest part of the Gulf Shore settlement lies between Baily's Brook and Arisaig Pier, embracing nearly the whole of this table land, and extending up upon the side of the mountain – presenting much the same character of scenery as the back settlements of Wilmot and Cornwallis, as far as regards the mere formation and improvement of the earth. But in the appearance of the Farm Houses, and in all that comes under the head of neatness, order and taste in rural economy, the settlers of the Gulf Shore are sadly deficient. We will not say that they deserve the character of Barbarians given to them by some of our public declaimers, but certain it is that in too many cases the very qualities which make them valuable pioneers, viz. their ability to endure hardship, to live on the humblest fare, and to be satisfied with the smallest amount of comfort that can be had on this side of actual starvation, are so incorporated into their mental organization, that they do not forsake them when they are raised to a degree of comparative comfort and independence. Artificial wants do not appear to come in upon them, as their means of supplying them increase; and instead of supplanting their old log houses with buildings of a more roomy and comfortable character, as the settlers in other parts of the Province do so soon as their circumstances have sufficiently improved, many of them still reside, with families of ten or a dozen children, in the same shielings which afforded them shelter when their infant clearing was commenced. Many of the farms are extensive, and nearly all of them as productive as any to be found within the Province; but the eye looks in vain for the neatly painted cottage, the bending orchard, or the tasty garden, which elsewhere give the richest charm to a fine agricultural district. Time and a more general diffusion of education will, however, work changes which we cannot but think are now 'devoutly to be wished.'[68] Of the female portion of the Gulf Shore population we shall

68 Shakespeare *Hamlet* III.i.64

say nothing, but we have heard the Inspecting Field Officer speak in raptures of the fine, steady, and truly martial appearance of the men, who are nearly all tall athletic fellows, ranging from five feet ten to six feet four, and exhibiting such an array of limbs as would give to an enemy a fair promise of a day's sport, with the bayonet or claymore.

Arisaig Pier, of which the gentle Reader may have heard something while seated in the Lobby of the Assembly during the discussion of grants for its erection or repair, is a long wharf, strongly built of wood and stone, extending inwards from the southern side of a small curved point of land, which stretches out from the shore into the waters of the Gulf, and affords a shelter for small vessels, and a good place of shipment and deposit for the produce of the agriculturists, and the supplies which they need in return. – This is a useful public work, and is of great service to the settlers upon the Gulf Shore; as, with the exception of Merrigomish, there is scarcely anything like a Harbor from Cape George to Pictou. A short distance beyond the Pier stands the Catholic Chapel, a handsome wooden structure, the size of which gives you a more distinct idea of the amount of neighboring population than can be formed by the most attentive observation of the country through which you have passed. The worthy pastor who presides over this numerous flock lives upon the hill side, a short distance above his Church; and by his unvarying kindness and liberality, extended through a long course of years to the rich and the poor, has earned quite a reputation for hospitality. Indeed the readiest way to affront him is to go by his door, without making a call.

There is a curious-looking rock which is pointed out to you in this neighborhood, called the Frenchman's Barn, from the circumstance of a French sloop of war having fired upon it, during some of the wars of the olden time, under the supposition that it was a building erected and inhabited by the English. After passing the Pier, we still keep the road round the shore for about six miles, through an unbroken line of settlement. The farms are not, however, equal to those we have left, the table land having dwindled to a very narrow stripe. No Bay or Harbor pierces the mountain ridge, and the only place that even approaches to the character of an inlet is one which bears the ominous name of Malignant Cove. The place, however, deserves a better appellation, and we could advise those who busy themselves in substituting English names, which mean nothing, for Indian names, which have invariably an appropriate and sometimes an exquisite significance, to correct so palpable a misnomer. The sloop of war *Malignant* was on her passage to Prince Edward's Island, in the fall of 1779, to bring away some troops, and was overtaken in the Gulf by a tremendous gale from the north east, accompanied by a heavy snow storm. Only fancy, thou gentle Traveller, who, on a sunny evening in July, art sauntering along upon thy steed, with nothing to do but ruminate, and feast thy eyes upon the scenery – only fancy for a moment that thou art upon the deck of a man-of-war, with a snow storm, a gale ahead, and such an iron-bound, shelterless shore as this, under your lee! We have heard the account from the lips of an elderly gentleman, who was at that time acting as Pilot of the Ship, and who, we hope, may long live to relate the story; and thus it was: All that the skill of those in command, and the activity and hardihood of the sailors could accomplish, was done to rescue the vessel from her perilous situation – but every succeeding moment impressed more strongly the sad conviction upon their minds that they must be driven ashore somewhere. There was no harbor – no shelter to run to; to strike was to perish, and so assured were many of the sailors no ray of hope remained, that they turned into their hammocks, resolved to defeat the prognostications of the grannies, who had declared they should not 'die in their beds.' Many a time, in great emergencies, has a quick thought and a prompt action saved the lives of hundreds. The keen eye of the Pilot saw the little cove through the snow flakes; he threw his heavy coat upon the deck, seized the helm, and dashed the ship stem foremost into the inlet – the wind and waves assisting to convey her far up into its channel. The moment he found the bottom was soft, he roared out all was safe – and thus in an instant the prospect was changed from certain death to comparative safety and security. That night they succeeded in getting ashore, and having saved such articles as they considered valuable and necessary, erected camps, to shelter themselves from the inclemency of the weather. There were only two or three settlers at that time upon the Gulf Shore; and the sufferings of the people, before they could make their way to Merrigomish – Pictou, and thence to town, were very great. Many of them perished from fatigue, and many from the intensity of the frost – some lost limbs and were otherwise disabled, and the remnant succeeded in finding their way to Halifax, through the trackless and inhospitable wild, which the whole eastern country at that early period presented.

A sudden turn to the right now shuts us out from the Gulf, the Cove, and all their reminiscences; and for the next ten miles we travel on through a forest road, but thinly skirted with the rough improvements of a comparatively recent settlement. And after our long day's ride, having secured an excellent bed at Mrs. Simon's Hotel, in Antigonish, we are not disposed, just now, to ramble any further with the gentle Traveller, unless it be into the land of dreams.

XII

22 June 1831

Hail Muse, et cetera. – We left Juan sleeping.
Byron

Sweet and refreshing are the slumbers that the Traveller earns by his toils. He sleeps not as the idler and the ennuyé sleep – whose minds and bodies, as they know not exercise, never need rest. The warm perspirations – nervous twitches and horrible dreams of the dyspeptic are all unknown to him whose sinews are braced by locomotion, and whose mind is pleasingly employed by an endless succession of new ideas that spring up from the varying scenes among which his path is winding. 'Heaven bless the man', saith Sancho Panza, 'who first invented sleep – it wraps a man round like a cloak' – but had Sancho never taken the road – had he never left his native village of La Mancha – nor been jolted for hours upon the back of his mule, the world would never have been blest with a remark as expressive as it is appropriate. But think not, Oh! gentle Reader, that we have been asleep in Mrs. Simon's hotel since the 19th of August, 1830.[69] The recollection of the first night we passed there, after our ride from Copeland's, round the Gulf Shore, is still fresh upon us; and verily our memory is stored with many a pleasant countenance and many a lovely scene, that subsequently beguiled our onward journey; and it was our purpose long since to have introduced them to the gentle Reader – but we have not for months been able to catch him with leisure enough upon his hands to listen to Travellers' Stories. First came the general Election, with all its excitements, contentions and triumphs, to occupy his attention; then our Legislative sages were assembled, and all eyes were attracted by their sagacity, wisdom and wit;[70] and since they departed, there has been such a crumbling of ancient dynasties – such a disruption of obsolete fictions in morals and government, and such wars and rumours of wars – that the general mind has been so borne down with the accumulated novelties of Europe, that he must have been a bold man, who, relying upon his descriptive powers, would have weaned it off from such marvellous material to his own solitary Rambles.[71]

But now that our domestic politics offer but few attractions, and that we have supped full of European horrors, what say you, gentle Reader, to have a glance at the Village of Antigonish? Winter has passed away like a gloomy churl as he is – and Spring has thrown her verdant mantle over the land – the trout are leaping on the glassy lake – the birds are singing in the woodland – and the mountain streams, like captives just

69 Howe is referring to the gap of ten months between the publication in the *Novascotian* of this chapter and the last one. Apparently more and more of his time was being taken up by his writing on public affairs.

70 A provincial election had been held in the autumn of 1830, and the new Assembly had been convened on 8 November of that year. Howe keeps his political leanings out of the *Rambles*, but is openly delighted about the victory of the Reformers in Pictou when he writes to his wife from that town in October 1830: 'never was there a more glorious triumph than that which we have obtained.'

71 Some of the stirring events in Europe to which Howe alludes would have been the revolt against Dutch rule in Brussels and the subsequent invasion of Belgium by the Dutch; the resignation of the Duke of Wellington as prime minister; the rioting of agricultural labourers in England; the gaining of independence by Greece; the struggle for the Reform Bill in the British House of Commons, its rejection by the House of Lords, and related riots in British cities; the attempts at national unity in Italy and their suppression by Austria; and uprisings in Poland against the Russians.

released, come leaping and bounding into the vallies, while all, 'Mixed in one mighty scene, with varied beauty glow.'[72]

Antigonish is the Shire Town of the County of Sydney, and, as we find it duly set forth in Haliburton's Statistical tome,[73] owes its name to the Indians; the word signifying, 'River of Fish' or, as some have it, 'Forked River.' The same veracious writer says 'It is situated about a mile above the head of the Navigation on Antigonish River, and a short distance beyond the junction of the north and west branches, on a spot of ground that is elevated but a few feet above the streams that environ it. It is one of the prettiest villages in the eastern Section of Nova Scotia, and the neatness and simplicity of its appearance amply compensate for the absence of bolder scenery. It has but one principal street which is serpentine, extending half a mile from east to west, and containing about 45 dwelling houses, exclusive of other buildings.' All this is substantially true, but men will form different ideas of the beauty of a face or a scene – and perhaps there is nothing that more entraps us into a disappointment than exaggerated descriptions of either. In the face of the grave authority we have quoted, and of the many verbal testifiers to the neatness and loveliness of Antigonish, we are almost afraid to express any difference of opinion – but yet we must acknowledge there was a dash of disappointment in the feeling with which we surveyed it on the morning after our arrival. We think we come near the truth when we say that it is not so neat as it might be, nor so beautiful as it will be. Many of the Buildings in the Village have never been painted or whitewashed – and many of those which have, stand in eminent need of retouching. There are a few exceptions, but they are not sufficiently numerous to entitle the Village to the claim of neatness, or to relieve it from a sombre air that is at variance with the prosperity which the place enjoys. There is another disadvantage under which it at present labors. Though nothing can be more pleasing to the eye than an unbroken forest scene – nothing more sightly than our timber trees, when waving their proud branches in the wind – there is not a more unlovely spectacle than a recent clearing. Antigonish, which, we have

72 Byron *Childe Harold's Pilgrimage* canto I, xix, l.9

73 T.C. Haliburton's *An Historical and Statistical Account of Nova Scotia,* in two volumes, was printed by Howe in 1829.

seen, is built along upon an intervale, is nearly surrounded by hills – along the back range of several of these the woods are still standing; but the axe has been busy on those sides which slope upwards from the village, and stumps, burnt logs and sprouting underwood destroy the beauty of the scene. As these disappear before the plastic hand of improvement, and the eye, as it roves along the cleared and cultivated hills, is not offended by the debris of the forest, the scenery of Antigonish will have a charm for the Traveller's eye that it does not at present possess.

There are a few fine houses in Antigonish – and two or three neat cottages have been recently built around the borders. The Catholic Chapel is the largest building in the eastern country. and yet is not more than sufficient for the accommodation of the numerous body which make up its weekly congregation. The Rev. Bishop Fraser,[74] who is the head of the Catholic Church, resides at Antigonish – and sets a very praiseworthy example to all clerical dignitaries, by his unostentatious establishment – the frankness of his manners – and the active spirit of Christian benevolence that marks the discharge of his duties. You will often meet him some ten or fifteen miles away down the shores, or in the depths of the forest, visiting some poor Highlander, or administering the last rites of his church to the rude and unlettered Indian. And though you hear not the rumbling of his chariot wheels, nor ever wake to find him the object of a noisy salute, you cannot fail to hear, as you pass along through his parish, the blessings breathed by the poor and helpless upon his name.

The old Presbyterian Meeting House is quite a small building – a new one of large dimensions was begun some time since, but has never been completed. It would be an ornament to the village if finished – as it is, it rather detracts from, than adds to its appearance. The Court House and Gaol, which in most of our country towns are comprised in the same building, have, in general, about as many attractions for a traveller as they would have for a thief. Antigonish has its own, but it does not differ much from other edifices of the same order. There are

74 William Fraser (1779-1851) came out from Scotland to Nova Scotia as a missionary in 1822. In 1826 he was created second vicar apostolic of Nova Scotia and titular bishop of Tanen. In 1842 he became the first Roman Catholic bishop of Halifax.

also the usual variety of mills, stores, taverns, and blacksmith's shops scattered along, not forgetting the offices of two or three Attornies.

Situated as this village is, in the heart of a fine agricultural district which is steadily advancing under the active industry of a hardy and laborious population, it cannot fail to rise in importance as the country around it improves. Within ten or twelve years, the number of buildings has been more than doubled – and as every season brings into its market numbers who come with the first fruits of a new clearing – or others, who having visited it in that character for a time, appear with the independent tread and well-filled team of the substantial freeholder, its growth, though gradual, will be steady – and if it does not astonish us by a rapid advance, there is no danger of any decline. As regards navigation, it labors under the same disadvantage as Truro. Rivers flow through it, and the tide water into which they debouche comes within a mile of the town – but produce must be sent that distance by land, and then be carried in boats, before it is shipped for transportation by sea. This is an inconvenience, but one which the villagers have endeavoured to lessen by making an excellent road to the boat landing, and a tow path for some distance round the shore, until deep water is obtained. There is a good story, which they tell in those parts, about this matter; and as it serves in some measure to illustrate the advantages of having a Legislative Body, which, residing always in the capital, must nevertheless sit in judgment upon every crossroad and tow path in the country,[75] we shall relate, without at all vouching for its authenticity. The head of the harbor was formerly split into several channels, by the tide flowing up, and the rivers flowing down, with that sort of eccentric impulse which bodies of water usually possess. Neither of those channels afforded a very safe navigation – as old stumps, drift wood, and sunken stones were scattered about in 'most admired disorder.'[76] It was therefore proposed to clear the nearest channel to the margin of the Antigonish shore – and, by widening, deepening, and removing

75 The 'Legislative Body' to which Howe refers here is the Council, not the Assembly. Members of the Council did indeed live in or near Halifax; exceptions were rare, and even when a councillor from another part of the province was appointed, his infrequent attendance at Council meetings impaired his effectiveness.

76 Shakespeare, *Macbeth* III.iv.110

obstructions – and blocking up some of the other channels, to confine the waters to this passage, and make it safe for boats and scows. For this purpose subscriptions were raised, and an application was made to the Legislature; a sum was granted by the House in aid of the work – but when it came before the Council, it was thrown out with contempt and indignation. 'What – vote money for clearing sticks from a river – we might as well give a sum to clear the *River of Styx*. Besides, the thing is not upon the main Post Road – the Judges never have to travel over it – we never saw it – must be a humbug – wont give a farthing, &c., &c.' Thus things went on – the people petitioning to be laughed at – and, of course, admiring the wisdom and facetiousness of their rulers; until a member of the Council, who happened to arrive at Antigonish, was persuaded to go and look at the situation of the harbor, and to judge for himself of the nature of the plan. A glance was sufficient to create conviction – he wondered at his own ignorance, and the obstinacy of his colleagues. The petition was forwarded at the ensuing session – and upon the solemn asseveration of the traveller, the Council was persuaded of the utility of the design, and passed the grant of money.

XIII

13 July 1831

Leaving Antigonish behind us, we take the road to St. Mary's, prepared for a pretty solitary and rather uninteresting ride of forty miles. Being struck with astonishment, as we passed out of Antigonish, at seeing an Attorney ploughing his own field by the road side, we cannot refrain from recording the circumstance, for the honor of the profession; and expressing a wish that the example thus set may be very generally followed. To plough furrows upon the brows, and to harrow up the feelings of the poor devils who get into their hands, is the everyday business of the profession; and we really think its members should endeavour to confer some benefit upon the country, by turning up the land in their hours of recreation. Perchance, if they learn from experience how hard the pittance of the poor is earned, the information may be more serviceable to their clients than all the law in their Libraries. The tree of true legal knowledge should always bear the fruit of mercy; but too often, those who, like Adam, approach its branches in the hope of becoming wiser, find their little fields and pleasant gardens swept away in a night, and themselves consigned to never-ending toil, and the bitterness of vain reflections.

The fashion of the present day runs strongly against pluralities; and while we read with delight the vigorous attacks of the British Press against these accumulated corruptions, and sometimes venture to assail such as we find springing up in our Nova Scotian capital, the gentle reader will perhaps be amazed to learn that there is scarcely a country village in the Province where some half a dozen public functions are not discharged by the same individual. This arises not from the value of the offices making them acceptable boons to individual favorites, but from the trifling amount of their emoluments rendering it absolutely necessary that they should by given to some one person, that the public may be served, and their servant at the same time live by his labor. Like the bundle of sticks in the fable, he that depends upon one of them, will find it a poor support, but when united, there is strength and safety in the combination. – You will discover a Postmaster who is also a Major of Militia, and Magistrate for the County, Clerk of the Peace, and Commissioner of Roads, and who may be seen on a warm day bustling in his shirt sleeves around an Office, lined with the indicia of his several appointments, while the jargon of the incomers would almost put Caleb Quotum himself into a fever.[77] During half an hour that we sat in such a place, in a certain Eastern Village, we are positive we saw as many strange animals as were ever gathered into the Ark, and heard as many discordant sounds as issued from the Tower of Babel. 'Have you ever a Letter for me, yer honor?' roared a stout Irishman, with his hat cocked on one side of his head, that he might

77 Caleb Quotum is a parish clerk in *The Review; or, The Wags of Windsor* (1798), a play by George Colman.

leisurely scratch the other. 'What name, what name?' asked the Postmaster. 'Sure ye know my name, for your honor roared it loud enough on the p'rade that day, when I tossed my musket on the wrong shoulder, in the drill.' – 'Oh! Sullivan – aye, I remember Jerry Sullivan; no, there is no letter for you.' 'Jist have another look, if you plase, yer honor; I writ home that I was in America, and I know they'd be sending a letter after me long ago.' 'There is none, I assure you', and away goes Jerry, grumbling that the Postmaster 'could make letters for everybody but him.' Then we have a Highlander disputing the payment of his County Rates, and swearing that, as the Council and Assembly had quarrelled, all the laws had been swept away; and that as there was to be no money laid out upon the roads, he would not pay any taxes. A merchant seeking a summons – a farmer inquiring after a grant – and a fisherman with a broken head, to make affidavit concerning a fray, were other features of the scene, and left upon our minds an abiding impression of the pleasures and labors of Nova Scotian pluralities, from the enjoyment of which, should we ever retire to the interior, may Providence in its infinite mercy defend us.

The first ten or a dozen miles of the St. Mary's road is dull and wearisome, and with such reflections and recollections as these did we endeavour to beguile it. – There are two roads leaving Antigonish, which run into each other at about that distance, and, like many a foolish Traveller before us, we chose the worst, merely because it was the shortest. The old road, we have been informed, is tolerably good, and winds along through some of the finest farms of the Upper District. The other is a new one, recently explored, wet and muddy enough in some places, and plentifully strewed with roots, which, when they run along upon a soft surface, form natural traps for the legs of a horse. As a general rule, we should advise all Travellers through a new country, whether pedestrians or equestrians, if their time is their own, and they wish to see the country over which they are passing, to abide by the old roads, wherever there are two to choose. In the early settlement of this Province, our ancestors walked as the crow flies – straight onwards, over all the mountains that lay in their course. The ground on the highlands was dryer than round the base of the hills, and afforded a better view of surrounding objects, by which alone the

Traveller was to find his way. From these old roads, therefore, follow them where you will, the best views of scenery are to be obtained; and perhaps the best views of our rural society also; because they lead you to the cottages of those who have been long enough upon their farms to get the comforts of life around them, and to have acquired something of that softness of manners which insensibly follows in their train. The new roads, on the contrary, carry you along the low grounds, from which you can see nothing but lines of trees that fence you in from 'all the world beside', save and except the hut of the recent settler who has but little leisure to waste, and but slender cheer to bestow, on the eager appetite or curiosity of the Traveller.

From such a dreary pathway as this, we at length emerged into a more open clearing, and almost immediately enjoyed one of the finest scenes that Nova Scotia can present to a Traveller's eye. – If the gentle reader has had the good fortune to see Captain Moorsom's Sketches of the Province, he may remember a drawing of the Lochaber Lake, accompanied by a record of the Artist's feelings on first beholding it.[78] If we remember right, the gallant soldier's acquaintance commenced with the west end of the Lake: we burst from the forest upon its eastern extremity; but look upon it from what point you please, the impression upon the mind is one of surpassing loveliness; and though many a year of toil may glide over our heads, and many a pleasant spot be presented to our eyes, we never shall lose the lineaments of the beautiful Lochaber, with the noble forests by which it is surrounded. The Lochaber Lake owes nothing to the labors of industry and art; its beauties are its own; the scene is essentially the same that it was a hundred, or perhaps a thousand years ago; except that the wild deer bounds not across the path, and the birds fly somewhat nearer Heaven.

There is scarcely a scene in the Province that we can call to mind which has not a mixed character. There may be a fine sheet of water or a noble belt of forest – a pleasant hill side, or a far extending intervale; but man and his labors, his plantations and improvements, are so

78 *Letters from Nova Scotia; comprising Sketches of a Young Country* (London 1830), by Captain William Moorsom. The engraving of Lochaber Lake to which Howe refers shows a rough track through stumps and underbrush, two crude cabins in the foreground, and in the middle distance a pastoral scene of cattle feeding in a meadow by the lake.

blended with them, that we are at a loss to decide whether they owe most to art or nature, and can form no definite idea of what they would have been, had the axe of the settler never subjected their charms to mutilation. We have often endeavoured to overpower the effects of these associations – to recall the original features; to restore in imagination the rocks and trees; swell out the shrinking rivers; and spread over the land its broken garb of thick but varied foliage. But ever and anon, just when we fancied we were most successful; when we were about to people the wilderness we had created with the dusky forms and gleaming eyes that erst were moving among its branches – the smoke of a dozen chimnies; the streaks of some score of dirty gables; the roar of a bull, or the bark of a dog, roused us from our reverie, and forced upon us the consciousness of change, and the impossibility of discovering a scene of any extent into which man, with his devastating improvements, had not intruded. Our ride along the Lochaber convinced us of the hastiness of this conclusion, and our heart bounded with delight (let the utilitarians say what they will) when we found that there really was one beautiful spot of our country upon which no hand could be seen, save that of the all-wise and glorious creator.

Let the Reader fancy he sees a long narrow Lake, extending about five miles, scarcely ever exceeding a hundred yards in breadth, and in some places so narrow as to be nearly shrouded with foliage; and here and there, by some slight bend, leading him to believe he is approaching its termination. Both sides of the Lake are inclosed by long ranges of hills, running parallel with it; sometimes thrown back from its shores with a gentle slope, at others, jutting out into the waters, and casting the reflection of the stately and unbroken forest of hardwood trees far down into its bosom, on the glassy and unruffled surface of which the sunbeams of a summer noon are quietly reposing. Let him fancy such a scene as this spread out before him, with nothing above, below or around, to remind him of the bustling, busy world, save and except his own unworthy person, and the wearied beast which he bestrides, and then let him wonder not, that we have lingered so long upon our recollections of the sylvan Lochaber.

A few straggling settlers have set themselves down upon the shores of the Lake; but as they are few, and are located at a considerable distance from each other, some views of great extent may be had, in which not a tree has been felled, or the least sign of cultivation is visible. We are conscious, however, that we have looked upon their unbroken loveliness for the last time; the County of Sydney is rapidly filling up with agriculturists; the land along the lake is excellent in quality, and being completely sheltered by the hilly ranges, offers too many attractions of a different character from those on which we have dwelt to be long neglected. It has been nearly all taken up, and in a very few years the forest will have fallen beneath the axe, and the shores of the lake will be changed into a flourishing farming district. Speaking as an economist rather than a tourist, we have here another instance of the folly of granting, either to individuals or corporate bodies, very large and unwieldly tracts of land. – On the northern margin of the lake a block of 5,000 acres has been set apart for the use of the College at Windsor, and in a few years, while the country around it becomes cleared and improved, there it will lie, like the Governor's grant in Merrigomish, and Desbarres' grants in Cumberland, a nuisance and obstruction to the general progress of cultivation.[79]

Being forced to stop at a cottage to rest and refresh our horse, we left him to masticate his oats, and springing into a canoe, spent an hour most agreeably in paddling around the lake; and never did we find it so difficult to tear ourselves from a scene or experience in a higher degree the full powers of sylvan enchantment.

XIV

27 July 1831

The valley of the Lochaber will, at no very distant day, be one of the most fruitful – as it will assuredly rank among the most beautiful, of

79 See note 59. The land grant of 5,000 acres was made to King's College, Windsor, in 1813. The present settlement of College Grant derives its name from the original grant, as did College Lake, the name originally given to Lochaber Lake. Des Barres'

the agricultural districts of the Province. Like the vale of Annapolis, it is protected on two sides from the high winds, and lying far inland, is subjected to no fog from the sea. The Lake, of which we have formerly spoken, emptying itself into the St. Mary's River, might, with some canal excavation, furnish a free outlet to the ocean, through which the products of the country could be conveyed to market. Many years will elapse before such an improvement is attempted, but it is one which is too strongly marked out by the hand of nature to be of very distant accomplishment.

The ride from the extremity of the Lake to the Forks of the St. Mary's River is not very interesting. There are a few farms and a mill or two, but no object of especial attraction. The west branch of the River runs off in a northerly direction, and extends to within a few miles of the head of the River Stewiacke; the east branch pierces the district of Pictou, and is supplied from a large Lake in the Township of Maxwellton. The Lochaber empties into this Branch, and just above the Forks a Lake of considerable size is formed, for some distance around which there is a rich and valuable intervale, partially cultivated, but in other spots studded with noble Elms and Beeches, which give it quite a parkish sort of character.

After a long ride over an indifferent road, an Inn is by no means the least attractive object in the scene; and that which holds out to the Traveller a prospect of food and refreshment on his arrival at the Forks of St. Mary's is not the most likely to disappoint his hopes. A clean cloth, a cup of good tea, homemade bread, fresh eggs, and though last not least, a slice of a fine fresh salmon, caught in the Lake not two hours previous, are not to be slighted by the wayfarer after a six hour's fast. Eating and drinking may be very vulgar and unsentimental employments, but we never met a lover of nature, who, after feasting his eyes with some twenty miles of her fair proportions, was not ready to feast on something more substantial. We have seen a Mineralogist drop his hammer to seize on a knife and fork, and a Botanist who preferred,

Grant in what is now Colchester County was a large tract extending inland six miles from Tatamagouche Harbour. Colonel Joseph F.W. Desbarres, who was later the Governor of Cape Breton and of Prince Edward Island, had been given the grant after the Peace of 1763. He attracted only a few settlers.

at the end of a long walk, the dissection of a duck to the dissection of a flower.

The Archibalds (a name by no means common elsewhere) appear to be spread all over the Eastern division of the Province. You find lots of them in Colchester – some in Pictou, and an equal proportion in Sydney County; our landlord at the Forks bears the name, and there are several others either settled upon the Branches or further down the River, the whole being descended, we believe, from a single stock. The Forks would be a fine location for a brace of sportsmen to spend a few weeks of the summer. There are lots of pigeons and partridges in the woods; ducks, salmon and trout in the lake – snipe and cock on the intervale; and a Bear or a Caraboo is no uncommon sight in the wide tract of pathless forest which stretches away to the westward.

From the Forks to Sherbrooke, the sea port and principal village of the Township, is about ten or a dozen miles and the road, which is none of the best, runs along on the eastern side of the River. After leaving the intervale at the Forks, we appear to strike suddenly in upon that belt of rough and sterile country which runs along the whole southern coast of Nova Scotia, here and there broken by patches of milder and more inviting aspect, but in general preserving one stern and unvaried outline. There is but little good land on either side of the River, and as a natural consequence, scarcely any cultivation. You ride along through a wilderness – the road over which you pass being almost the only evidence of man's industry. To the left a range of rocky hills, in some places very steep and rather picturesque, seems to shut you in from the eastward.

The River, which is a noble one about the breadth of the Annapolis, runs swiftly along upon the right, and being shaded by the hills, and overhung by foliage, its waters have a dark and mysterious character that has an effect upon the fancy – more especially, as in some places the abrupt swelling of the hills leaves but as little room for the Traveller as was to be had in the valley of Glendearg, and makes him fear, that like the jolly Friar, he may be taken at disadvantage, and plunged into the stream.[80] For a distance of four or five miles, the River is scarcely

80 The Vale of Glendearg is a fictional site in Scott's *The Monastery* (1820). Scott's description explains Howe's reference: 'The hills which ascend on each side of this glen are very steep, and rise boldly above the stream, which is thus imprisoned within their

broken by any obstruction to its course. This part of it is called the 'still water' – but, although that which is running with much velocity can scarcely be said to be 'still', there is an essential difference between this portion of the River, and others where the suddenness of the descent, or the presence of large rocks, give a restless and turbid motion to its volume. A bird perched on a rock, ready to pounce upon its prey – and a Trout leaping to the surface, as if to catch the last ray of the sun ere it sinks behind the hills, are the only living things that are likely to attract attention from the scenery over which we pass, and as the saddle gets wonderfully hard towards the close of a summer day., we are not sorry to find ourselves close on the borders of the village of Sherbrooke; although, we can see, by a first glance, that supper and a bed must be among the chief of its attractions.

Sherbrooke is a rough and unsightly cluster of wooden houses, built along a street running parallel with the eastern bank of the River, at the head of the Navigation, where its waters meet, and are lost in the tide which flows upwards about ten miles from the sea. This village is a creation of the Timber Trade, and like all its other children, has looked for two or three years past as if it were in a decline. At one time it was the scene of an active and profitable trade in lumber and new vessels, ten, of from fifty to one hundred tons, having been built there within a few years. In 1824, 25, and 26, fourteen cargoes of timber, amounting in the whole to 4155 tons, 63,460 feet of plank, besides, lathwood, spars, &c., were exported; and in 1827, 400,000 feet of sawed lumber, and 100 head of horned cattle were sent from this place to Halifax.*

There are now two or three small vessels on the stocks, and the whole business of the place appears to be their completion, and the rafting, securing and sawing of timber. The Harbor of Sherbrooke seems admirably adapted to this purpose; two points of land approaching so near each other across its channel, that booms are easily extended from one to the other, which arrest the progress of any logs which may hap-

barriers. The sides of the glen are impracticable for horse, and are only to be traversed by means of the sheep-paths which lie along their sides' (chapter 2). The 'jolly Friar' is apparently Father Philip, a minor character in the novel who is ill at ease when obliged to travel through the glen at night.

* Haliburton's Statistics [Howe's note]

pen to break adrift. There is an excellent Saw Mill at the lower extremity of the village, which is supplied with water through a sort of canal, cut for a distance of a quarter of a mile, to the margin of a Lake. The accommodations at St. Mary's are about equal to its outward appearance – and our steed having loosened a shoe, we were forced to row across the harbor to borrow a little coal from a gentleman superintending the rigging of a Brig, before we could get the Smith to secure it.

Although this village has at present rather a desolate look, still, as it recovers from the shock of 1827,[81] and as the country above it becomes populous and improved, it must become an entrepôt for the supply of the settlers, and an outlet for the produce of the country. Indeed, it must live by commerce or manufactures, for there is scarcely land enough around it for a garden.

XV

3 August 1831

He who would be a successful Traveller, must rise with the sun, and to horse, ere the mist has risen from river and lake. If the day be warm, he can then afford to lye by for an hour or two at noon; if it rains, he may linger in some cottage till the shower is over, and if the road be narrow and rough, he is not forced to gallop over it at the imminent risk of his neck. Leaving Sherbrooke behind us, we retrace our steps some 15 miles, until we pass the Forks, the intervale and the Lake, which we described in a former No., and strike into the right of the road leading to Antigonish, and bending our course due east, plod on towards Guysborough, our anticipations somewhat damped by the result of the previous day's hard riding, and the meagre attractions of

81 A financial crisis which occurred in England in 1825-6 had serious effects on Nova Scotian trade, making 1827 the worst year of the post-war depression in the province. Shipping firms went bankrupt, lumbering and shipbuilding were brought to a halt by lack of markets, and the whole economy suffered badly.

the lumbering village of Sherbrooke.[82] After leaving the Antigonish road, that on which we are travelling dwindles to a mere bridle path; in some places nearly overgrown with shrubs and wild berry bushes, in others clogged by a fallen tree, and for many miles as rough and wearisome as a traveller need desire. We have heard that one of the successful candidates for the County of Sydney nearly jeopardized his election last fall, by his apprehensions of the condition of this highway; and as he is a man of some bulk, we can readily forgive what to others less acquainted with the journey would seem like an undue care of his person; for unless your beast be singularly sure-footed, both eye and hand are necessary to the security of your neck.

For many miles along this road the land is very indifferent, which is evidenced by the old and abandoned clearings – broken fences and dilapidated log huts that skirt the way. There are but few settlers upon it, and although a feed of oats may be procured at a little cottage some ten miles from the intervale, no other refreshment, save perhaps a potatoe, need be solicited, as if it were it would scarcely be obtained. When within about eight miles of Guysborough the prospect begins to open – and something like cultivation glads the sight as you approach the Salmon River Bridge, but upon the whole we think we may venture the assertion, that there is but one attraction between Sherbrooke and Guysborough – and that is the good breakfast you get at the intervale, a slice of the salmon, whose virtues we have elsewhere recorded, included as a matter of course.

Well was it for us that we remembered the value of early rising, for had we folded our hands with the sluggard in the morning, we should scarcely have reached Guysborough at night. The dark, heavy clouds, which, since noon, have been gathering up on the horizon, have gradually increased in density and extent; in vain are the rays of the sun shed out upon them – they may temper but cannot subdue; and as the great dispenser of light and heat sinks downwards in the heavenly arch, the

82 Sherbrooke, though still a small community, is now a more pleasant place than when Howe first visited it. It is still a lumbering centre but also has become known for the good sports fishing in the area. Its main attraction to the traveller is a small-scale pioneer village which the provincial government, using old buildings, has started to develop in one part of the town.

black vapours thicken around and seem to threaten his retreat. Now they roll heavily onwards; and now that we have got to a part of the road shut in on both sides by the forest, they appear to bow themselves almost to the tops of the trees – a flash of light, a peal of thunder, and down comes the rain in torrents – pattering merrily upon the beech leaves, and drenching the Traveller to the skin; and as a tired horse cannot be forced into exertion, there he must sit, chilled, chafed and lugubrious, while the 'bottles of the skies'[83] are emptied upon his devoted head. But thanks again, say we, to the good thought that roused us with the lark, for we have but a mile or two more to travel in this uncomfortable plight, and before we are quite drowned, we enter the village of Guysborough, shrouded in mist and smothered in showers; and, by the advice of a fellow wanderer, betake us to the most respectable public, over which Squire Christian Miller presides, and to which we would, in all seriousness, recommend those who are curious in the details of the Seven Years' War, or are insufficiently acquainted with the merits of Frederick the Great.[84]

Oh! how the countenance of the wayfarer falls, when on casting aside his wet and comfortless garments, and betaking himself to his valise, he finds that however good leather may be to fortify a Town, according to the School Boy Fable, it is not always a sufficient protection to dry stockings and shirts.[85] But what evil is there in this life for which the kind hand of woman has not a remedy? doleful indeed must be his

83 'Who can number the clouds in wisdom? or who can stay the bottles of heaven?' Job 38:37.

84 Christian Miller or Müller (c 1751-1841) was born in Germany, where he served as a soldier and attained the rank of sergeant-major. As a member of the 60th Regiment, he had 250 acres of land granted to him on the south side of Chedabucto Bay. He soon moved to the nearby village of Guysborough and became a prominent member of the community, holding the office of sheriff for Sydney County and, as Howe testifies, keeping the best inn in the area.

85 An allusion to an old fable, credited to Aesop, about a town in danger of a siege. When the townspeople meet to decide what material is best for fortification, the mason recommends stone, the carpenter oak wood, the currier leather. Howe's source was probably a schoolbook, for an anonymous rhymed version of the tale appeared in many schoolbooks of the early nineteenth century. The last two lines run as follows: 'A currier, wiser than both these together, / Said, "Try what you please, there's nothing like leather."'

plight to whom she brings not comfort and consolation. A man need not travel as far as Ledyard[86] to acquire the privilege of sounding her praises, and so sudden was our transition from the plight in which the shower had left us to that in which, by her aid, we were suddenly transformed, that stretching ourselves in a large armchair in front of a blazing fire, we fell fast asleep, and was just dreaming of half-drowned mariners, snatched from the billows by kind damsels to share the warmth and comfort of their cots, when we were roused to behold our gallant host, charging by the side of the mighty Frederick at the battle of Prague, and to listen to such an account of the whole campaign as we are satisfied is not stored up in any other head in the Province of Nova Scotia.

Having experienced some disappointment in the appearance of Antigonish and Sherbrooke, we had made up our minds to expect but little from any part of the County of Sydney, and hoped to find in Guysborough a tolerable Fishing Settlement with but few charms for the eye, and very little deserving of attention. The praises of Windsor, of Horton, of Truro, had been loudly sounded in our ears – we had listened to and read many rapturous descriptions of Annapolis, Digby and Antigonish, but never heard Guysborough mentioned, unless in connection with pickled fish and oil; and when we ascended one of its highest elevations on the morning after our arrival, were agreeably surprised and delighted with the wide, varied and beautiful view which it affords. Chedabucto Bay, one of the finest sheets of water of which the Province can boast, stretches away seawards a distance of 25 miles; and on both sides of it, as far as the eye can reach, farms, clearings and cottages are scattered along on the lines of coast which form its east and western boundaries. This Bay terminates in Milford Haven, a beautiful Basin, on the eastern side of which the Township of Guysborough is laid out, that of Manchester occupying the opposite shore. Milford Haven winds its way for about twelve miles above Guysborough, and

86 John Ledyard (1751-88) was a noted traveller who set out to walk from western Europe to eastern Asia. After walking around the Gulf of Bothnia (a distance of 1500 miles) in the depth of winter, he continued to St Petersburg, averaging thirty miles a day, and then on to Yakutsk. Howe had already written an account of Ledyard's exploits in the *Novascotian* for 23 October 1828.

the scenery along the whole course of it is highly picturesque and beautiful.

From the Manchester side of the Haven, a point of land extends about half way across, and partially closes it in from the sea – and at the landward extremity of Guysborough another long point, extending in an opposite direction, and studded with handsome cottages, gardens and orchards, adds much to the beauty of the scene. – Indeed every step you take – every turn of the eye – furnishes some new combination of land and water, some scenic grace that was not at first observed; and the result of the whole survey satisfies the Traveller that there are few places in the Province whose natural beauties and great commercial advantages are more agreeably blended.

XVI

19 October 1831

Guysborough was settled by about 200 persons, who belonged to the Civil Department of the Army and Navy, at the evacuation of New York. Their first place of refuge had been Port Muttoon, in Queen's County; but after suffering much in that quarter, they obtained a grant of 53,850 acres of land, and removed to the shores of Chedabucto Bay, where they found a part of the Duke of Cumberland's regiment, that had landed there about a month before. The Town and Township were shortly after laid out, and were named in honor of Sir Guy Carleton, who was, at that time, Commander-in-Chief of His Majesty's forces in North America.*

Guysborough reminded us of Chester; and although there is no very strict resemblance between the two places, they have these traits in com-

* Haliburton. The following passage, which we extract entire from the same volume, may not be uninteresting, as illustrating the early history, and in some degree, accounting for the present condition of Guysborough: – 'To each of the settlers, both a town and farm lot were assigned, and also a share in the rear divisions. At first they

mon: – both are built along the land rising from an arm of the sea – from both you look out upon a beautiful and extensive Bay – and each is spread over a space of ground sufficient for the area of a large city. The history of Shelburne is well known. Guysborough and Chester partook of the same sudden rise – the same unsubstantial prosperity, rapid decline, and premature desertion. Each had enow of blighted hopes and broken hearts for its early portion; and for a long while we might have applied Scott's motto to either –

> A pleasant place it was in days of yore –
> But something ails it now – they say 'tis curst.[87]

Chester was, for many years, a deserted village, but is now reviving. Guysborough declined for about forty years, until, having reached the extreme point of depression, a reaction commenced, and since then, trade has been revived and extended; agriculture has been more systematically and more successfully pursued; new buildings have been erected, and the old Town lots, which, for a long time, would scarcely be taken as a gift, have been steadily rising in value. A Gentleman informed us that he had, seven years ago, purchased several for two or three pounds, which were now worth from twenty to thirty; and we think that the great natural advantages of Guysborough assure us of the accomplishment, even in our day, of the fondest hopes that the first

all erected houses, and settled on the town plot; and during the succeeding winter, cut down the adjoining timber. In attempting to burn the wood (the usual mode of clearing land) the fire spread with such violence and rapidity, that most of the houses were destroyed, and they were compelled to seek refuge from its fury in the water. Notwithstanding this disasterous occurrence, they were still unwilling to separate and settle upon their farm lots, but rebuilt their houses and remained together until the Government allowance of provision ceased, when many appalled by the difficulties of subduing the wilderness, removed from the Province. Those who remained were compelled to make the attempt after suffering the severest privations, in consequence of the difficulty of procuring supplies from Halifax, and in a few years the town was nearly deserted. In this derelict state, inhabited by only a few merchants and mechanics, it continued until within the last ten years, during which it has partaken of the general growth of the country.' [Howe's note]

87 These lines appear as the general motto on the title page of Scott's *St Ronan's Well* (1824), where they are attributed to Wordsworth. They are lines 123–4 of Wordsworth's poem 'Hart-Leap Well' (1800).

settlers entertained of its ultimate growth and prosperity. The village contains an Episcopal Church, a Roman Catholic Chapel, a Methodist Meeting, Court House, and some schools, the largest and best of which was, at the period of our visit, under the management of a gentleman named Catheray, whose education and abilities had conferred upon it a very high character. There may be from 30 to 40 dwelling houses in Guysborough, but there are a great many stores, barns and outhouses, which help to fill up the scene. A few of the stores are roomy and extensive, and there are several good wharves, at which vessels of heavy tonnage may be accommodated. Gardening is a favorite amusement, as well as a great auxiliary to domestic comfort, in Guysborough; and without being contented, as some of our villagers are, with sowing carrots and cabbages and devouring them, some attention is paid to a tasty arrangement and agreeable disposition in the internal economy of these little plantations. Flowers are fostered and trained by the fair hands of some, 'Themselves the fairest flowers',[88] and we have it from good authority, that the Temperance Society would never have taken root in the place, had not the delicious currant wine, which the ladies make, reconciled their husbands to the abandonment of more ardent but less palatable beverage. The Society of Guysborough is peculiarly grateful to the feelings of a Traveller – being frank, intelligent and hospitable.

About a quarter of a mile below the Town, and commanding the narrow entrance to the harbor, is an old fortification. This stronghold was, we believe, originally built by Monsieur Denys,[89] who had obtained from the Crown of France a grant of all the eastern division of Acadia. Here he lived, for some time, carrying on the fur trade, and enjoying, so far as the savages would allow him, the rights of sovereignty over the 'fowl and the brute', the trees of the forest and the fish in the bay.

88 A rephrasing of Milton's line describing Eve, 'Herself though fairest unsupported Flow'r,' *Paradise Lost* IX, l.432.

89 Nicholas Denys (1598-1688) was a French trader who engaged in various business enterprises in Acadia. In 1654 he was appointed Governor of the Gulf of St. Lawrence district from Canso to Gaspé and of Newfoundland.

By-and-by came one Girondiere,[90] who set up a claim to the country, seized Denys' vessel and supplies, and drove him into a law suit which cost him 15000 crowns, a great deal more, we should be inclined to believe, than the whole territory was worth at the period. Subsequently, when this little fort was held by Montorgieul,[91] the successor of Denys, it was forced to stand a seige by a strong force of English and Provincials under Sir William Phipps, – the besieged defended themselves so bravely, that the assailants were forced to set the place on fire before they could oblige them to capitulate. – We know not whether it was ever put into thorough repair; if it was, time, the great besieger of all sublunary things, has again reduced it to a state of piteous dilapidation. The embankments shew the form and outline of the ancient fortress – a part of the platform, an old sentry box, some rusty shot and two or three honey-combed guns, are all the indicia they bear of the pomp, pride and circumstance of war. Nothing could have been better chosen than the site of this battery; it has a perfect command of the narrow entrance of the harbor, and a few heavy guns would, if properly sheltered, endanger the safety of any vessel attempting to approach the town. There is one set of feelings which these ancient erections force upon the mind, and we envy not the man who can tread over their ruins without emotion. They were the first spots on which the hand of civilization was laid in its struggle with a savage and uncultivated wilderness. Whether English or French, it was here that the pioneers of the old world commenced the course of improvement which ensured to us and our posterity a free and happy home. – The hearts of these adventurers once beat as high as our own, on the very spot where we recline, and the bones of many of them are mouldering in the soil over which we ramble. We reap the fruit of their labors – we gather the rewards of their dangers, privations, and toils; let us never disturb their ashes by our tread, without yielding to their memories the tribute of a tear.

90 La Giraudière is the usual form of the name. Little more is known of this man's life than his rivalry with Denys.

91 Dauphin de Montorgueuil (died 1694), a naval officer and lieutenant to Villebon at Port Royal before he assumed command of Fort Saint-Louis de Chedabouctou (Guysborough).

Index

'Acacia Grove' 81n
Acadian Magazine 64
Acadian (newspaper) 3, 37, 38
Acadians 111–13
Albion Mines (Stellarton) 157n, 159ff
Alger, Cyrus 90n
Alger, Francis 90n
Annapolis County 93ff
Annapolis-Cornwallis Valley 11, 13
Annapolis River 96
Annapolis Royal 10, 103–5
Annapolis Township 94ff
Antiburghers 146
Antigonish 10, 182ff
Arisaig Pier 180

Barney's River 177
Bailey's Brook 178
Barry, John A. 97n
Bedford Basin 55
Bible Hill (Truro) 130, 138
Blackwood, Robert, the Rev. 125n
Blair, Robert 78
blockhouse (McAlpine's) 106n
Bloody Creek (Annapolis Co) 103
Bloomfield, Robert 171n
Boone, Daniel 72n
bridges 19
Bridgewater 10
Bridgetown 97ff; Sunday School 100–1
Burns, Robert 84
Byron, Lord 37, 58, 64, 71, 75, 184

Campbell, Thomas 37–8
Cape Breton 11
Carriboo Bog 94
Cervantes M. de 79, 182
Chateaubriand 50
Chester 200–1
Chezzetcook 146n
Chipman's hill (Truro) 129
Citadel (Halifax) 9, 53
Clare 111ff
coal mines (Stellarton) 160ff
Cochran, Sir Thomas 56n
Coffin, Sir Isaac 152n
Coleridge, S.T. 37, 109
College Grant 192n
Colman, George 119, 188
Combe, William 164n
corduroy roads 19–20
Corn Laws 119n
Cornwallis Township 79ff
Curran, John 62n

Darwin, Erasmus 169n
Davies, W.H. 162n
Dennison, Sherman 169n
Denys, Nicholas 202
Des Barres' Grant 192n
'Digbies' 108n
Digby 106ff
Digby Gut 109
Digby Neck 110
Dutch Village 146n

East River (Pictou Co) 158–9, 168
'Eastern Rambles' 3, 11–12
Eastern Stage Coach Company 24, 26, 27, 83–4, 121–2
election of 1830 183n
Emancipation Bill 124n

Falmouth 71
farmers: idleness of 81ff, 95–6; extravagance of 83, 85, 87–8, 101, 140–1
Fraser, William, the Rev. 185n
Frenchman's Barn 180
French River 39, 174

Garrick, David 119
Gaspereau Valley 73ff
Gay, John 117
Glower, Charles 109
Goldsmith, Oliver 117
Governor's Grant 170n
Governor's North Farm 53n
Granville Township 101–2
Gulf Shore 13, 150, 178–82
Guysborough 10, 198ff

Haliburton, T.C. 29, 41, 42, 57n, 73, 110n, 184, 195, 200
Halifax 9–10, 53
Hemans, Mrs Felicia 38, 60, 72, 153
Herschel, Sir William 166
Hogg, James 126n
Homer, John 97n
Horton 76
Horton Corner 77
Horton mountains 71ff
Howe, Catharine Susan Ann 4, 7
Howe, John, sr 34, 42
Howe, Joseph: business trips for *Novascotian* 4–9; letter to his wife 4ff; on inns 29–30; his verse 31; education 34ff; tastes in literature 36ff; tone and purpose of the sketches 39ff; politics and religion 39–42; local patriotism 42; egalitarianism 42
Hume, David 140

innkeepers 28–9
inns: Hiltz's (Windsor Road) 25, 59n, 62n; Mrs Wilcox's (Windsor) 25, 27, 66n; Mrs Fuller's (Kentville) 25, 27, 79; Mrs Davis' (Annapolis) 27; Fultz's (Lower Sackville) 27, 58n, 59, 123; Blanchard's (Truro) 27, 127–8; Terfry's (Newport Corners) 63n; Fletcher's (Truro Road) 124n; Shultz's (Truro Road) 124n; Hill's (Stewiacke) 125n; Archibald's (West River) 144; Copeland's (French River) 6, 174; Murray's (Barney's River) 177; Mrs Simon's (Antigonish) 182–3; Archibald's (St Mary's Forks) 193–4; Miller's (Guysborough) 183
iron smelter (Annapolis Co) 105–6

Jackson, Charles Thomas 90n
Jeffery, Thomas N. 62n

Keats, John 37
Kempt Road (Halifax) 53n
Kentville 10, 77ff
Kentville Falls 90–3
King's College (Windsor) 65

La Giraudière, monsieur 203
land grants 170, 175
Lawrence Town (Annapolis Co) 96
lawyers 61n, 187–8
Ledyard, John 199n
legends, lack of in NS 33, 92
Legislative Assembly 21–2, 141, 174, 183
Legislative Council 174, 186
Liverpool 15, 18
Lochaber Lake 190–2
Lochaber Valley 13, 192–3
Lunenburg 13
luxuries, imported 85–7, 101
Lynds, Jacob 141n

mail courier, Cumberland 128n
Malignant, sloop, shipwreck of 181–2
Malignant Cove 180–1
McCulloch, Thomas 40, 42, 147, 155, 157
Merrigomish 174–7
Miller, Christian 198

Miller, Joe 62n
Milton, John 36, 55, 202
Minas Basin 65n
Montgomery, James 79
Montorgueuil, Dauphin de 203
Moore, Thomas 37, 54, 59, 83
Moorsom, Captain William 9–10, 17, 18, 19–20, 26, 28–9, 31–4, 190, 57n, 62n, 66n, 86n, 108n, 176n, 190
Mortimer, Edward 142n, 146
Mortimer's Point (Pictou) 146
Morton, John Elkanah 107n
'Mount Rundle' 159
Mount Tom 142
Musquodoboit Valley 11

Negroes 55–7
New Glasgow 10, 158
North Mountain (Truro) 130
'Norway House' 147
Nova Scotia: population 10; towns 10; area covered by the *Rambles* 10–13; shipping 13–14; land routes 14–18; stagecoach travel 22–7; roadbuilding 20–2; inns 27–30; economic state of, 99n, 196n
Novascotian 3, 7

Ogleby, Lord 119n
Old Barns (Truro) 132–3
oratory 100

pedlars 171–3
Phipps, Sir William 104, 203
physician, country 91
Pictou Academy 40, 146n, 147, 154ff; museum 155ff
Pictou 39, 40, 144ff
Pigeon, Captain 103
pioneers, reflections on 133
pluralities 188–9
politics 39–40, 174n, 183n, 186
Pope, Alexander 98, 168, 177
Port Royal (Annapolis Royal) 103–5
Prescott, Charles Ramage 81n
Prince's Lodge 57n
Prior, Matthew 165

railway, at Albion Mines 160
religion 40–2
representation (political) 141n
roads: Great Roads 14–16; western 14, 17; eastern 14; northern 14, 16; Annapolis-Shelburne 14; Liverpool-Chester 15, 17–18; Pictou-Straits of Canso 15; Windsor-Chester 13; Antigonish-Straits 16; Musquodoboit-St Mary's 17; bridle paths 16; new cuts 16, 189; British 20; statute labour on 21; commissioners for 21–2; Assembly grants for 22, 174n
Rocking stone (Spryfield) 89

Sandemanianism 40
Scott, Sir Walter 336–7, 73, 93, 104, 146, 194, 201
Scots, Highland 152–3, 178
Shakespeare 36, 69, 70, 74, 76, 78, 81, 82, 110, 128, 165, 179, 186
Shelley, P.B. 37
Sherbrooke 11, 195–6, 197n
Sheridan, R.B. 78
shipbuilding 14, 99, 107, 175, 195
Shubenacadie canal 124n
Sigogne, Jean-Mandé, Abbé 111–13
Sissiboo (Weymouth) 109–10
Sleigh, Colonel 15
Smith, Isaiah 22
Smith, Richard 159n
Smollett, Tobias 85
Spenser, Edmund 36, 92
Spike, James 3
statute labour 21
Stellarton, coal mines 160ff
Stepsure, Mephibosheth 140n
Sterne, Laurence 37, 50, 69, 71
Stewiacke River 126
St Mary's church (Church Point) 112n
St Mary's Forks 193–4
St Mary's River 194–5

Sydney 10
Sydney County 150n, 192
Symmes, Captain John Cleves 165n

Tasso, Torquato 120
timber trade 99n, 151–2, 176
Tonge, Grieselda 38–9, 66–9
travel, by stagecoach 22–9, 52, 83, 121–2; by steamboat (Annapolis-Digby-Saint John) 14, 105n, 122; *see also* roads
Trenck, Frederick von der 170n
Truro 10, 127ff; falls at 135–7

Uniacke, Richard John 63n

Walton, Isaac 74
West River (Pictou Co) 143–4
'Western Rambles' 3, 10–11
Western Stage Coach Company 23–4, 26, 27, 52n, 121–3
Wilmot Township 94–6
Wilson, John 126n
Windsor 64ff
Windsor Street (Halifax) 53n
Witter, Ezra 23
Wolfville 53n
women, frivolity of 69–71, 87–8, 140–1
Wordsworth, William 37

Young, Arthur 20
Young, George 3
Young, John ('Agricola') 42

CANADIAN UNIVERSITY PAPERBOOKS

Some other titles in the series

3 *The Rideau Waterway*, revised ed.
ROBERT LEGGET

7 *The Bruce Beckons: The story of Lake Huron's great peninsula*
W. SHERWOOD FOX

16 *The Great Migration*
EDWIN C. GUILLET

30 *Pioneer Days in Upper Canada*
EDWIN C. GUILLET

36 *The Englishwoman in America*
JAMES R. SUTHERLAND

40 *Toronto during the French Régime: A history of the Toronto region from Brulé to Simcoe, 1615–1793*
PERCY J. ROBINSON

47 *Pioneer Travel*
EDWIN C. GUILLET

53 *The Incredible War of 1812*
J. MACKAY HITSMAN

85 *Highland Settler: A portrait of the Scottish gael in Nova Scotia*
CHARLES W. DUNN

96 *Pioneer Settlements in Upper Canada*
EDWIN C. GUILLET

100 *Life in Ontario: A social history*
G. P. DE T. GLAZEBROOK

131 *Beyond the River and the Bay*
ERIC ROSS

Milton Keynes UK
Ingram Content Group UK Ltd.
UKHW031029291024
450383UK00001B/16

9 780802 061836